D0758038

OMNIVM
LVX
CIVIVM
MDCCCLII
MDCCC
LXXVIII
BOSTON
PUBLIC
LIBRARY

Fryderyk Chopin
Pianist from Warsaw

FRYDERYK CHOPIN

PIANIST FROM WARSAW

WILLIAM G. ATWOOD

New York COLUMBIA UNIVERSITY PRESS *1987*

Library of Congress Cataloging-in-Publication Data

Atwood, William G., 1932–
Fryderyk Chopin: Pianist from Warsaw.

Bibliography: p.
Includes index.
1. Chopin, Frédéric, 1810–1849. 2. Pianists—
Biography. I. Title
ML410.C54A77 1987 786.1'092'4 [B] 86–12986
ISBN 0–231–06406–3

Book design by Laiying Chong

COLUMBIA UNIVERSITY PRESS
NEW YORK GUILDFORD, SURREY

PRINTED IN THE UNITED STATES OF AMERICA

THIS BOOK IS SMYTH-SEWN.

This book is an expression of thanks to
DR. WIKTOR LABUNSKI (1895–1974),
a respected teacher and pianist—also from Warsaw

CONTENTS

PREFACE

THE MAIN FOCUS of this book is the concert career of Fryderyk Chopin, the complex and intriguing genius so widely known today for his masterful compositions, his ardent patriotism, and his notorious love affair with George Sand. He was, at the same time, one of the most legendary piano virtuosos of the nineteenth century. In an age that clamored for thunder and bombast on one hand and wallowed in cheap sentimentality on the other, his consummate refinement set him apart. Repeatedly he was referred to by press and public alike as the "sylph" or the "Ariel" of the piano because of his light, almost ethereal touch. Although he had his critics, some of whom could be incredibly vicious, most of his contemporaries admitted that he remained unmatched when it came to pure artistic sensitivity. True, Henri Herz, Sigismond Thalberg, or Franz Liszt might rival him in technical proficiency and certainly outstrip him in the art of showmanship, but as for the quintessential qualities of musicianship, Chopin stood out as the pianists' pianist.

Yet with all these virtues Chopin rarely appeared on the concert stage. From the age of seven when he made his debut in Warsaw's Radziwiłł Palace until the age of thirty-eight when he appeared for the last time in London's Guildhall, he played in probably no more than fifty public concerts altogether. Why, in view of his great popularity, did he choose to display his pianistic abilities on such a limited scale?

First of all, Chopin was an aristocrat by nature if not by birth,[1] which led him to prefer the exclusiveness of a salon to the motley milieu of a public concert hall. No doubt he was repelled by the tawdry level of taste that prevailed in many of the musical events of his era. Liszt, who always envied the ease with which Chopin was accepted by the nobility, once snorted that the Polish pianist had "a very clear sense of his superiority."[2] This observation, though born of jealousy, was nevertheless accurate. From childhood on, Chopin reveled in the adulation of the *haut monde* which he gradually came to expect as his due. His fragile temperament thrived in the security of that inner circle where he felt understood and appreciated.

Second, Chopin's emotional makeup was not well suited to the life of a virtuoso, which, then as now, requires a special blend of talent and toughness. While his most successful colleagues were often driven by a spirit of competition and exhibitionism, Chopin's own nature was entirely different. For him, playing in public was always an ordeal. The very prospect of it would incapacitate him for days in advance. "I am not fitted to give concerts," he once told Liszt, "the public frightens me, I feel suffocated by its panting breath, paralyzed by its curious glance, mute before those unknown faces."[3]

More often than not, when he did muster up the courage to appear in public he was greeted with the complaint that his playing was "too soft" or "too delicate" to be truly impressive. The gossamer beauty of his exquisite style was frequently lost in the cavernous recesses of a large concert hall. Only in the intimacy of a salon or drawing room was he heard at his best. This delicacy of style—a third reason for Chopin's aversion to the life of a virtuoso pianist—was to become even more marked in later life as tuberculosis gradually sapped his strength away.

Here we come to the subject of Chopin's health, which, perhaps more than anything else, was the factor that restricted his concert career. Even as a child he was never robust, but his youthful energy and ambition initially compensated for his physical frailty. By the time he reached Paris he began to suffer from regular bouts of so-called "influenza," "bronchitis," "laryngitis," and "neuritis," all of which were, in reality, the early manifestations of his fatal consumption. The slowly progressive ravages of this disease were to hamper him from carrying out the arduous tasks required of a professional pianist in his day. At a time when agents or managers were practically unknown, it took a hardy individual to stand up to the rigors of arranging a concert. Among the chores this entailed were bargaining for the rental of a hall, finding ways to publicize the program, securing outlets for the sale of tickets (concert halls rarely had a box office), cajoling other musicians to "assist" him, and often having to recruit and rehearse an orchestra or chorus.

Many of these preparations stemmed from the extraordinary surfeit which characterized an early nineteenth-century concert. Far from being the pristine cultural event one might expect, these affairs presented a veritable hodgepodge of artists and instruments, not unlike a variety show on television today. At times, actors as well as musicians were included on the bill. Once Chopin found himself assigned to fill in the gap between a dramatic monologue by a retired actress and some scenes performed by a troupe from the Paris Vaudeville Theatre. Often his contribution to a program was a minor one, such as taking the bass part of a piano duet. In only a third or fewer of the concerts where he appeared was he actually the featured attraction. Most of the time he merely served as an "assisting artist" in a grand potpourri of musical numbers that could well comprise guitar solos, trumpet duets, male quartets, six-piano ensembles, and pump organ demonstrations. At these lengthy performances it was not uncommon for the overtaxed audience to stroll about, talk, and even eat. The sedate solo piano recital as we know it today was not introduced until 1839 (by Liszt) and did not gain widespread popularity until the latter half of the century.

As Chopin's early enthusiasm for the concert stage began to wane, he continued to give small impromptu musicales night after night in the fashionable salons of the rich and titled wherever he happened to be. Such occasions (even if we could document them all) would be far too numerous to fit into a work of this size. Nevertheless, I have provided accounts of a few of these private soirées (including appearances at court) where reliable information is available.

While we may anticipate that the future will bring to light further concerts in which Chopin participated, the ones recorded in these pages probably represent the vast majority of those in his career. Because these concerts span a thirty-year period, from 1818 to 1848, they extend over the greater part of Chopin's brief thirty-nine-year existence. In reviewing them along with the circumstances in which they took place and the events that link them together, this book has evolved into a biography of sorts, but one with a different emphasis from those preceding it.

At this point I would like to mention that since Chopin virtually abandoned the concert stage during his nine-year liaison with George Sand (when he played in public only twice—at the Salle Pleyel in 1841 and 1842), this volume serves essentially as a complement to my previous one, *The Lioness and the Little One: The Liaison of George Sand and Frédéric Chopin.*

PREFACE

To acknowledge in print the kindnesses of the many people who helped me in the preparation of this book would be impossible. However, I would like to mention the special contributions of a few, including Krystyna Olszer and Regina Gelb, whose instruction and assistance maneuvered me through the intricacies of the Polish language, Hugh Taliaferro and Michael Legutko, who provided a number of illustrations for the book, and Glen Loney, who located several of the reviews found in the appendix.

. . . Chopin, the sylph of the piano, the ineffable artist,
attached to this mortal world by the merest touch of a finger
and nourished by dreams from on high.
Listen to Chopin play!
It is like the sighing of a flower, the whisper of the clouds,
or the murmur of the stars.

Le Ménestrel, *February 20, 1848*

• CHAPTER ONE •

Żelazowa Wola and Warsaw 1810–1818

A LOVE OF MUSIC was one of the bonds that drew Chopin's parents together when they first met in the quiet village of Żelazowa Wola, Poland, not far from Warsaw. There they lived and worked in the small manor house of Count and Countess Skarbek. The household was run simply since the count's penchant for gambling had left the family in reduced circumstances. Many evenings after dinner, Nicholas Chopin, a native of France and tutor to the Skarbek children,[1] would play the flute or violin while his future wife, Justyna Krzyżanowska, accompanied him at the piano or sang. She was a distant cousin of the Skarbeks and occupied a rather ambiguous position in the house, somewhere between a domestic and a poor relation.

After the couple's marriage in 1806, music continued to be one of their favorite pastimes, and they naturally encouraged their children to share this pleasure with them. The oldest child, a daughter, Ludwika, learned to play the piano quickly and was the first to give lessons to her younger brother, Fryderyk, the only son of the family, born March 1, 1810. The two subsequent daughters, Izabela and Emilia, probably benefited from her instruction also, but Fryderyk was her most avid pupil.

As the boy's musical talent became apparent his mother took over his training. By the age of six he had exhausted her resources, and the family decided he needed some professional guidance. By then the Chopins were living in Warsaw where Nicholas had become master of French language and literature at both the Warsaw Lyceum and the Cadet School of Artillery and Military Engineering. Among his acquaintances in the city was a sixty-year-old Czech pianist and violinist, Wojciech Żywny, who had already given Ludwika a few lessons and was now asked to provide instruction for her brother as well.

The amiable but eccentric Żywny preened himself on having studied with Kuchar, a pupil of Johann Sebastian Bach. While this may have been true, it didn't alter the fact that he wasn't a terribly gifted musician. Still, his ability had once earned him the title of court pianist to Prince Sapieha even though his appearance and manners were anything but courtly. Fat, toothless, and unkempt, he had a ruddy nose and reeked of snuff. In his bedraggled wig and outdated clothes he looked like a clownish anachronism from the previous century. His chatty joviality, though, charmed young Fryderyk and won the affection of the entire Chopin family.

Day after day Żywny coached his new pupil in the works of Bach and Mozart with Haydn and Hummel as supplementary models. He had little use for Beethoven, while anything Italian was quite beyond the range of his Teutonic tastes.[2] When the lessons were over he often lingered on to gossip with the Chopins in his peculiar amalgam of German, Czech, and Polish. He knew if he talked long enough he would eventually be invited to dinner.

Far from being a genius in his own right, the garrulous old Żywny was nevertheless capable of nurturing the one placed in his care. Besides introducing Fryderyk to the works of baroque and classical masters, he stimulated his originality by encouraging him to improvise. With some help at first, the boy was soon jotting down his early improvisations, and by the age of eight he had published his first composition, a "Polonaise for Piano-Forte" dedicated to "Mademoiselle, the Countess Victoire Skarbek," a daughter of his father's onetime employer.

The Warsaw press was quick to call attention to this precocious achievement. "The composer of this Polish dance, a young lad barely eight years old, is the son of Nicholas Chopin . . . and a true musical genius," the *Pamiętnik Warszawski* announced in 1818. "Not only does he play the most difficult piano pieces with the greatest ease and the most extraordinary taste, he is already the composer of several dances and variations, each of which has thoroughly astonished the connoisseurs, especially in view of his tender age."[3]

Certainly Żywny did all he could to let the world know about his brilliant pupil whom he enthusiastically touted as a "new Mozart." Before long, word of the boy's marvelous abilities reached the Grand Duke Constantine Pavlovitch, brother of the czar and Supreme Commander of the Kingdom of Poland.[4] There was probably no one as heartily detested in Warsaw as the brutal and sadistic grand duke, who made no secret of his contempt for the Poles.[5] He subjected his soldiers to excruciating all-day parades and his officers to such humiliation that several were driven to suicide. His mental instability often turned him into a "raging hyena"[6] and drove him on wild shooting sprees through the streets of Warsaw. Moments after such an outburst he was apt to lapse into a depression and beg for the sound of music. On one of these occasions he asked to hear young Chopin. Since no one dared oppose his whims the boy was brought to the Belvedere Palace, where he so enthralled the maniacal prince he was summoned back time and again.[7]

Before long the grand duke found himself in competition with other members of the city's aristocracy who also took to inviting the gifted child into their drawing rooms. Among those vying for his presence were Prince Sapieha (Żywny's former patron), Count Potocki, Prince and Princess Czartoryski, and the Czar's own viceroy, General Zajączek. Eventually it was to be one of his highborn admirers, the Countess Zofia Zamoyska, who arranged for his first public performance in February 1818.

• CHAPTER TWO •

Warsaw and Bad Reinerz 1818–1828

MME. ZAMOYSKA'S SALON in the so-called Blue Palace on Senatorska Street was one of the most fashionable in Warsaw and her family one of the most distinguished in Poland. She was a daughter of Prince Adam Czartoryski, a statesman and diplomat of such extraordinary finesse that Czar Alexander I not only appointed him Russia's Minister of Foreign Affairs but allowed him to become the lover of the Czarina with his full knowledge and tacit approval.

Mme. Zamoyska herself was an energetic and public-spirited lady who had recently founded the Warsaw Charitable Society to aid victims of the Napoleonic Wars. In Poland alone there were thousands who had been maimed, orphaned, or left penniless by the horrible events of the previous decade. Instead of just handing out alms the countess established vocational schools and workshops to teach these unfortunate people the skills they needed to earn a living. She also created reading rooms with instructors for the illiterate which led, in time, to the founding of the Warsaw Public Library.

In 1818, confronted with the problem of raising money for her organization, Mme. Zamoyska sought the advice of Julian Ursyn Niemcewicz, a prominent poet-politician who was president of the Charitable Society that year. Between them they decided the society should give a concert. According to Niemcewicz, it was Mme. Zamoyska who first thought of putting a child prodigy (like the seven-year-old Chopin) on the program to attract an audience. In a whimsical account of the affair which he published some years later, Niemcewicz gave a tongue-in-cheek version of how all this came about: "If we give a concert we can have little Chopin sing [*sic*]," the countess supposedly claimed.

> His tender age will certainly draw a big crowd. He's already nine [*sic*]—but wait! I've got a splendid idea! We'll get everyone's curiosity piqued by printing in the announcements that he's only three! Just imagine! A three-year-old child playing some great concerto on the clavichord, crossing his tiny hands over each other, first to the right and then to the left — oh! Nobody can resist it! . . . On the other hand, when little Chopin walks on stage, everyone will see that he's really not so little after all. What will happen then? Oh dear, I'd better talk this over with the society.[1]

As it turned out, the announcement in the *Gazeta Korespondenta Warszawskiego i Zagranicznego* on Saturday, February 21, 1818, didn't make any of these extravagant claims attributed to the countess. It read simply:

> On the coming Tuesday, the 24th of February, a vocal and instrumental concert for the benefit of the poor will take place in the theater of the Radziwiłł Palace, given by the best-known musicians of this capital as well as some newly arrived artists, namely Mlle. Vicini on the violin and Messrs. Kaczyńscy, Arnold, Brice, Feuillde [*sic*], etc., whose delightful talents bring much pleasure to their public. Music, which touches our spirits with its tender melodies and delicately arouses our feelings, cannot help but contribute to the relief of human suffering. As to the particulars of the concert, these will be posted. Tickets at the usual prices will be available at the box office of the French Theater.

The French Theater, where tickets were sold, had been located in the Radziwiłł Palace since 1801. It was often used for public events like the one being planned by Countess Zamoyska, but by 1818 it had fallen into such disrepair that the concert for the Charitable Society was among the last functions ever held there. The whole palace, in fact, was in a sorry state of decay since its owner, Prince Karol Radziwiłł, lived outside Warsaw and took little interest in it. He was too busy overseeing his vast estates, which covered an area half the size of Ireland. In his absence troupes of professional actors were allowed to rent space in the palace, first Germans and later French (hence the so-called French Theater). In 1785 part of the building was leased out for furniture storage. Finally in 1818 the government acquired the entire structure with the intention of converting it into administrative offices and headquarters for the governor general, Józef Zajączek. Massive renovations were required for this, but they were not begun until later in the year, well after Mme. Zamoyska's concert.

In February 1818 the palace still retained its original baroque facade and sat in shabby grandeur along the east side of the Krakowskie Przedmieście, one of Warsaw's main thoroughfares. The crumbling old building was just one of many great palaces that lined this elegant boulevard which ran from the royal castle through the city's finest residential area, known as the Cracow suburb. The Chopins themselves lived only a few blocks south of it in another of these grand establishments, the Kazimierzowski Palace, which then housed the Warsaw Lyceum and its faculty.

For Fryderyk's first public appearance his Czech teacher decided he should play the piano concerto in E minor by another Czech composer, Adalbert Gyrowetz. His choice wasn't based entirely on chauvinistic considerations since Gyrowetz, in his lifetime, was a highly respected composer whose best works were often confused with those of Haydn.

For some reason Mme. Chopin didn't attend her son's concert debut. She did see to it, though, that he was impeccably dressed for the occasion in a black velvet jacket with short pants, white stockings, and a broad lace collar which she herself had made. All decked out in his new finery the young virtuoso, less than a week away from his eighth birthday, told his mother good-bye and made his way up the Krakowskie Przedmieście accompanied by his father and the fusty old Żywny.

On their arrival at the Radziwiłł Palace they found that Mme. Zamoyska hadn't really considered her "little Chopin" enough of a curiosity to fill up the French Theater after all. There, waiting in the wings, was another pianist she had invited, a heroic young man named Charles Arnold who was once honored by the city fathers of Cracow for jumping, fully clothed, into the Vistula River to save a drowning boy.

A number of other musicians were there also, including Hyacinthe Brice, the first tenor at St. Petersburg's French Theater. Although the poor man stuttered he nevertheless managed to beguile his listeners with "his pleasant and skillful singing and his simple and natural acting."[2] Along with these two foreign artists were Warsaw's own Kaczyński brothers, one of whom was a violinist and the other a cellist. Years later Chopin often played chamber music with them, and in 1830 he wrote an Introduction to his Polonaise for piano and violoncello for the cellist brother.[3]

As the legendary account of this concert would have us believe, Fryderyk rushed home that evening to tell his mother what a great impression he made, not with his playing but with her white lace collar. While this hackneyed tale has an air of fiction about it, the fact remains that Chopin as an adult was notoriously obsessed with his grooming. In Vienna he was visited daily by a hairdresser, and in Paris he fussed constantly over the cut of his trousers and the color of his waistcoats. It was his famous white gloves, however, that came to be his special sartorial signature.

By contrast, Nicholas and Justyna Chopin were unpretentious people, hardly inclined to encourage such vanity in their young son. Żwyny could bluster all he wanted to about his "new Mozart," but they weren't about to let the boy be spoiled prematurely by too much attention. Possibly for this reason they didn't allow him to play in public again for five years.

In October 1820 a nine-year-old Hungarian prodigy named Franz Liszt made his concert debut in the town of Öldenburg near the border between Austria and Hungary. For the next seven years his father paraded him back and forth across Europe in a series of grueling exhibitions. By Februry of 1823 he had already played in more concerts than Chopin ever would in his whole lifetime, but the price of such an early success was high. Liszt saw little of his mother and seldom enjoyed the companionship of children his own age. Not only did this affect him emotionally, it deprived him of a proper education, which was a constant source of embarrassment to him in later years.

Chopin's parents never felt tempted to take advantage of their son's gifts in a similar way. Nicholas Chopin made a comfortable living and didn't need extra money. Besides, he and his wife prized their family life too much to disrupt it for the sake of long, arduous concert tours. They took pride, though, in seeing Fryderyk display his talent in many of the private salons of Warsaw.

In the fall of 1818 he even played for the Empress Maria Feodorovna, widow of Czar Paul and mother of the reigning czar, Alexander I. She had come to Warsaw that year to visit her second son, the Grand Duke Constantine. Like him, Maria Feodorovna was a strong-willed person, often accused by historians of helping to assassinate her husband in hopes of controlling the government inherited by their son Alexander.

During the course of her official duties in Warsaw, the dowager czarina was taken to the Lyceum where Chopin played for her. After his performance the young pianist presented her with copies of two polonaises he had just written and inscribed to her.

Since these polonaises, along with his other childhood works, have been lost we cannot judge Chopin's early ability as a composer. As a pianist, though, he was advancing so rapidly that by 1822 Żywny had to admit there was nothing more he could teach him. Only the year before, a new music school had been established in Warsaw by a man named Józef Elsner,[4] a prolific if somewhat pedestrian composer, married to one of the prima donnas of the Warsaw Opera. With Żywny's blessing he was chosen to be Fryderyk's new teacher.

Elsner, a Silesian by birth, had studied in Breslau before becoming first violinist in the Moravian town of Brno and subsequently conductor at Lwów in eastern Poland. While such credentials were respectable enough, Elsner enjoyed pretending he was a Swede, descended from the royal Vasa family which ruled Poland in the sixteenth and seventeenth centuries. Apart from this small conceit the man was a perfectly worthy individual. Since he had been trained primarily as a violinist, Elsner taught Chopin more about theory and composition than piano technique. This may have been just as well since it left the boy free to develop his own unique style of playing.

Scarcely a year after Fryderyk began his studies with Elsner he appeared in public again at another of the Warsaw Charitable Society's benefit concerts. By coincidence it too was on a February 24. This time Mme. Zamoyska and Niemcewicz (who was still president of the society) left the organization of the concert to Józef Jawurek, a professor at the Musical School and conductor of its orchestra. The Chopins had known Jawurek for many years and were often invited to his home for evening musicales. Like Elsner, Jawurek composed a number of long-forgotten orchestral and vocal works. However, for the program he was to conduct in February of 1823, he selected works of others, including overtures by Mozart and Paër, a concerto by Crémont, excerpts from Haydn's *The Four Seasons*, and a septet by an unspecified composer. The piece Chopin played for the occasion was a piano concerto by Ferdinand Ries, a German pianist and composer who once studied with Beethoven.

By 1823 the Charitable Society had already been lodged in permanent headquarters of its own on the Krakowskie Przedmieście for nearly four years. These new accommodations, only a few doors north of the Radziwiłł Palace, were in a building that had belonged to the Zamoyski family since 1732. From 1801 to 1805 the exiled Louis XVIII of France found refuge there through the kindness of his aunt, Ludwika Zamoyska, the daughter of Louis XV and Maria Leszczyńska. Later, a group of Carmelite nuns occupied the premises until 1819 when the government suppressed their order and forced them to leave. At that point Countess Zamoyska turned over the building to the Charitable Society, and in 1822 a portion of it was converted into a small concert hall.

In the opinion of the *Kuryer dla Płci Pięknej* (Courier for the Fair Sex), Jawurek's concert on February 24 was more outstanding than the society's earlier ones that season.[5] Chopin's talent, it noted, "aroused everyone's admiration . . . . We can confidently say that we have not heard a virtuoso to date in our capital who could overcome such astonishing difficulties with so much ease and accuracy or render the incomparable beauty of the Adagio with equal feeling and precision."[6] In closing, the critic compared Chopin with Liszt, who was then creating a sensation in Vienna. "Our capital possesses his equal, if not his superior in the person of . . . young Chopin," he contended proudly.

For the time being that was praise enough to satisfy the twelve-year-old Fryderyk. But the day was soon coming when he too would long to create a sensation in Vienna.[7]

Over the next two years Chopin continued to study with Elsner. There was no doubt that he possessed incredible talent, but so far no decision had been made as to his future. Except for his music lessons the boy lacked any formal education. His parents and possibly some private tutors were the only teachers he had known.

In the fall of 1823 Nicholas Chopin decided it was time for Fryderyk to enter the Lyceum, where he would be required to study a variety of subjects including history, literature, mathematics, and the natural sciences. Since the Chopins lived in an academic world, surrounded by cultivated friends, they expected their son to be brought up in a manner suitable to such an environment. Little did they suspect that the educational advantages they provided for him then would eventually smooth his way into the polished societies of Paris and London years later.

Fryderyk's entrance into the Lyceum didn't create any drastic change in his life. With his father on the faculty and their apartment full of student boarders, he already knew almost everybody in the school. The Lyceum, in fact, was literally his home since the Chopins lived on the second floor of one of the school buildings.[8]

Around this time Fryderyk began taking lessons on the organ from a member of the Conservatory faculty, Wilhelm Würfel, and during his second year at the Lyceum he became the official school organist. His main love, though, remained the piano, and he continued to write short pieces for it including mazurkas, variations, and a polonaise.

Besides the piano and organ, several new instruments, the aeolopantaleon, the aeolomelodikon, and the choraleon, also occupied Fryderyk's attention in 1825. The first of these, the aeolopantaleon, was invented by a cabinet maker named Długosz, while the other two were the creations of Professor Jacob Fryderyk Hofman, a naturalist who established the University of Warsaw's mineralogy museum and botanical garden (situated just behind the Chopin's apartment). A local manufacturer named Brunner offered to construct these new inventions since his rival, Bucholz, was already turning out similar ones known as the melodikordon, the melodipantaleon, and the orchestrion.

The aeolomelodikon, which attracted particular attention in 1825, was a species of organ with a keyboard and foot pedals. The latter activated a pair of bellows and forced air through metal cylinders into large tin trumpets. According to its promoters, the quality of sound produced by the instrument could fluctuate from the reedy tones of a clarinet to the sharp blast of a brass ensemble, while the volume it generated was enough to drown out a chorus of fifty singers backed up by an orchestra of fifty pieces!

This amazing product of Professor Hofman's ingenuity gained so much notoriety that it aroused the interest of the czar himself. When he visited Warsaw in May of 1825 to open the nation's Diet he expressed a desire to hear the aeolomelodikon. Accordingly, its inventor (who happened to be a good friend of the Chopins) got the fifteen-year-old Fryderyk to demonstrate it for him.

Czar Alexander I was the third member of Russia's Romanov family that the young Chopin played for. Born in 1777, he was an offspring of the Enlightenment and came to the throne in 1801 with a headful of liberal ideas. His victories over Napoleon made him a hero throughout Europe, while his role in creating constitutional governments for France and the so-called "Congress Kingdom of Poland" made him seem a true champion of freedom.[9] However, most of his progressive notions never got beyond the stage of grandiose pronouncements, and he gradually turned into a confused despot, plagued by conflicting aspirations.

Toward the end of his life, when Chopin played for him, the czar had become so immersed in spiritual matters he found little time for affairs of the state. Much of his piety (he helped to found the Russian Bible Society and bore calluses on his knees from hours of prayer) was fueled by the guilt he felt over his father's assassination. He had known about the plot to murder him but did nothing to forestall it. Eventually his troubled conscience led him to seek comfort from holy men of every persuasion. As head of state he was obliged to uphold the doctrines of the Orthodox Church in public, but privately he felt a strong attraction to many of the Protestant sects, especially the Quakers and the Lutherans. This perhaps explains why it was decided to have Chopin play for him in Warsaw's Evangelical Church. More likely, though, it was because the aeolomelodikon had already been installed there by its Protestant inventor.

The Evangelical Church was a circular, Pantheon-like structure, unique in predominantly Roman Catholic Warsaw. Members of the city's German Protestant minority had begun its construction nearly fifty years earlier, and in the interim the church had become one of the capital's favorite tourist attractions because of the spectacular view from the lantern tower on top of its dome. Many of Chopin's friends, including Elsner and the headmaster of the Lyceum, Samuel Linde, belonged to the congregation. Chopin himself had gone there often to hear its choir perform under the direction of Józef Jawurek.

In 1825 the building was still not completely finished, and the lack of any stained glass in its windows allowed shafts of bright yellow sunlight to spill across the immaculate white of its sanctuary. The chaste simplicity of the neoclassical interior provided an atmosphere of religious calm in which Chopin's music made a moving impression on the devout czar. As an expression of his pleasure, Alexander rewarded both the young performer and the instrument's manufacturer, Brunner, with a diamond ring.

Six months later the czar died at Taganrog near the Black Sea. For years rumors circulated that his "death" was, in fact, a fabrication and that the deeply religious autocrat had actually retreated to Siberia where he lived out the rest of his life as a hermit. Today these stories are generally discredited. Nevertheless, when Alexander's coffin was exhumed and opened in 1865 it was found to be empty!

The two other Warsaw-spawned instruments with which Chopin experimented in the spring of 1825 were the aeolopantaleon and the choraleon. Not only did he play them at several private homes around the city, he also gave a public exhibition of the former at a Conservatory concert on May 27 that year.

The aeolopantaleon was something of a musical mule, half-aeolomelodikon and half piano. The choraleon, on the other hand, was a super-organ which could produce "cresendo, decrescendo, forte, piano, staccato, legato, and tremolando." In short, it was able to "express everything." so the advertisements read.[10] One of its virtues was the ability to "ennoble the art of religious singing" with "increased solemnity, dignity, and grandeur."[11] This tempted Elsner to add it to the score of his cantata based on the anthem "God Save the King" which he planned to present at the Conservatory concert that May. Since Chopin was one of the few people familiar with the new instrument it is likely he was elected to perform the choraleon part for Elsner's work.

By 1825 the four-year-old Conservatory was already well established in its quarters just below the royal castle on the Krakowskie Przedmieście. It occupied the former church and cloisters of St. Clara, abandoned since 1819 when the Bernardine sisters were transferred out of Warsaw. To make room for the benches and desks of the new school, the convent's altars had to be moved out and its stone crypt markers ripped up. Departments for piano, voice, woodwinds, brass, and string instruments as well as counterpoint and declamation were set up, and by 1823 the institution had attracted a student body of 164, 56 of whom were female.[12]

The May 27 concert, although held in the Conservatory, was yet another of the Warsaw Charitable Society's affairs. Again it was organized by Józef Jawurek, who conducted the orchestra and chorus. The program, given "with the permission of the authorities"[13] (an accepted fact of life in Russian-run Poland), began at seven o'clock:

1. Overture composed by Józef Nowakowski,
   a student of composition at the Conservatory
2. Concerto for pianoforte [in F minor, the first Allegro]
   composed by Moscheles [played by Chopin]
3. Duet from the opera *Achilles* composed by Paër
   [sung by Mlle. Weinnert and M. Suzurowski]
4. Concerto for violin, first Allegro, composed by Rode
   [played by M. Frankowski]
5. Chorus composed by Beethoven with accompaniment
   provided by the choraleon
6. Rondo Brillante composed by Hummel
   [played by Mlle. Sredulanka]
7. Fantasia on the aeolopantaleon [played by Chopin]
8. Cantata composed by Józef Elsner,
   professor of the university and rector of the Conservatory[14]

Free copies of the texts to Elsner's cantata and the Beethoven chorus were passed out at the door. Altogether 200 people showed up to hear a cast of 140 musicians perform. Among those present was Prince Antoni Radziwiłł, governor of the Grand Duchy of Poznań, who had come to Warsaw for the session of the Diet. He was married to a

Prussian princess and enjoyed enormous wealth and influence. In addition he happened to be a great music lover who played the cello and composed.[15] According to the *Allegemeine Musikalische Zeitung,* he was very complimentary of the concert, especially Elsner's cantata.[16] The great "taste and feeling"[17] with which Chopin played that night must also have been noted by the prince, although it was not until some years later that he expressed any real interest in the boy's talent.

Because the concert as a whole received such an enthusiastic response, the performers were encouraged to repeat their success shortly afterward on June 10.

The second performance (also for the benefit of the Warsaw Charitable Society) was distinguished by the presence of two foreign artists passing through Warsaw that spring: a flutist named Otto Kresner and a singer known only as Mme. Bianchi. The latter, it has been claimed, was Antonia Bianchi, Paganini's volatile mistress, a jealous little spitfire given to smashing her lover's violin cases in her frequent fits of rage. However, this assumption seems untenable in view of the fact that Antonia Bianchi was eight-months pregnant and living with Paganini in Palermo in June 1825. On July 23 of that year she gave birth to their only child, a son named Achille. The Mme. Bianchi touring Warsaw in the spring of 1825 is therefore, more likely to have been Carolina Crespi Bianchi, the wife of Eliodoro Bianchi, a prominent tenor who sang lead roles in several of Rossini's early operas. She and her husband met in Paris where they were both under contract at the Théâtre-Italien. In 1807 they were married and returned to Italy shortly afterward. Later, following the birth of two children, they separated and Mme. Bianchi was forced to resume her vocal career. According to Fétis, she was an attractive woman endowed with "a beauty superior to her talent."[18] By the time of her arrival in Warsaw she would have been in her mid-to-late forties and, as the *Allgemeine Musikalische Zeitung* noted, her voice had already lost its "youthful freshness."[19] Of the two arias she sang on the stage of the Warsaw Conservatory it was only in the second one that she really hit her stride.

From an artistic point of view Herr Kresner's flute variations came off much better. "Still quite a young man," Kresner, a royal chamber musician from the Saxon court in Dresden, was "an excellent flutist" who played with "great dexterity" and a "beautiful tone."[20]

Once more Chopin improvised on the aeolopantaleon and ran through the Allegro from Moscheles' F-minor concerto. In the words of the *Allgemeine Musikalische Zeitung,* he was a "complete master" of the new instrument and displayed extraordinary originality in his improvisations.[21]

With a few exceptions the rest of the concert was similar to the one on May 27.[22]

Since Fryderyk's rare public performances had so far been entirely for charitable purposes, Nicholas and Justyna Chopin had never received any financial benefit from their son's talent. By contrast, Adam Liszt was reaping healthy profits from his offspring's widely advertized concert tours. In March of 1825 he rented the largest auditorium available in Paris, the Opéra itself, so young Franz could play before a crowd of thousands. During the summer of that year, when Fryderyk was sent off to vacation in the country, his Hungarian counterpart was hustled across the English Channel to be ogled by audiences in London and Manchester. Later, while Chopin went sight-seeing around Danzig and Torun, Liszt entertained King George IV at a command performance in Windsor Castle.

That fall when Chopin returned to his last year in the Lyceum, Liszt scurried back to Paris for the rehearsals of his new opera, *Don Sanche,* which was to premiere there on October 17, just five days before his fourteenth birthday. Chopin's musical achievements were scarcely as conspicuous as Liszt's, but his dedication to music was every bit as intense, and sometime during the school year he decided to make it his career. The following September he planned to enroll in the Warsaw Conservatory as a full-time student.

During the winter of 1825–26 he developed painful, swollen glands in his neck which the family physician, Dr. Malcz, treated with the application of leeches. When his younger sister Emilia came down with similar symptoms she received the same treatment. Both children responded nicely, and by spring Fryderyk was well enough to take his final examinations and graduate.

Shortly afterward Emilia took sick again, but this time she got no relief from Dr. Malcz's leeches. In July the family decided to take her (as well as Fryderyk, who still looked pale from his winter's illness) to Bad Reinerz, a popular health resort in Prussian Silesia just north of the Bohemian border.[23] The mineral water there had a high iron content which was reputed to cure a multitude of ailments. Elsner had gone to the spa for a rest in 1818 and recommended it, as did Chopin's godfather, Count Fryderyk Skarbek, who was spending some time there that very summer. Because of the expense of the trip Nicholas Chopin felt compelled to remain in Warsaw with Izabela while he sent the seventeen-year-old Ludwika along with her mother to help care for the other two children.

Reinerz was a small town nestled among low, wooded mountains on the floor of the narrow Bystrzyca River valley. Its snug setting was deceptive since the river valley actually lay at an altitude of over 1,700 feet. This, in the minds of the local inhabitants, was the reason for the healthfulness of its clear, crisp air.

The town had a long history going back many centuries. In the 1500s it flourished as a center of iron mining. Then in 1605 a paper mill, built along the river, became the economic mainstay of the community until the middle of the eighteenth century, when the area's spring water was analyzed and found to have "medicinal" properties. After that Reinerz's reputation as a spa blossomed rapidly. Soon a cluster of pavilions, inns, and bathhouses sprouted up around the springs, a kilometer or so up the valley from the once-quiet village. For those who flocked to the new resort a "cure" evolved, similar to those popular in the neighboring Swiss and Carpathian spas. This consisted of a combination of waters from the warm and cold springs[24] taken in conjunction with large quantities of sheep's or goat's milk whey.

In 1821 an uncle of Felix Mendelssohn opened up several foundries in Bad Reinerz but soon converted them into bathhouses to accommodate the increasing numbers of sick and infirm that poured into the village each year. When the fourteen-year-old Felix came for a visit in 1823, he gave a concert for wounded veterans of the Napoleonic Wars in the spa's new theater (or Kursaal) built along the banks of the river the year before. Besides being used for plays and concerts, it served as a "strolling hall" or assembly room where visitors gathered to mill about and chat while sipping the curative waters. In the evening it became a scene of merriment with music and dancing for those sound enough to disport themselves in such a lively fashion.

On the third of August the four Chopins arrived at Bad Reinerz, one of 314 families to come to the bustling resort that summer.[25] Accustomed to the Mazovian plains around Warsaw, they were overwhelmed by the beauty of Lower Silesia's mountainous terrain. At the foot of one of its scenic slopes they found a modest guest house just across the river from the new theater. It was owned by a Herr Bürgel, who rented them several rooms in which they lived for the next five weeks.[26]

During that time the family followed the daily routine recommended for ailing visitors. At six o'clock in the morning a noisy fanfare by one of the local bands inaugurated the day's activities and set the spa in motion. For the Chopins this meant getting up and walking to the Summer Spring, which was housed in a pleasant octagonal pavilion with Doric columns. Although it was very near Herr Bürgel's house it was often difficult to reach. The park surrounding the pump room was usually muddy on the best of days and turned into a veritable lake whenever it rained. For ladies in large, billowy skirts this presented grave—sometimes insurmountable—problems. Those who succeeded in navigating the treacherous approach were rewarded by further discordant blasts from another band inside the pavilion.

At the spring the Chopins filled up their glasses and joined the ritual parade of cure seekers meandering around the premises. A carnival-like atmosphere pervaded these early morning assemblies, since it was the fashion for the strollers to wear masks and costumes as they swilled down the waters and peered about at one another's outfits.

After breakfast at eight o'clock Fryderyk liked to explore the wooded trails around the village until lunch, which was followed by a repetition of the masks, costumes, and endless promenading along the tree-lined *allées* between the village and the springs.[27] Throughout the afternoon and evening the bands blared on with relentless jollity. Their steady din tired Chopin, who longed for a piano to break the monotony. He had little luck in finding one, though. "Can you believe, Sir?" he wrote Elsner. "There isn't a single decent piano here. Everyone I've tried so far is more of an aggravation to me than a pleasure."[28]

Surprisingly enough, only a few days after writing this Fryderyk found himself giving two concerts on one of those wretched pianos he had complained about. What prompted him to do this was the death of a fellow visitor to Reinerz, a Bohemian cloth merchant named Josef Čor. He had come to the spa only a short time before with his children, who were now stranded in a strange town far from home. Since this tragedy had occurred the very day of the Chopin's arrival, they could never have known the dead man. Still, it was easy enough for them to sympathize with the plight of his children. Should anything happen to Mme. Chopin, Fryderyk and his sisters would face a similar predicament. To raise money for the orphans' return to relatives in Bohemia, Fryderyk consented to grapple with the dilapidated instrument on the stage of the local theater[29] in two concerts given on August 11 and 16.[30] What he played on these occasions in uncertain. One account claims he performed several études and a funeral march of his own composition,[31] while another states that an "aristocratic Polish lady" sang several songs on the program.[32] The *Kurjer Warszawski,* which received news of the concerts later in the month, merely commented on the "magnificent talent"[33] and laudable generosity of the youthful pianist.

When the Chopins finally returned home it was nearly the middle of September. The trip to Reinerz had been good for Fryderyk. As he told Elsner, "The fresh air and whey have been such a help to me I am a completely different person than before."[34]

• CHAPTER THREE •

VIENNA
1829

FROM THE FALL of 1826 until June of 1829 Fryderyk was a student at the Warsaw Principal Music School, a division of the Conservatory headed by Elsner.[1] There he continued to study with Wilhelm Würfel, who had started giving him organ lessons while he was still at the Lyceum.[2] These lessons soon came to an end, however, when Würfel left Warsaw to become a conductor at the Vienna Opera.

Early in his first year at the Conservatory Chopin got sick again. By spring he didn't seem any better, and his parents thought of taking him back to Bad Reinerz. As it turned out, these plans never materialized. On April 10, 1827, Emilia Chopin died of tuberculosis at the age of fourteen. Not long afterward the bereaved family moved from the Kazimierzowski Palace to an apartment across the street in the Krasiński Palace, where the memory of her death was less vivid. Even then Justyna Chopin never fully recovered from the blow and always dressed in mourning for the rest of her life.

It was in that year marked by illness and death that Chopin composed his scintillating variations on the aria "La ci darem" from Mozart's *Don Giovanni*. Soon this remarkable work was to establish his reputation as a composer all over Europe. On its publication in 1830 Robert Schumann burst out with his celebrated comment: "Hats off, gentlemen—a genius!"[3]

Up to 1827 Fryderyk's world had been one of limited horizons. Outside of his trip to Bad Reinerz and short excursions to Torun and Danzig he had never traveled beyond the boundaries of the little Kingdom of Poland. Then in the summer of 1828 an unexpected offer to visit

Berlin gave him a glimpse into the musical life of one of Europe's largest cities. That September he accompanied Feliks Jarocki, a professor of natural history at the University of Warsaw, to an international congress of naturalists in the Prussian capital. Although Alexander Humboldt was the major attraction of the conference, Chopin ignored him and the other scientists for the chance to attend concerts and operas and to gaze on such musical celebrities as Mendelssohn and Spontini.

Back home that fall he experienced the tremulous sensation of love for the first time. Its object was a young voice student from the Conservatory named Konstancja Gładkowska. Because he was too reticent to express his passion, their "romance" remained little more than an exercise in fantasy.

On his graduation from the Conservatory in the spring of 1829, Chopin was anxious to get out and see more of the world beyond Warsaw. Italy and Paris especially attracted him, but to visit such places required money beyond what his father's limited means could provide. One way of financing such a trip was to apply for a travel grant from the government. Nicholas Chopin's petition for one, however, was curtly refused. Without this help the best he could do was to send his son off to Vienna for a few weeks that summer.

Once in the Austrian capital Fryderyk looked up Würfel, his former organ teacher, who welcomed him warmly and introduced him around the city. In only a matter of days he had met men like Karl Czerny (the pianist and composer who taught Liszt), Graf and Stein (two of the city's foremost piano manufacturers), Tobias Haslinger (a music publisher), J. L. Blahetka (a newspaper critic), and Count Wenzel Robert Gallenberg (the director of one of Vienna's leading theaters).

Chopin was dazzled. So was Vienna. "I don't understand it," he wrote his parents, "but all the Austrians are amazed at me and I am just as amazed at them for being amazed at me."[4] Haslinger wanted to publish his compositions, Graf and Stein lent him pianos, and everyone insisted that he give a concert. Count Gallenberg even volunteered the use of his theater. At first the idea of a concert frightened Chopin. He hadn't touched a piano in weeks and didn't dare appear before the discriminating Viennese without some preparation. To refuse, Würfel told him, would be a disgrace to both his teacher and his family, while Haslinger teased him for being a coward. Eventually their pressure broke down his resistance. "What young artist in his right mind could miss such an opportunity?" he conceded.[5]

In his naïveté Chopin didn't realize that many of his boosters were, in fact, trying to exploit him. Haslinger, for instance, had no intention of paying for his musical scores. He expected the composer to be thankful just to see them in print.[6] Gallenberg's attitude was the same; he was only too glad to have Chopin play in his theater as long as he didn't ask for any share of the proceeds. Similarly, Graf and Stein offered him their pianos more in the hope of getting a little free publicity than out of any real generosity.

When Fryderyk finally chose August 11 as the date of his concert, he had only three days to prepare for it. While he used the precious time to practice, Würfel posted announcements and helped Gallenberg work out the details of the program.

Vienna, which seemed such a wondrous city to a Warsaw youth in 1829, still had in many respects the appearance of a walled town from the Middle Ages. Surrounded by a moat, it was dominated by the spires and domes of its great churches. The Kärnthnerthor Theater where Chopin was to perform had been founded in 1708 as one of the two "imperial and royal" establishments maintained by the Hapsburgs for dramatic and musical productions.[7] It was so named because of its location next to the Kärnthner gate from which a bridge led across the moat to the countryside south of Vienna.[8] The city's court opera originated there and was run for over a century by various impressarios, most of whom were Italian. Besides opera, other musical events also took place there, including the premiere of Beethoven's Ninth Symphony on May 7, 1824.

After Barbaja, the last of the Italian managers, left the Kärnthnerthor in the spring of 1828, the house remained dark until January of 1829 when it came to life again under the direction of Count Gallenberg, a ballet composer of some note. The interests of the new manager were reflected in his selection of the opening number for Chopin's concert: Beethoven's overture to the ballet *The Creatures of Prometheus*. Initially this was to have been followed by Chopin's Rondo à la Krakowiak, but during the first rehearsal the orchestra rebelled at having to learn a new score. Even if they had been willing to try it, the manuscript was so illegibly scribbled out they couldn't have read it. In the end the stage manager suggested that Chopin forget his Rondo and substitute an improvisation. To everyone's relief he agreed.

Since no musical program was complete in those days without at least one assisting artist, Würfel and Gallenberg solicited the help of a singer, Fräulein Charlotte Veltheim. She was reputed to have a "charming, supple, and cultivated voice" as well as a "brilliant style."[9] Apparently she was also a lady of considerable stamina who could sing Agathe in Weber's *Der Freischütz* one night and then appear with Chopin the next.

Unlike so many gargantuan programs of the period, Fryderyk's Viennese debut was unusually short. The whole affair—or "Musical Academy" as the Austrians called such events—was, in effect, no more than the prelude to a comic ballet, *The Masked Ball*, which was the real attraction of the evening.

Starring in the ballet was the nineteen-year-old ballerina Fanny Elssler, whose spectacular feats were probably responsible for drawing most of the audience to the theater that night. She and her sister Therese were special favorites of Count Gallenberg and often appeared on his stage.[10] Fanny, who had not only more talent but a better figure than her sister, made her debut at the Kärnthnerthor Theater in 1818.[11] Subsequently she studied in Italy where her beauty led to a liaison with the prince of Salerno, a brother of the king of Naples. In 1827 she was back in Vienna where she bore the prince a child and soon afterward attracted the attention of Napoléon's son, the duke of Reichstadt.[12] Although their relationship seems to have been purely platonic, it stirred up enough gossip to make Fanny one of Vienna's most titillating celebrities when she shared the following program with Chopin on the evening of Tuesday, August 11, 1829.[13]

Overture from the ballet *Prometheus*
by Herr L. van Beethoven

Variations Brillantes on a theme by Mozart,
composed and played by Herr Friedrich Chopin
Aria from the opera *Bianca e Faliero,* composed by Herr Rossini
and performed by Fräulein C. Veltheim

Free Fantasy on themes from *La Dame Blanche* by Boïeldieu
and the Polish song "Chmiel" by Herr Friedrich Chopin

Rondo with Variations and chorus from the opera *Pietro il Grande,* composed by Herr Vaccaj and performed by Fräulein C. Veltheim

Intermission

The Masked Ball, a comic ballet in two acts

The theater was far from full when Chopin walked on stage shortly after the Beethoven overture.[14] High above him, in the five tiers of balconies that ringed the large hall, were many vacant seats. As the discordant whine of instruments being retuned gave way to the subdued clapping of the meager audience, Chopin sat down at the Graf piano, looking pale and nervous. Next to him was a foppish page turner whose brightly rouged cheeks made his own seem all the more washed out.

Moments later, Chopin's face was flushed with excitement as he listened to the wild applause that greeted the first of his Mozart variations. The uproar was so great he could barely hear the orchestral bridge leading into the second variation. At the end of the piece nothing would quiet the crowd until he came back for a bow.

After Fräulein Veltheim's aria he returned to improvise on a theme from Boïeldieu's recent opera *La Dame Blanche* and aroused such enthusiasm the stage manager sent him back to improvise some more. This time he chose a Polish folk song, "Chmiel" (The Hopvine), which was a favorite at country weddings. When he finished, the entire house was on its feet cheering—even the orchestra members who had been so antagonistic to him the day before.

Elated, Fryderyk could hardly wait to write his parents. "I was overwhelmed with bravos," he exclaimed. "My friends and comrades stationed themselves through the hall to pick up comments from the audience. Celiński[15] can tell you how little criticism there was. The worst remark was one Hube[16] overheard a lady make: 'What a shame the young man doesn't cut a more stylish figure onstage,' she said. If that's the biggest objection I have to put up with, I really can't complain."[17]

Certainly he had no complaint to make about the newspaper reviews which raved over his "delightful artistic accomplishments,"[18] his "effortless executions,"[19] and the "clarity"[20] that pervaded his every phrase. According to *Der Sammler,* he was nothing less than the "brightest meteor on the musical horizon."[21] There was one fault, however, which some people did find with his playing: it was too subdued. "In general," he admitted to his family, "I'm told here I don't play loud enough."[22] In the words of the *Allgemeine Theaterzeitung,* "His touch, though clean and firm, had little of the brilliance which our [Viennese] virtuosos . . . exhibit."[23]

Back in Poland the *Gazeta Warszawska* reported that Chopin had been acclaimed "a second Hummel" in Vienna and that "distinguished personages"[24] had called on him to give another concert there—which is exactly what he did.

Among the "distinguished personages" anxious to hear Fryderyk again was Count Moritz Dietrichstein, an intimate of the emperor. Since it had long been whispered that Dietrichstein was the natural father of Sigismond Thalberg,[25] a fantastic seventeen-year-old pianist and the latest pet of Viennese society, his interest in Chopin may have been motivated by personal considerations.

Another of the prominent individuals who visited him after his concert was Count Moritz Lichnowsky, a brother of Beethoven's patron, Prince Karl Lichnowsky. He invited the young pianist to dinner and urged him to play again in Vienna but on a piano with greater volume. He even offered to lend him his own.[26]

Count Gallenberg also pressed him to give a second performance at the Kärnthnerthor Theater, hoping to make more money on him now that he had excited such notice the first time around. When Fryderyk finally consented, it was less out of deference to these pleas than to public opinion back home. "I wouldn't want them saying in Warsaw, 'What? He gave one concert and then left. Didn't he make a good impression?'"[27]

For his second appearance Chopin was determined to play his Rondo á la Krakowiak, which meant recopying the manuscript so the orchestra could read it. With the concert set for August 18 there was less than a week to do this, and he asked a friend, Napoléon Tomasz Nidecki, to help him. Ironically, Nidecki, also a former pupil of Elsner's, had come to Vienna on one of those government travel grants the Polish Ministry of Education had denied Chopin earlier that spring.

While the new program was similar to the first one in its general outline, Gallenberg made several changes in its content. A young violinist, Joseph Khayll, who played a polonaise by Mayseder, replaced Fräulein Veltheim, while Lindpaintner's overture to *Der Bergkönig* opened the program instead of the one by Beethoven. Again a ballet followed the concert.

To Chopin's delight the audience on August 18 was larger and even more enthusiastic than the earlier one. "If I was well-received the first time," he wrote his parents, "things went still better yesterday. . . . The orchestra was crazy about my Rondo. Everyone from the conductor[28] to the piano tuner thought it was marvelous. Even the ladies loved it."[29] So did Adalbert Gyrowetz. The sixty-six-year-old composer whose concerto Chopin had played in Warsaw eleven years earlier was observed in the audience that night, applauding avidly and shouting loud bravos.

Once more the newspapers were full of favorable comments. Both the *Wiener Zeitschrift für Kunst, Literatur, Theater, und Mode*[30] and the Leipzig *Allgemeine Musikalische Zeitung*[31] called Chopin a pianist "of the highest order," while the *Allgemeine Theaterzeitung*[32] found him unique among contemporary virtuosos because he seemed more concerned about interpreting fine music than just showing off his technique. Some of the critics, however, weren't as impressed with his Rondo as the audience had been. One complained that it lacked "variety" and found its chromatic style "difficult to appreciate."[33] Such remarks, though, hardly diminished the overall success of the evening.

On August 19, the day after his concert, Chopin set out for Poland. Vienna had been a test flight for the fledgling musician, and now that he had felt the strength of his artistic wings he welcomed the chance to rest and recoup his forces. Inevitably Warsaw was bound to seem small and provincial compared with Vienna, but just then he didn't have anywhere else to go. The Austrians had been liberal enough with their acclaim but not with their money, and the funds his father had given him were almost gone.

• CHAPTER FOUR •

WARSAW
1829–1830

ON HIS WAY HOME Chopin stopped in Prague for three days. There he was urged to give a concert but replied that there wasn't enough time to arrange one. The real reason, though, was his fear of getting a bad reception. In Prague not even Paganini had been able to make an impression on the city's exacting public.

From Prague he moved on to Teplice where he donned the white gloves he had carried on stage in Vienna and paid a visit to the castle of the local burgrave, Prince Clary-Aldringen.[1] There he spent the evening improvising on themes from Rossini's *Moses* and *The Barber of Seville* as well as several Polish songs. The young Clary princesses were quite taken by him and begged him to stay, but his coach left at five o'clock the next morning and he couldn't tarry. After a brief rest in Dresden he continued on through Breslau to Warsaw where he arrived on September 12.

Less than a month later he had already grown restless at home and began making plans for another trip. Italy and Paris were again considered as possible destinations. "One thing's for sure," he wrote his friend Tytus Woyciechowski, "I'm not staying in Warsaw. . . . You have no idea how dreary it is here. It it weren't for my family I simply couldn't stand it."[2]

In October he escaped for a few weeks, first to his godmother's estate near Kalisz and then to the nearby hunting lodge of Prince Antoni Radziwiłł, who by now had recognized the young man's genius. Briefly it looked as if Chopin might have found himself a rich patron, but nothing came of it.

Throughout November Chopin remained at loose ends. For lack of anything to do he often wandered in and out of the city's coffee houses, listening halfheartedly to the conversations going on around him. Far stronger than the coffee was the heated talk of revolution that brewed in these meeting places. The new czar, Nicholas I, had proved to be a worse dictator than his brother, Alexander. In Poland his policies were becoming intolerable.

As an antidote to boredom that fall, Chopin started work on a piano concerto.[3] He had never tackled anything of this dimension before and he found it a difficult task. Every day he secluded himself in a quiet little retreat on the top floor of his parents' apartment and labored over it. At night he would attend whatever musical event the city had to offer or go to the homes of friends where conversation and chamber music were the two chief amusements.

The musical season in Warsaw was a far cry from what he had seen in Berlin and Vienna. The Polish capital wasn't part of the established concert circuit in the early nineteenth century, although artists like Paganini, Henrietta Sontag, and Angelica Catalani did make appearances there from time to time. In its remoteness Warsaw lacked the large opera houses, concert halls, and sophisticated audiences of the more cosmopolitan European cities.

One institution in Warsaw that strove to improve its musical life was the Merchants' Club or Resursa, which held regular Saturday concerts. It originated in 1820 to provide "suitable collective recreation and organize gatherings for the presentation of professional matters and current affairs."[4] Among its founders was the versatile Professor Hofman, botanist, mineralogist, and inventor of the aeolomelodikon and choraleon. During the 1820s the club was located in the Zajdler Palace[5] on the city's busy Miodowa Street.

In the fall of 1829 Chopin attended a number of events at the Resursa and may even have played his Mozart Variations there on November 21.[6] The following Sunday evening (November 22) a musical comedy, *The Millionaire Farmer,* written by a German composer, Drechsler, opened in Warsaw. Chopin saw it and thought it abominable. Three days later another operetta, based on the same story and called *The Millionaire Peasant,* premiered at the city's National Theater. Its composer, Józef Damse, was a friend of Chopin, and one of its songs, entitled "Miotełki" or "Brooms," became such a hit that Jan Nowakowski, who sang it during the show's long run, took to making up new lyrics for it with each performance. Chopin liked the tune so much he decided to improvise on it when he was invited to play at the Resursa on Saturday, December 19, 1829.

That same evening he had to double as accompanist to a M. Capello who sang an aria from Paër's *Achilles*. The other singer on the program, M. Dorville, a "French theatrical artist,"[7] performed the aria "Santinel," accompanied by Carlo Soliva, director of the voice and dramatic art section of the Conservatory. A quintet by Beethoven opened the concert. One of its members, Józef Bielawski, first violinist of the Warsaw Opera and a professor at the Conservatory, returned to play a solo number in the second half of the program.

A large crowd was present for the performance which Stanisław Koźmian of the *Kurjer Warszawski* called "one of the most enjoyable events in our capital."[8] Chopin's ingenious improvisations thrilled the audience so much that Koźmian felt obliged to chide him for not sharing his talent more often with his fellow countrymen who took such pride in him. The triumphs of Vienna, however, had made Fryderyk yearn for something more than playing popular tunes in the small auditorium of a businessmen's club.

Like Chopin, the Resursa too aspired to better things. Only the night before he played there, a committee of the club's members met and voted to move from their cramped quarters at the Zajdler Palace into the empty Mniszech Palace on Senatorska Street. Six months later, on July 1, 1830, the doors of the new Resursa were opened for the first time. Since Chopin was to leave Warsaw for good the following November it seems unlikely that he ever played there.

The Christmas festivities of 1829 were the last Chopin spent with his family. He loved the social bustle of the season with its ancient customs and lovely carols,[9] but such holiday distractions made it hard for him to concentrate on his new concerto. The orchestral score in particular gave him trouble, and he couldn't seem to come up with the effect he wanted. Even when he finished it around the end of January, he wasn't sure it was good enough to play in public. To hear how it sounded he rehearsed it with a small orchestra and tried it out on a group of friends at his parents' apartment on Sunday, February 7.

This trial run was intended to be a private affair, but in a small city like Warsaw it made the papers. A critic from the *Gazeta Polska* was there and admired the piece, calling it "beautiful" and full of "new ideas."[10] Still Chopin wasn't happy with it and spent the rest of the month revising the manuscript.

On March 3 he invited an even larger audience to a second rehearsal of the concerto, again in his family's apartment at No. 5 Krakowski Przedmieście. Karol Kurpiński, a director of the Warsaw Opera, conducted the orchestra, and this time the composer was satisfied with the results.[11] At the end of the performance old Żywny sat with tears in his eyes, while Elsner beamed with pride as he listened to the rising murmur of compliments that filled the crowded room. Everyone was ecstatic. In the newspapers Chopin was hailed as the "Paganini of the piano"[12] and his concerto was compared with those of Beethoven.[13]

Fryderyk now felt no need for further rehearsals and began making plans to present his finished work to the general public in the grandest and most important hall in Warsaw, the National Theater on Krasiński Square.

This theater had been established in 1765 by the country's last Polish king, Stanisław Augustus Poniatowski. In keeping with its "national" character, all performances given there were required to be in the Polish language. Later, toward the end of the century, after the partitions of Poland, the theater became a focal point for the preservation of Polish culture and helped hold together a people who were no longer a nation.

The theater's first home was a building called the Operalnia in the Radziwiłł Palace compound. Soon, through funds from the royal purse, a more suitable structure was erected for it on Krasiński Square. Its plain exterior suffered from heavy, almost clumsy proportions, but inside was a graceful oval auditorium surrounded by a three-tiered horseshoe of curtained boxes capped by an open gallery. Rows of benches originally covered the front half of the parterre, although in Chopin's time these may have been replaced by more comfortable seats. Behind them was a large area of standing room. It was on the stage of this theater that the great musicians of the period performed whenever they came to Warsaw. For years Chopin had gone to hear them; now he was about to join their ranks.[14]

"The justifiably admired Mr. Szopę [Chopin], whose excellent talent is comparable to that of the greatest virtuosos, is to give a piano concert shortly in the National Theater, playing works of his own composition," the *Kurjer Warszawski* announced on March 8, 1830.

A week later every ticket had been sold, and on Wednesday, March 17, after a morning rehearsal with the orchestra, Chopin made his professional debut in Warsaw. He was twenty years old—no longer a student or merely a gifted amateur. His career as a concert artist had officially begun, and for the first time in his life he was to receive a share of the house receipts.

Nearly 900 people watched that night as the orchestra members took their seats and began to warm up their instruments. Moments later Karol Kurpiński strode onto the stage and signaled them to attention. With the opening bars to Elsner's opera *King Leshek the White,* the following program began.

1. Overture to *Leszek Biały* Elsner
2. Allegro from the Concerto in F minor Chopin
3. Divertissement for French horn Görner
4. Adagio[15] and Rondo from the Concerto in F minor Chopin
5. Overture to *Cecylja Piaseczyńska* Kurpiński
6. Variations (sung by Mme. Meier) Paër
7. Grand Fantasy on Polish Airs Chopin

When Chopin's Grand Fantasy brought the concert to a close the hall rang with applause, but the loud ovations left the young pianist disappointed. In his mind he had failed to produce the effect hoped for. The audience, he felt, clapped merely out of politeness. The problem, Kurpiński told him, was that his piano didn't project a brilliant enough sound to carry through the theater.[16] Elsner agreed. From where he was sitting the piano's bass register was barely audible and others, in the back of the parterre, claimed there were times when they couldn't hear anything at all.

Luckily the music critics had better seats and extolled the young pianist's performance. The *Pamiętnik dla Płci Pięknej* (Album for the

Fair Sex) described him as having "both a genius for composition" and a "truly masterful technique."[17] "Each stroke of the keys . . . is an expression of the heart."[18] the *Gazeta Warszawska* wrote, while the *Dekameron Polski* hailed him as "a new Mozart."[19] The *Powszechny Dziennik Krajowy* (Daily National Standard) went even further and ranked him not only with Mozart but Bach, Handel, Gluck, Cherubini, and Beethoven as well.[20]

Review after review echoed Warsaw's pride in her native son. One critic, Maurycy Mochnacki of the *Kurjer Polski,* however, complained about the weak tone of Chopin's playing and suggested that he try to muster up a bit more energy in subsequent performances.[21] The *Powszechny Dziennik Krajowy* also noted the softness and delicacy of his style but didn't find them objectionable.[22]

On the whole those who attended the concert were enthusiastic about the young artist and clamored to hear him again. Since Chopin was anxious to redeem himself for what he thought was a poor showing, he readily complied and scheduled another concert to be given on March 22.

The five days between the two concerts were frantic once for Fryderyk, who had to search out new musicians, rehearse program changes, and find a different piano to play on. The instrument he eventually selected was a Viennese one belonging to a Russian general named Diakov. It had more volume than his own piano, which he had used on March 17, but even it was subject to the poor acoustics of the theater, where sounds got swallowed up in the wings of the stage or lost in dead pockets scattered around the orchestra and boxes.

Because he felt his Grand Fantasy on Polish Airs hadn't come across well Chopin decided to replace it with his Rondo à la Krakowiak, also based on Polish themes. The entire program, whether intentional or not, had a definite nationalistic favor. All but one of the works on it were written by Polish composers. Patriotic sentiments were running high in Warsaw that spring as Czar Nicholas continued to tighten his grip on the country. The bloody uprising of November 30 was only eight months away.

The city, however, was peaceful enough on the night of March 22 as the National Theater filled up with a crowd even larger than the one five days before. Except for a repetition of the Concerto in F minor the program was entirely new:

PART I

1. Symphony by Nowakowski
2. Allegro from the Concerto in F minor, composed and played by F. Chopin
3. *Air Varié* by de Bériot,[23] played by Bielawski
4. Adagio and Rondo from the Concerto in F minor, composed and played by F. Chopin.

PART II

1. Rondo à la Krakowiak, composed and played by F. Chopin
2. Aria from *Helena and Malwina* by Soliva, sung by Mme. Meier
3. Improvisations by F. Chopin

After the Rondo à la Krakowiak Chopin's audience called him back onstage four times. Then, in keeping with the growing surge of national ferver, they shouted for him to improvise on some popular Polish songs. The two he chose were "There Are Strange Customs in the Town" and "Cruel World." At their close the crowd rose and cried out for a third concert to be given in Warsaw's Town Hall, which had an even greater seating capacity than the National Theater.

Such enthusiasm was thrilling but it caused Chopin some pangs of conscience. In his final improvisations he had played the showman in order to please his audience. "To tell the truth," he confessed, "that's not how I felt like doing things, but I knew that's what they wanted more than anything else."[24]

Two days later in the *Kurjer Polski* Maurycy Mochnacki castigated Chopin for wasting his time on such improvisations. That sort of thing, he claimed, was best left "to lesser talents."[25] In his opinion the young pianist was better off playing his own compositions, which had all the freshness of improvisations with considerably more polish.

Most other critics, however, were thoroughly delighted with Chopin's performance and acknowledged him to be a genius. He revealed "the touch of a master," the *Kurjer Warszawski* reported.[26] More important to some of his reviewers, he was a *Polish* genius. As one wrote, "Fate has blessed the Poles with M. Chopin just as she gave the Germans Mozart."[27] Comparisons with Mozart were certainly nothing new to Chopin, but such effusive compliments still embarrassed him, and he dismissed them as "utter nonsense."[28]

It was harder, though, to dismiss the many admirers who now smothered him with adulation. A childhood friend, Alexandrine de Moriolles, sent him a laurel wreath which even in 1830 was a rather outmoded piece of headgear. In addition, the music publisher Sennewald wanted to put out a series of engravings with his portrait, and two newspapers printed a poem in his honor.[29]

Later that spring a student from the Conservatory, Antoni Orłowski, came out with a collection of waltzes, mazurkas, and galops based on themes from Chopin's new concerto. The results were of such mediocrity that their intended tribute emerged as a tasteless caricature. "He only did it to make money!" Fryderyk snapped and refused to let him publish them.[30]

By mid-April Chopin had had his fill of hero worship. "I don't want to read anything more about myself or listen to any of the gossip that's going around about me," he announced once and for all.[31]

A third concert in the Town Hall was out of the question. Such a huge auditorium would only accentuate the delicacy of his playing, and he had heard enough criticism of that already. Furthermore his experiences over the past year had made him aware that he wasn't really comfortable in front of large audiences. They intimidated him. "You have no idea what torture I go through three days before having to play in public," he confided to Tytus.[32]

Another reason for his lack of interest in a third concert just then was a new concerto he had started working on that spring. For the time being this was to take precedence over all else.

By the middle of May Chopin had finished the first movement of his second concerto and began to think of trying it out in a preview at home later that month. If all went well he might even play it in public before the season was over.

That year Czar Nicholas was coming to open the Polish Diet in June, and many social and artistic events were planned for his visit. This was to be the first session of the nation's parliament since 1825 when Fryderyk played the aeolomelodikon for the czar's brother, Alexander I. Now he presumed he would be asked to play for the new monarch. If he pleased him sufficiently there was a chance he might still get that government stipend denied him the year before.

When Nicholas arrived in Warsaw ahead of schedule on May 20, Chopin didn't have his new concerto ready. All the same, he prepared himself for a summons from the court—or at least an invitation to participate in one of the numerous concerts being arranged for the czar's entertainment. He waited in vain. As the weeks passed it became apparent that he had been deliberately ignored, and he soon guessed why. "People are astonished that I'm not taking part in any of the festivities," he wrote Tytus, "but to me, it's no mystery at all."[33] Since his return from Vienna he had often been seen with friends like Mochnacki, Zaleski, and Lelewel who were under surveillance by the czar's agents. These young radicals, whose inflammatory discussions he had often heard in the Warsaw coffee houses, were considered dangerous by the Russian government. Not only did Chopin associate with them in public, he was a frequent visitor to their homes, where they aired their discontent even more vehemently. No wonder he was out of favor with the imperial entourage that spring.

The suspicion that he was on the government's "black list" only increased Chopin's dissatisfaction with life in Warsaw. He was now more determined than ever to leave Poland as soon as possible. Since he had already earned 5,000 złotys from his two concerts in March, he could afford to travel on his own without the need of any government assistance. Before he left, though, he was anxious to finish the last two movements of his new concerto, and for the next few months he rarely let anything tear him away from this project.

Toward the end of June Barbara Meier, one of the leading singers at the Warsaw Opera, asked him to appear in a concert with her on July 8. She hadn't been well that spring and hoped to raise enough money from her concert to get away for a rest. At first Chopin was tempted to say no. A few weeks earlier he had already turned down a similar request from a blind flutist, but he couldn't bring himself to refuse Mme.

Meier. Not only was she a close friend of Elsner's wife (who also sang at the Warsaw Opera), she had been kind enough to assist him in his last two concerts.

Since Haslinger had just published his Mozart Variations in Vienna that summer and they were about to appear in the Warsaw music stores, the composer decided to give them a little advance publicity by playing them on Mme. Meier's program.

Unfortunately, few people were to hear his performance. The czar's departure at the end of June left Warsaw exhausted from all the flurry surrounding his state visit. On the Thursday of Mme. Meier's concert the great oval hall of the National Theater contained only a sprinkling of souls. Such a pitiful turnout couldn't have subsidized much of a trip for the ailing singer, who may well have been forced to recuperate at home.

Later in the summer Chopin again interrupted work on his concerto, this time to visit Tytus Woyciechowski, who owned and operated a large farm near Potuszyn. Ever since he first came to live with the Chopins as a student at the Lyceum, Tytus had been an idol to young Fryderyk. Two years his senior, the rugged, good-looking Woyciechowski possessed a keen appreciation of the arts and could even play the piano in a passable fashion. Chopin's affection for him had all the intensity of an adolescent crush—or, as some have suggested, a homosexual attachment. Whatever the case, the fact remains that in the summer of 1830 Chopin still fancied himself so enamored of Konstancja Gładkowska that he cut short his visit with Tytus to rush home for her operatic debut as the lead in Paër's *Agnese*. The rapport which he had finally established with his "ideal" over the past year, however, remained limited. While he was far too timid to make an outright declaration of his love, he did, at least, have the courage to invite her to sing at his next concert in the National Theater—whenever that might be.

For months now Chopin had been unable to set a specific date for this concert which he regarded as his definitive "farewell" to Warsaw. The truth was, he couldn't bring himself to break away from home yet. "If I leave I'm afraid I'll never see this house again," he told Tytus. "I keep thinking I'll die abroad. How awful if that were to happen far from home. How terrifying not to see any familiar faces around my deathbed."[34]

Toward the end of the summer Chopin's new concerto was finished and he had no excuse for delaying his concert any longer. Still, he waited nearly another month before testing it out on friends in two private rehearsals at home. For economy's sake he delegated the orchestral accompaniment to a string quartet. The result didn't suit him, so on Wednesday, September 22, he held a third rehearsal with a full orchestra. Only a few hours before it began he wrote Tytus nervously, "My second concerto . . . is so original I'm afraid I'll never learn to play it right."[35]

That evening, to his surprise, everything went smoothly. "A large gathering of artists and music lovers . . . received the work with great pleasure," the *Kurjer Warszawski* related.[36] "Its originality and graceful conception, its abundance of imaginative ideas, its perfect orchestration, and last but not least, its masterful execution delighted the audience." In short, the concerto was nothing less than "a work of genius," the *Powszechny Dziennik Krajowy* asserted.[37]

Such encouraging remarks led Chopin to choose October 11 as the date for his long-deferred concert. Konstancja Gładkowska was naturally among the first to hear about it since she had promised to be on the program. One of her classmates, another voice student, Anna Wołkow, was also asked to perform, and their professor, Carlo Soliva, agreed to conduct the orchestra. From past experience Chopin had discovered the type of piano best suited to the acoustical peculiarities of the National Theater and again chose a Viennese one made by Streicher.

On the Monday evening of the concert every seat in the house appeared to be taken as Chopin waited tensely backstage for the following program to begin.[38]

1. Symphony by Görner
2. Concerto in E minor, Allegro
   composed and played by Chopin
3. Aria with chorus by Soliva, sung by Mlle. Wołkow
4. Concerto in E minor, Adagio and Rondo,
   composed and played by Chopin

INTERMISSION

5. Overture from *William Tell* by Rossini
6. Aria by Rossini, sung by Mlle. Gładkowska
7. Grand Fantasy on Polish Airs,
   composed and played by Chopin

At the end of the Allegro from Chopin's concerto the house broke out in "a storm of deafening bravos."[39] Mlle. Wołkow, "dressed in blue like a darling little angel,"[40] then sang her aria, after which Chopin returned to play the last two movements of his concerto. As he rose to take his bows a crowd of well-wishers thronged the stage to congratulate him.

During the second half of the program he fidgeted impatiently until it came time for Konstancja's aria. Following the applause for the *William Tell* overture she stepped forward, "dressed entirely in white with a crown of roses" on her brow,[41] and sang the cavatina from Rossini's *La Donna del Lago*.[42] Once more the auditorium swelled with applause. In its wake a delirious Chopin led his young "ideal" triumphantly offstage.

A moment later he was back at the piano to finish the program with his Grand Fantasy on Polish Airs. Afterward the crowd cheered wildly and called him back four times. "For once," he told Tytus, "I knew what I was doing, the orchestra knew what it was doing, and the audience understood it all. . . . There wasn't a single 'Boo.'. . . It was the first time I ever played so effortlessly with an orchestra."[43]

The *Kurjer Warszawski* labeled Chopin's new concerto "sublime" but offered no comment on his playing.[44] The city's other papers maintained a strange silence. Perhaps this was due to pressure from the government, which now counted Chopin among those seditious youths who opposed its policies. Throughout the country swiftly mounting tensions were causing Russian authority to be challenged more and more openly each day. Warsaw may have given the czar a warm reception in June, but the nation was now moving headlong toward a confrontation with its political masters.

• CHAPTER FIVE •

Breslau, Vienna, and Munich 1830–1831

THE DAY AFTER his concert Chopin wrote Tytus of his preparations to leave for Vienna. A week earlier he had bought a trunk, laid out his clothes, and bound up the manuscripts he wanted to take with him. "All that's left," he said, "is to say good-bye and that's the hardest part."[1] The pain of separating from his loved ones was lessened by the pleasure of traveling with Tytus, who planned to meet him in Kalisz and accompany him to Vienna.

Even so, the anguish of departure was so great, Chopin dragged out his farewells for a full three weeks. Only toward the end of this period did he find the courage to tell Konstancja good-bye. When he did she responded with a short verse for his album. It closed with these lines: "Strangers may give you louder praise and greater accolades / But one thing is certain: they can never love you more than we do."[2]

The young girl's expressions of "love" were, in reality, nothing more than the conventional rhetoric of the period. She admired Chopin but was not at all "in love" with him and hadn't the vaguest idea of the secret emotions which tormented him.[3]

On Monday, November 1, a large farewell dinner was given in Chopin's honor. It took place on the eve of his departure, and what might have been a long-faced affair turned into a boisterous celebration with singing and dancing that lasted late into the night.

The next morning Fryderyk was finally forced to face the moment he had dreaded for so long. After the inevitable tears and embraces he climbed into the coach and set off toward Kalisz.

The last farewell, however, wasn't over yet. As his carriage pulled into one of the western suburbs of Warsaw a crowd of young men flocked around it and burst into song. They were Conservatory students whom Elsner had assembled to perform one of his cantatas, written as a special tribute to his departing pupil. Once more there were tears and sad embraces.

Some 150 miles later, in the town of Kalisz, Tytus boarded the coach and the two friends traveled on to Breslau where they arrived around six o'clock on the evening of November 6. For Chopin, who had been there twice before (on his trips to Bad Reinerz and, later, Vienna), the Silesian capital on the banks of the Oder River was a familiar sight. Like Vienna it was ringed by a system of moats linked to the river. It too still preserved a medieval appearance, especially in its central square, where the Gothic town hall was surrounded by houses with colorful facades and high-peaked gables similar to those in Warsaw's old marketplace. For years the city had been under Prussian control, although it once belonged to Poland and a large Polish population still lived there.[4]

Through Elsner, who was a native of Silesia, Chopin had a number of contacts in Breslau. It wasn't until his second day there, however, that he got around to looking anyone up. On the night of his arrival he and Tytus settled into the Golden Goose Inn and immediately rushed off to the theater to see Raimund's comedy *The Alpine King*.[5]

On the following morning, which happened to be a Sunday, they went to the cathedral, hoping to find the kapellmeister, Josef Ignaz Schnabel. He was an old friend and colleague of Elsner. Some fifty years earlier the two of them had studied together in Breslau and later served as violinists at the local theater until Elsner's departure for Vienna in 1789. Afterward Schnabel became director of the city's orchestra and devoted much of his time to composing—mostly ecclesiastical works. Each year during the musical season he conducted three programs a week. On the Sunday Chopin looked him up, the old kapellmeister insisted that he come to a rehearsal for one of these concerts the next morning.

In the meantime he and Tytus passed the rest of the day exploring the sights of Breslau. That night they returned to the theater for a production of Auber's *The Mason and the Locksmith*. Like *The Alpine King* the evening before, it was a mediocre performance.

So far Chopin didn't have a very good impression of musical standards in the Silesian capital. All the same, he hurried off Monday morning to meet Schnabel and see what his orchestra was like. The rehearsal took place in the city's Resursa, a rather small but handsome neo-classical building on what is known today as Theater Square. Inside he found "a small group gathered there . . . including the members of the orchestra and the soloist, a certain amateur pianist named Hellwig who had been practicing Moscheles' Concerto in E-flat major."[6]

When Schnabel saw Chopin come into the hall he interrupted Herr Hellwig to let his guest try out the piano. It had been over a year since he had last heard Chopin play, and he was staggered by the incredible virtuosity with which the young man now dashed off a series of variations for him. So was the wide-mouthed Herr Hellwig, who felt so intimidated by Chopin's amazing talent that he fled from the room and refused to play at the concert that night.

This unexpected turn of events created a crisis for Schnabel, who now begged Chopin to take over as soloist. After a few moments' hesitation he accepted. How else could he make amends for the awkward situation he had inadvertently caused? Back at the Golden Goose he retrieved a copy of his new concerto and hastily read over the last two movements of it with the orchestra. To his dismay nobody seemed impressed by it. In fact, Tytus overheard one of the musicians comment that the young Pole didn't have much of a knack for composing even though he was a wizard of a pianist. This lack of enthusiasm eventually led Chopin to play only the final Rondo of the work. In lieu of the deleted movements he offered an improvisation on a theme from Auber's *La Muette de Portici*.

As for the timorous Herr Hellwig who was to have been the main attraction on the program, Schnabel coaxed him back on stage by letting him show off his skills as a singer rather than a pianist. His rendition of Figaro's aria from Rossini's *Barber of Seville,* however, proved to be so atrocious, Chopin didn't even bother to commend the poor man for his singular versatility.

The concert closed with an overture by the orchestra, after which a supper and a dance followed. Schnabel tried to talk Fryderyk and Tytus into staying, but they took only a bit of bouillon and went back to their hotel around nine o'clock.

From the few remarks Chopin heard at the end of the concert he knew he hadn't scored a tremendous success with his Prussian audience. "Except for Schnabel, who was obviously delighted and who kept hugging me and chucking me under the chin, none of the Germans knew what to say," he wrote his family. "Tytus got quite a kick out of watching their reactions. They were clearly astonished but didn't dare show it since I wasn't anyone famous. They couldn't make up their minds whether my composition was good or not."[7] As in Warsaw and Vienna he again heard criticisms of his "light touch."[8]

The coolness of his reception in Breslau left Chopin rather miffed. "They're a dreadful bunch, these Germans here," he complained.[9]

Seven months later, while in Vienna, he received word that Schnabel had died on June 16, 1831. In gratitude for his many years of service to the musical life of Breslau the kindly old kapellmeister was honored by the performance of no less than six requiem masses.[10]

The trip from Breslau to Vienna took nearly two weeks. After three days on the road, Fryderyk and Tytus reached Dresden, the capital of Saxony. Here as in Breslau there were many Poles, since the electors of Saxony had ruled as kings of Poland for much of the eighteenth century.

Briefly he thought of giving a concert there, but all the theaters were booked and he refused to wait for an opening. "I have no time to waste in Dresden," he commented curtly.[11]

From Dresden Chopin and Tytus moved on to Prague where they stayed for several days. Finally, at nine o'clock on Tuesday morning, November 23, they arrived in Vienna. For the first few days there they took rooms at the City of London Hotel in the Fleischmarkt until they found cheaper accommodations in the Golden Lamb Hotel near the Prater. Even the latter proved beyond their means, and shortly afterward they settled into lodgings on the third floor of a building in the Kohlmarkt near the center of town.[12] Here, for only a small sum, they had a three-room apartment "furnished in an attractive, elegant, even sumptuous manner."[13] To add to their luxury Konrad Graf sent over one of his pianos, recalling how much Chopin had admired them the year before.

As it turned out, Graf was one of the few people in Vienna who still remembered the young Polish virtuoso. In the fifteen months he had been away Chopin found his former triumphs all but forgotten, and it looked as if he would have to rebuild his reputation there from scratch.

The blow of this setback was soon reduced to insignificance by catastrophic events which took place in Warsaw on November 29. That night, students from the Cadet School (where Chopin's father once taught) attacked the Belvedere Palace in an attempt to capture the Grand Duke Constantine and overthrow the government. Fryderyk knew many of those involved and sympathized with their cause, but the brashness of their action frightened him. Their valor was no match for the military might of the Russians.

While he fretted over the situation, Tytus dashed back to Warsaw to join the insurgents. Later Chopin raced after him but the chase was futile. He had waited too long to catch up. Shortly afterward his parents wrote, urging him not to come home. He didn't have the strength for physical combat and could be of little value as a soldier. In the long run, they argued, he was more apt to bring glory to his country by staying where he was and cultivating his talent in the safety of Vienna.

Their advice was sensible but Chopin, by then, was so confused and distraught he no longer enjoyed Vienna. Each day he grew more and more discontented there. Wherever he went he heard disparaging remarks about Poland. Most of the Austrians made no secret of their support for the Russians. One day in a coffeehouse he overheard someone comment that the good Lord made a colossal blunder in ever creating the Poles to begin with.

In this hostile environment Chopin gave up any thought of a concert for the time being. Instead he distracted himself with a host of petty diversions. By day he took German lessons, sat for his portrait, lunched with friends, and strolled around the city. In the evening he attended concerts, dinners, and soirées. Back home at night, though, he couldn't escape his loneliness and often sat for hours improvising at the piano. Occasionally he jotted down his musical ideas, only to tuck them away in his trunks for some future publication. Since Haslinger still refused to pay him anything for his works, he planned to wait and sell them elsewhere. "From now on," he resolved, "I'm through working for nothing!"[14] The only thing he published on this trip to Vienna was his Introduction and Polonaise Brillante for piano and cello, opus 3, which he sold to Mechetti in 1831. It was dedicated to Josef Merk, first cellist of the Vienna Opera, a professor at the city's Conservatory, and one of the finest musicians Chopin had ever known.

No matter how busy he kept himself Fryderyk was still unhappy in Vienna. As Christmas passed and the New Year arrived he grew even more dejected. He had come to Vienna to further his musical career, but so far the trip had been nothing but a waste of time. The new director of the Kärnthnerthor Theater, Herr Duport, offered to let him play there again, but—like Count Gallenberg—without any percentage of the take. Chopin declined.

Few other offers came his way. There were just too many pianists in Vienna then. Besides, tastes were changing and in 1830 all the Viennese wanted to hear were waltzes by Strauss and Lanner. Nobody seemed to care about "serious" music anymore.

At last in April 1831 Chopin finally got a chance to play on a program given by a singer, Mme. Garcia-Vestris. Although her reputation wasn't great she had sung at the Théâtre-Italien in Paris and now hoped to fill up Vienna's stately Redoutensaal next to the famous Spanish Riding School.[15] This grand hall in the Hapsburgs' sprawling palace compound, the Hofburg, was designed primarily for social events like court receptions and fancy dress balls. Fifteen years earlier, during the Congress of Vienna, it had swarmed with ministers and monarchs in some of the most glittering festivities ever witnessed in all of Europe. On March 29, 1828, Paganini made his Viennese debut there. Now three years later it was still in such demand for concerts and fashionable assemblies (*Redouten* in German) that it had to be booked well in advance.

The time chosen by Mme. Garcia-Vestris for her concert was noon, April 4, the Monday after Easter. To assist her she brought together a collection of nine supporting artists, among them "Herr Chopin" who played portions of his E minor concerto as an unaccompanied piano solo. He was probably recommended to Mme. Garcia-Vestris by some of the other musicians on the program. Josef Merk, for example, and the horn-playing Lewy brothers, Josef and Edward, were acquaintances of his with whom he liked to perform chamber music while in Vienna.

Of the singers, at least two, Sabine Heinefetter and Franz Wild,[16] were also known to Chopin. He had heard them often and considered them the mainstays of the Vienna Opera. The third singer that day was Sabine's younger sister, Klara. Exceptionally gifted but emotionally unstable, both sisters eventually ended their days in the grim confines of a nineteenth-century "lunatic asylum."[17] The other performers that afternoon were two professors of violin at the Vienna Conservatory, Josef Böhm and his pupil Georg Hellmesberger.

Attendance at the concert was poor, and one almost wonders if the stage may not have been more crowded than the hall itself. Certainly the event did little to raise Chopin's spirits or increase his reputation in Vienna.

Not even the warm breezes of May or the soft veil of green which soon covered the slopes of the Danube could cheer Chopin up that spring. In Warsaw the struggle against the Russians continued. Why didn't he go back to help? "Why can't I at least serve as a drummer boy?" he cried bitterly.[18]

As much as he tortured himself with such thoughts he still lingered on, hoping to repeat the successes of his first visit. His hopes were encouraged by one of his Viennese friends, Dr. Johann Malfatti, a dedicated music lover whose Polish wife delighted Chopin with her Polish cooking and her Polish chatter. The doctor had once taken care of Beethoven and was now physician to the imperial family. Through connections in the Hofburg he tried to get Fryderyk an invitation to play at court. However, the death of the king of Naples, a first cousin and onetime brother-in-law of the Austrian emperor, imposed a period of mourning on the Hapsburgs and thwarted his efforts.

Toward the end of spring it was clear to Chopin that he had no future in Vienna. He was anxious to leave but two things held him up. First of all, he had spent most of the money from his Warsaw concerts, and second, the precarious political situation in Europe then made travel anywhere a risky business. With Warsaw still under siege it was foolish to return there, while trouble in Italy put an end to any thoughts of visiting the peninsular states. In France conditions were still unsettled from the previous year's "July revolution." Nevertheless many Poles, found Paris a friendly haven and had even established a government in exile there. This alarmed the czar who, as king of Poland, prohibited any further emigration of his Polish subjects to France.

By June the idea of getting out of Vienna had become such an obsession with Chopin that he showed little interest when another opportunity to play in public came his way. "The concert I'm supposed to be in the day after tomorrow . . . might as well not take place at all as far as I'm concerned," he commented indifferently.[19] What he was referring to was a benefit concert in the Kärnthnerthor Theater on June 11 for Dominique Mattis, one of the lead dancers in the imperial corps de ballet.

As might be expected the principal fare of the evening was a ballet, with Chopin and a male quartet serving merely as an appetizer to this musical feast. Two members of the quartet were twenty-year-old medical students who went on to make significant careers for themselves in music. The bass, Josef Staudigel, created the role of Elijah in Mendelssohn's oratorio fifteen years later, while the tenor, Josef Alois Tichatschek, was chosen by Wagner to sing in the premieres of two of his early operas, *Rienzi* (1841) and *Tannhäuser* (1845).[20]

Since an orchestra was available for the concert Chopin decided to repeat his E minor concerto which he had played as a piano solo that April in the Redoutensaal. Below is a reconstructed version of the program:

1. C. M. von Weber: Overture to the opera *Euryanthe*.
2. Fr. Chopin: Concerto in E minor.
   First part played by the composer with orchestral accompaniment.
3. Vocal quartet sung by MM. Staudigel, Emminger,
   Ruprecht, and Tichatschek.
4. Fr. Chopin: Concerto in E minor. Romance and Rondo played by
   the composer with orchestral accompaniment.

[Intermission]

5. Count Wenceslas de Gallenberg: Ballet, *Theodosia,*
   with the participation of Mlle. Fanny Elssler and her two sisters.

The ballet which climaxed the program had never been given before. It was written by Count Gallenberg specially for Fanny Elssler with subsidiary roles for her younger sisters, Therese and Anna. As the ballet's suffering heroine, Fanny was said to have "reached the height of tragedy."[21] Unfortunately the composer wasn't able to see her moving performance since he had been forced to leave Vienna because of financial lossses incurred through his management of the Kärnthnerthor. In 1831 he and his lovely wife, Giulia Guicciardi (to whom Beethoven dedicated his *Moonlight* Sonata), were living in Italy. No doubt the countess welcomed this move which finally broke up the liaison between her husband and Therese Elssler. As for Therese, she soon forgot her Austrian count and fell in love with a Prussian prince who eventually made her his morganatic wife.

In spite of all their beauty and talent the Elssler sisters had little luck in drawing a crowd to the Kärnthnerthor Theater on a warm June evening when most Viennese preferred to be off in the country dancing and sipping May wine in the hillside villages surrounding the city. The house receipts failed to cover the expenses, and none of the performers were paid. Even the "beneficiary," Herr Mattis, had to go home with his pockets empty.

Although the *Allgemeine Theaterzeitung* found Chopin's concerto full of "depth and originality" and complimented the "technical skill" and "expressive style" of his performance,[22] Fryderyk was far from pleased. His return to Vienna had been a mistake and he felt a failure. "My only desire is to fulfill your expectations," he wrote his family, "and up to now I haven't been able to do that."[23] If he ever hoped to, he had to get out of Vienna. But that required money which he didn't have and was too embarrassed to ask for. Instead he instructed his parents to sell the diamond ring which Czar Alexander had given him. The recent events in Warsaw now made it a symbol of Russian oppression, and he no longer valued it.

By the end of June a wave of cholera which began in India had swept westward across Russia and Poland into Austria. To get out of Vienna now Chopin needed not only a passport but a health certificate as well. With Dr. Malfatti's help the latter was no problem, but getting a passport was another matter. As Chopin suspected, the Russian authorities wouldn't let him go to Paris. For the moment he settled on Munich as an alternative and left his passport at the police station for validation. When he returned to pick it up he was told it had been lost and he would have to apply for a new one. This time he asked to have his destination changed from Munich to London, which would take him through Paris en route. Then at the suggestion of friends he got the French ambassador to sign his new passport, hoping this would influence officials in Paris to let him stay there despite Russian prohibitions.

While these preparations were going on, Chopin waited impatiently for the money from the sale of his ring in Warsaw. When he finally had all his travel documents in hand he was so anxious to leave he asked his father to forward the money to him in Munich. In the meantime he borrowed 450 Rhineland florins from a Viennese banker named Stein.[24] Then just as he was ready to go, his traveling companion, Norbert Alfons Kumelski, a young naturalist from Warsaw, got sick.

Eventually, on July 20, the two men set out for Munich. There they were held up again because the money from Chopin's father still hadn't arrived. To pass the time until it came Fryderyk cast about the city in search of its musical life. Among the musicians he ran into were Felix Mendelssohn and Josef Hartmann Stunz. Like himself, Mendelssohn was merely a visitor in the Bavarian capital, while Stunz, a thirty-eight-year-old Swiss composer and conductor, had been directing the city's Royal Opera since 1825. He was a former pupil of Salieri in Vienna and a very competent musician. However, the slow, plodding pace of his conducting made him unpopular in Munich where the public perferred a livelier beat to its music.

In 1831 Stunz also led the local Philharmonic in weekly concerts every Sunday at noon. These were held in the Odeon, a splendid new hall built three years earlier in one of the city's most exclusive districts. It faced on the Hofgarten just north of the royal Residenz and had entrances on both Odeons Platz and Wittelsbacher Platz. Its main floor contained several elegant "saloons" of various sizes. The largest of these (where the Philharmonic played) was a striking auditorium "in pure Grecian style, having a double row of pillars opposite each other."[25] Between them ran a long gallery with "an oval ending for the orchestra, adorned with busts of the celebrated composers."[26] Overhead was an ornate ceiling with three large frescoes portraying scenes from the life of Apollo.[27]

While Chopin was in Munich Stunz invited him to play at one of these Sunday concerts. Because it was late summer and many people were out of town, the concert may not have been given in the "grand saloon" described above. The fact that one of the newspapers[28] directed concertgoers to the Odeon's secondary entrance on Wittelsbacher Platz suggests that a smaller room was used for the performance—perhaps one of those on the second floor, later occupied by the city's Conservatory. It is even possible the Philharmonic members themselves were away on vacation then since the only available review fails to mention the presence of an orchestra.

As he had done at his last two concerts in Vienna, Chopin again played his E minor concerto. Stunz, who was a proficient pianist (he always conducted the Philharmonic from a piano at the center of the stage), could well have supplied the orchestral portion of the concerto on a second piano.

In any event the music critic for *Flora: A Journal of Entertainment* was impressed with Chopin's "outstanding virtuosity" and the "lovely delicacy" of his playing.[29]

Other artists on the program that day included a Herr Bayer who sang a Schubert cavatina with piano and clarinet accompaniment. The clarinetist was a twenty-year-old virtuoso named Heinrich Bärmann for whom *Flora*'s reporter predicted a great future. Unfortunately the young man's career was cut short by his early death twelve years later. A vocal quartet, written by Stunz and sung by Herr Bayer along with a Mme. Pelligrini and two other gentlemen named Lenz and Harm, completed the midday program.

Shortly after the concert the money from Chopin's father arrived and he was able to head on toward Paris. Luckily he was traveling away from the cholera epidemic which by then had wreaked havoc in Austria and was beginning to creep across the Bavarian border. In the previous month 60,000 people had fled Vienna. Most took refuge in the mountains of Switzerland and the Tyrol, while the Austrian court secluded itself in Schönbrunn Palace behind boarded windows. Businesses were closed and infected houses burned to the ground. Everywhere the smell of smoke was mingled with the stench of decaying bodies. Many of the sick developed tetanus which left them in a *rigor mortis*-like state resembling death and caused them to be swept into living graves.

All this, however, lay far behind Chopin as he and Kumelski wound their way through the cool Bavarian forests into the neighboring kingdom of Württemberg early that September.

CONSERVATORY, WARSAW

JOSEF ALOIS TICHATSCHEK

FRYDERYK FRANCISZEK CHOPIN

CZAR ALEXANDER I

NATIONAL THEATER ON KRASIŃSKI SQUARE, WARSAW

PROTESTANT CHURCH, WARSAW

KÄRNTHNERTHOR THEATER, VIENNA

DOMINIQUE MATTIS

JOSEF STAUDIGEL

JOSEF MERK

KURSAAL, BAD REINERZ

RESURSA, BRESLAU

THE PHILHARMONIC SOCIETY'S HALL, MUNICH
(WITTELSBACHER PLATZ ENTRANCE)

PRINCE DE LA MOSKOWA

ERMINIA TOMÉONI

FRANÇOIS JOSEPH FÉTIS

CONSERVATORY, PARIS

SALLE DES CONCERTS,
PARIS CONSERVATORY

• CHAPTER SIX •

PARIS
1831–1832

TOWARD THE END of the first week in September the travelers from Munich stopped for a few days in Stuttgart, the capital of Württemberg. There they learned that Warsaw had finally fallen to the Russian troops of Field Marshal Paskevich after nine months of bitter fighting. Prince Adam Czartoryski tried to bring a peaceful resolution to the uprising, but extremists ignored his pleas for a compromise. In desperation he sought help from France, England, and Austria but was rebuffed by all three.[1] Without external aid the insurrection was doomed, and by the summer's end Russia had again trampled her western neighbor into submission.

When Chopin heard the news his nerves snapped and he became hysterical. In his feverish imagination he pictured his loved ones destitute, maimed, and starving. Why had he done nothing to stop this? Why did others have to die while he sat idly by? Frantically he poured out his anguish onto the pages of his journal.[2] In a torrent of chaotic scribblings, he cursed the Russians, accused God of being a Muscovite, and railed against the French for not going to the defense of the Poles.[3]

While Warsaw suffered badly during this period, it was far from the scene of utter annihilation that Chopin feared. Both his family and Konstancja survived without physical harm. Prince Czartoryski escaped and took refuge in Paris. Many less fortunate patriots, though, found themselves packed off to Siberia, while those who remained in Poland were faced with privations and had to endure countless indignities. For his victory over the Poles, Paskevich was honored with the title of prince of Warsaw and given virtual control of the nation. His rule was one of harsh repression. He suspended the Polish constitution, closed all the universities (including the Warsaw Conservatory), and confiscated the property of anyone associated with the uprising.

When Chopin recovered from the shock of this news he realized there could be no turning back now and booked himself on the next stagecoach to Paris. From that point on he was alone since Kumelski had left him to go to Berlin. He was alone, that is, except for the thirteen or fourteen other passengers crammed into the big lumbering vehicle that rattled slowly westward out of Stuttgart. Some miles beyond, at the French border, the diligence was stopped by gendarmes whose duty it was to seize any goods that might be contaminated by the cholera. From there Chopin moved on to Paris where he arrived around the middle of September.

The sight of this vibrant metropolis swirling vertiginously around a giant bend in the Seine electrified him the moment he saw it. At that time Paris was not just the political heart of the French nation, it was the intellectual and artistic capital of Europe. By comparison Warsaw looked like an overgrown village and Berlin a grandiose ghost town. Even Vienna, with all its sophisticated elegance, was little more than a pale reflection of the incredible magnificence of Paris. The Parisians themselves added to the luster of their city. There, with pen in hand, were writers like Victor Hugo, Balzac, and Stendhal. Daubing away at their easels were Delacroix, Ingres, and Delaroche. Keyboards rang out to the touch of Liszt, Hiller, and Kalkbrenner, while the voices of La Malibran, Pasta, and Nourrit echoed through opera houses and concert halls all over the city. The music they sang was written by men like Cherubini who ran the Conservatory and Rossini who directed the Théâtre-Italien. Of course Paris also teemed with outstanding men of science, politics, philosophy, and other fields, but they were peripheral to the artistic world in which Chopin's interest lay.

The astonishing freedom—not to say licentiousness—that prevailed in Paris bewildered Fryderyk, who had grown up in the restricted atmosphere of Russian-dominated Poland. Even in his travels, the Germanic stiffness of cities like Berlin and Vienna left him unprepared for the Gallic insouciance of Paris where, for a few francs, he could buy pornography on a street corner or gape at the lavishness of a Meyerbeer opera. Both left him equally flabbergasted.

Amid all the sordid novelty and startling grandeur of the city Fryderyk discovered many familiar faces from the Warsaw he had left behind. Among the Polish émigrés who flooded Paris then were old friends like the Czartoryskis, the Platers, and the Potockis. Also there were the Wodziński brothers who once boarded in his parents' home and two former classmates from the Conservatory, Antoni Orłowski and Julian Fontana.

Ironically, if it weren't for the recent conflict in Warsaw Paris itself might have been a battlefield that year. When Charles X, the last of the French Bourbons, was overthrown in July 1830, Czar Nicholas I tried to persuade Prussia and Austria to help him restore the fallen monarch. While waiting for their decision he began massing forces in Poland to march on Paris. Only when he found himself obliged to use these troops to quell the revolution on his own doorstep did he give up the idea of attacking France.

Through letters of introduction Chopin brought with him, he soon broadened his circle of acquaintances in Paris beyond the city's little Polish colony. Dr. Malfatti had written Ferdinand Paër, Louis-Philippe's court director of music, about his arrival, and the acerbic old man treated him with unusual kindness. Thanks to his help Chopin was able to get a residence permit that allowed him to remain in Paris indefinitely. The possession of this document, however, put him in flagrant defiance of the Russian authorities and meant he could never return to Poland without courting grave consequences. From that moment on, Chopin was doomed to a life of exile.

Paër also helped him establish many musical contacts in the city. Through him he met Cherubini, the director of the Conservatory, and a number of the school's faculty members, including Pierre-Marie-François de Sales Baillot, a violinist of such fantastic technique he was considered by some to be a rival of Paganini. Besides teaching at the Conservatory Baillot also conducted at the Paris Opéra and was the leader of a string quartet that held the esteem of Paris for some twenty years.

While these contacts would prove valuable to Chopin later on, he was too excited during his first few weeks in the city to look beyond the moment. Instead he rushed deliriously around Paris, exploring its many wonders and indulging in its endless pleasures. Oblivious to the cost of all this, he spent extravagant sums on clothes, ate in expensive restaurants, hired private carriages, and attended the Opéra regularly. Soon the reckless young man was facetiously signing his diary, "Fryderyk Chopin, pauper."

In only one thing did he show any economy: his apartment, a snug little retreat on the top floor of a five-story building at No. 27 Boulevard Poissonnière. From this high perch he enjoyed a panoramic view of Paris, stretching from the windmills of Montmartre to the dome of the Panthéon. Beyond the rooftops in front of him lay the Conservatory; to the left, down the Grands Boulevards, were the Opéra and the Théâtre-Italien, while to the right were many of the city's famous theaters and music halls.

In his euphoria nothing could dampen Chopin's spirits that fall, not even the news that his "ideal," Konstancja Gładkowska, had just been married in Warsaw. Paris was his new love.

Eventually a bout of venereal disease, financial problems, and the influence of a new acquaintance made Chopin realize it was time to stop being frivolous and start thinking about his future. The acquaintance was Friedrich Kalkbrenner, a pompous forty five-year-old pianist and composer of humble origins and high-flown pretensions. According to those who knew him well he was a flashy dresser, an incurable social climber, and an inveterate name-dropper. One of his favorite boasts was that Louis-Philippe once offered him a title, which he declined. Heinrich Heine and Clara Schumann found him insufferably egotistical, while Mendelssohn called him a poseur—and worse still, a plagiarist.

Personal failings aside, Kalkbrenner was an exceptional pianist, at least from a technical point of view. He made his debut playing a concerto at age five and graduated from the Paris Conservatory at age thirteen. His approach to music, however, was rigid and pedantic. No one was more of a perfectionist than Kalkbrenner, but his playing lacked feeling and his concerts were models of sterile precision. Nevertheless, Chopin virtually threw himself at his feet the first time he heard him. All other pianists "are nobodies compared to Kalkbrenner," he exclaimed.[4] "He is the only person whose shoelaces I am not worthy to untie."[5]

In response to this adulation Kalkbrenner suggested that Chopin become his pupil and outlined a three-year course of study for him. When Elsner and Chopin's parents heard this they were indignant. Such a proposal, they warned Fryderyk, ran the risk of destroying his unique talent.

In the end, Chopin tactfully declined Kalkbrenner's offer and the two remained on good terms. As a friend, rather than a teacher, Kalkbrenner proved to be enormously helpful. It was, in fact, largely through his advice and encouragement that Fryderyk finally succeeded in organizing his Paris debut that winter.[6]

Few people have ever been blessed like Kalkbrenner with the hands of an artist and the head of a businessman. In 1829 he became a partner in the firm of Pleyel et Cie., which published music and manufactured pianos. One year later the company opened a small concert hall at No. 9 rue Cadet, called the Salle Pleyel. It could seat up to 350 people and soon became one of the city's most eminent musical centers. With Kalkbrenner's influence Chopin was able to reserve the hall free of charge for a concert he hoped to give there early in December 1831.

Kalkbrenner even offered to lend his presence to the occasion by taking part in a performance of his Grande Polonaise and March for six pianos. Gratefully Chopin accepted his offer although he later began to have some misgivings about the work. "It's a crazy piece," he wrote Tytus. "Kalkbrenner will play on an immense pantaleon while I will have a little monochord piano."[7] The other four instruments were to serve as a quasi-orchestral accompaniment for the two solo ones.

Since Chopin had only been in Paris a short while he didn't know many people he could ask to fill the extra piano parts. Happily Mendelssohn, whom he had met in Munich that summer, was in town and consented to help out. He, in turn, cajoled a friend of his, Ferdinand Hiller, into doing the same. Like Mendelssohn, Hiller was of German-Jewish origins and a former child prodigy who made his debut at age ten playing a Mozart concerto. Since 1828 he had lived in Paris where he received only modest recognition for his efforts to revive and create music of a worthwhile nature.

For a fifth pianist Kalkbrenner recommended one of his pupils, George Alexander Osborne, a remarkable twenty five-year-old Irishman who had never taken a piano lesson until he was eighteen.

The difficulty of finding a sixth pianist forced Chopin to fall back on an old Warsaw colleague, Wojciech Sowiński, whom he scorned as "the height of artistic chicanery and stupidity,"[8] an idiot, "short of brains,"[9] who "bangs the piano, leaps all over the place, crosses his hands, and hammers away at the same note for five whole minutes with a clumsy finger that looks like it should be wielding the whip and reins for some farmer out in the Ukraine."[10] On the other hand Sowiński did have one redeeming feature: he was on the staff of the *Revue Musicale,* which would probably be writing up Chopin's concert.

Baillot, in addition to Kalkbrenner, also took an interest in Chopin's debut and offered the services of his string quartet. The other members of the group whom Fryderyk knew well by now all taught at the Conservatory and played with the orchestra of the Paris Opéra. The second violinist of the quartet, Jean-Jacques Vidal, conducted at the Théâtre-Italien as well and served under Paër in the king's orchestra. The cellist, Louis Norblin, shared with Chopin the distinction of having a Polish mother and a French father. Although he was born in Warsaw, Norblin spent most of his life in Paris where his fame as a teacher attracted such pupils as Jacques Offenbach and Auguste Franchomme.

The most unusual member of the group was undoubtedly the violist, Chrétien Urhan, a versatile Belgian who was equally accomplished on the violin and the organ. In his youth he aspired to be a monk until a week of silence in a Trappist monastery changed his mind. Throughout his life though, he remained devoutly religious and always carried something blue on his person in honor of the Virgin Mary. When the Empress Josephine heard him in Aix-la-Chapelle she had him brought to Paris where he became a prominent violist and permanent organist at the Church of Saint-Vincent de Paul. Whenever he had to play for ballet performances at the Opéra he always made a point of turning his back to the stage so as not to be tempted by the sinful sight of tightly clad bodies. Over the years he and Franz Liszt became good friends—perhaps because of their joint passion for things musical and mystical.

Since Baillot proposed to play a Beethoven quintet[11] at Chopin's concert he needed someone to take the extra viola part and chose Théophile Tilmant, a violinist who was also adept at the viola. Later Tilmant and his younger brother, Alexandre, formed their own string quartet which rivaled Baillot's for many years.[12]

To this plethora of artists, still one more was added: an oboist named Henri Brod,[13] who also taught at the Conservatory and played for the Paris Opéra. The softness and sweetness of tone for which he was noted suggest that he and Chopin may have been similar in temperament.

Such a full program would have satisfied most audiences of the period, but Fryderyk's plans for a "Grand Vocal and Instrumental Concert" called for singers as well, which was to cause him considerable trouble. Rossini at the Théâtre-Italien would gladly have released some of his cast for the evening but his assistant, M. Robert, objected. Determined to have vocalists, Chopin delayed his concert while he tried his luck at the Paris Opéra. When its cantankerous director, Dr. Véron,[14] also refused him he had to postpone his concert a second time.

Not until January did he finally succeed in finding singers to help him. That month he located three: Ernest Boulanger, Erminia Toméoni, and Mlle. Isambert. None were exceptional artists even though two came from prominent musical families. Boulanger's mother was a star at the Opéra-Comique, while Mlle. Toméoni's father had been a voice teacher, composer, and publisher in Italy. Already forty-nine years old (an age when many prima donnas would be considering retirement), Mlle. Toméoni still had hopes of singing on the stage of the Paris Opéra. Eventually in 1836 she made it, but only for a few weeks, since neither she nor the company's management lived up to each other's expectations. By then, according to the *Revue et Gazette Musicale,* her voice had lost its "color and charm" even though the middle-aged mademoiselle still looked "very seductive" when viewed face-on if not in profile.[15] Seven years later she died in a shipwreck on her way to Mexico.

Just when everything seemed to be in order Kalkbrenner took sick and the concert had to be put off again. For the fourth time Chopin reserved the Salle Pleyel, but the date he selected, February 26, 1832, didn't suit Mendelssohn, who had to bow out of the program.[16] To fill the breach Kalkbrenner called on another of his pupils, the twenty-one-year-old pianist Camille Stamaty.

For financial reasons Chopin was forced to give up the idea of hiring an orchestra. Even with Kalkbrenner and the Baillot quartet as drawing cards tickets weren't selling well. This was partly due to the fact that Pleyel insisted on charging 10 francs apiece for them when a ticket cost only 9 francs at the Opéra and still less at the Opéra-Comique (7.50 francs) and the Théâtre-Italien (6.50 francs). To make matters worse the cholera epidemic, which had continued its death march westward, now hovered at the gates of Paris. Already people were beginning to leave the city, and those who remained hesitated to go out in large crowds.

When the lights went down in the Salle Pleyel at eight o'clock on Sunday evening, February 26, the hall was only a third full. Conspicuous in the small audience were Felix Mendelssohn and Franz Liszt.[17] Most of those present were members of the Polish diaspora like Julian Niemcewicz, the poet Stefan Witwicki, the pianist Julian Fontana, the violinist Antoni Orłowski, and an aristocratic clique represented by Count Wojciech Grzymała, the Czartoryskis, the Platers, and others. This sprinkling of a hundred or so people was to hear one of the most historically significant concerts ever given in Paris.

FIRST PART

1. Quintet [opus 29, in C major]
   composed by Beethoven, performed by MM. Baillot, Vidal, Urhan, Tilmant, and Norblin
2. Duet sung by Mlles. Toméoni and Isambert
3. Concerto for piano [in F minor],
   composed and played by M. F. Chopin[18]
4. Aria sung by Mlle. Toméoni

SECOND PART

1. Grande Polonaise preceded by an Introduction and a March,
   composed for six pianos by M. Kalkbrenner and
   performed by MM. Kalkbrenner, Stamaty, Hiller, Osborne, Sowiński, and Chopin
2. Aria, sung by Mlle. Isambert
3. Oboe solo by M. Brod
4. Grandes Variations Brillantes on a theme by
   Mozart, composed and played by M. F. Chopin[19]

"All Paris was stupefied!" Orłowski exclaimed after the concert was over. Chopin "mopped up the floor with every one of the pianists here."[20] Liszt, of course, was hardly prepared to go that far, but even he had to admit it was an unforgettable night. Years later he acknowledged being "so delighted [with Chopin's performance] that the most vociferous applause seemed insufficient for the talent that was opening a new phase of poetic sentiment and presenting happy innovations in the substance of his art."[21]

Perhaps more objective than either Orłowski or Liszt was François Joseph Fétis, the founder and chief critic of the *Revue Musicale*. His enormous debts forced him to live outside Paris since a warrant for his arrest had been issued there. This meant he had to slip in and out of the city secretly in order to fulfill his duties, a risk he considered well worthwhile in the case of Chopin's concert. Seldom had he heard anyone play in such an "elegant, effortless, and graceful" manner.[22] But, like others before him, he complained about the extreme softness of the pianist's tone.

Fétis also admired the remarkable originality of Chopin's compositions, especially the concerto with its melodies that literally "sang out from the soul."[23] Strangely enough, though, he was offended by the feeling of spontaneity they conveyed. For Fétis this represented a structural flaw which he hoped age and experience would correct. Nevertheless he foresaw "a brilliant and well-deserved reputation" for this young newcomer on the Paris scene.[24]

Since Chopin's debut at the Salle Pleyel had been poorly attended he didn't make much money from it. However, he was still firmly resolved to settle in Paris. Now that he knew Cherubini and others at the Conservatory he hoped for an invitation to play with the Société des Concerts du Conservatoire. Two members of Baillot's quartet, Norblin and Urhan, had helped to found the organization, while another, Vidal, played in its orchestra. Each year from January to May this illustrious body gave a series of nine performances which were among the most important musical events of the season. They "exceed your greatest expectations," Fryderyk wrote enthusiastically. "Their orchestra is unsurpassable."[25]

On March 13 he sent a letter to the society's concert committee requesting "the favor of being heard" on one of its programs.[26] Considering his many connections at the Conservatory his request seemed to be a mere formality.

In the meantime he struggled along as best he could to make ends meet. In Warsaw Nicholas Chopin worried that his son's financial problems would keep him from concentrating on his music, and the whole family shared his concern. "Write me privately, if necessary," his sister Ludwika begged. "At least one of us should know how things really stand. Please, don't be mad. You know how we all fret over you."[27]

With a mother's intuition, Justyna Chopin avoided embarrassing questions and simply forwarded her son 1,200 francs out of her personal savings. The gift was welcome but it made Fryderyk feel bad for not having done more with his time in Paris. "It's a real problem to find students here and even harder to organize a concert," he complained.[28] This wasn't just an attempt to justify himself but the cold truth. "Things are miserable here," his friend Orłowski confirmed. "It's impossible for an artist to earn a penny, and the cholera is driving all the rich people off to the provinces."[29]

The first outbreak of the disease in Paris that March occurred near the Hôtel de Ville. Within three days 300 cases were reported, and a few weeks later the situation was desperate. Hospitals were crammed with three persons to a bed, and the number of dead mounted so rapidly the newspapers took to suppressing the true figures for fear of creating a panic.

On April 10, at the height of the epidemic, 2,000 people died in a single day. The city ran out of coffins, and bodies were stuffed into old sacks and "stacked pell-mell like so many lifeless bundles"[30] on carts, furniture vans, or any vehicle that could serve as a make-shift hearse. From her Left Bank apartment George Sand watched the grim procession of corpses arriving at the city's morgue on the Île de la Cité. "The worst thing about it all," she noted, ". . . is the lack of any friends or relatives accompanying these funeral wagons."[31]

Most of the bodies came from the working-class districts in the east of Paris where rumors had it that the epidemic was deliberately started by the rich to prevent a proletarian revolt. Louis-Philippe, the so-called "Citizen King," did little to quell such talk; he retreated into the safety of the Tuileries and abandoned his subjects. Of all the royal family, only the Duke of Orléans, the King's oldest son and heir, had the courage to go out and visit the city's hospitals.

As the disease worked its way through one quarter of town after another, every level of society soon became affected. No one ventured on to the streets without wearing a "cholera belt" lined with wool and impregnated with medicaments. These devices served to warm the kidneys and abdominal organs which were deemed especially susceptible to infection. The consumption of hot tea or charcoal-filtered water was also advised. At the Academy of Sciences papers were read on other remedies including the inhalation of oxygen, but still the cholera raged.

While some Parisians like the Rothschilds canceled their subscriptions to the Opéra, theaters like the Vaudeville and the Porte Saint-Martin continued to play to full houses. Even the Opéra itself was packed to capacity on Good Friday, April 20, for a concert by Paganini.[32] Those who attended found the foyer and corridors lined with huge vases of chlorinated water that gave off a pungent odor as their antiseptic fumes were fanned about by an elaborate ventilating system. Twice a day porters scrubbed down the steps of the building with still more of the disinfectant solution.

Outside, the streets were littered with discarded clothes, linens, and other personal effects of the dead and dying. Like vultures, the Paris ragpickers swooped down and battled the city's sanitation crews for possession of them.

At the Conservatory a group of public-minded professors raised 227 francs to aid the cholera victims, and on May 20 the Prince de la Moskowa took over the school's auditorium to give a charity concert for the same purpose. Such were the deplorable circumstances in which Chopin made his second public appearance in Paris.

Joseph Napoléon Ney, Prince de la Moskowa, was the twenty-nine-year-old son of Napoléon's famous Marshal Ney. Like his father he also achieved military distinction but not until some years later as a general under Louis-Napoléon, in 1853. Prior to that he was better known as a fashionable man-about-town, a big-time spender, and a musical dilettante of above-average talents. Among the things he wrote were a number of operas and other secular pieces, but his particular specialty was the composition of religious works. For his concert that May he intended to repeat a mass which he had written and performed at the Conservatory earlier in the summer of 1830.

Since he was married to Albine Laffitte (the daughter of Jacques

Laffitte, Europe's so-called "banker of kings and king of bankers") the prince could easily afford such grandiose productions as his mass. His wife's dowry had brought him a handsome twenty five million francs which her father willingly sacrificed in order to make Albine a princess. This was quite an astronomical price to pay for his daughter's entry into the aristocracy, but then the girl was rather difficult to dispose of. None too bright, she was even more extravagant than her husband and once had the paths of her garden covered with sugar instead of sand.

Chopin probably met M. de la Moskowa in one of the aristocratic salons they both frequented.[33] Although the prince must have been impressed with Fryderyk's talent he might not have invited such an obscure artist to play at his concert if it weren't for the lack of other pianists in Paris then. Virtuosos like Liszt, Mendelssohn, and Hiller had already left the city to avoid the cholera. The fact that the soloists for the mass, Mmes. Mori and Lavri and MM. Domange and Bellecourt, were as little known as Chopin would certainly point to a scarcity of musicians in Paris that spring.

Besides M. de la Moskowa's mass the lengthy program included two instrumental and two vocal solos. The latter were performed by a Mlle. Michel who "left something to be desired in the accuracy of her pitch"[34] and Henri Bernard Dabadie from the Opéra. Chopin and the oboist Henri Brod (who had taken part in Fryderyk's recent Paris debut) were the two instrumental soloists.

For his contribution to the program Chopin played the first movement of his F minor concerto with disappointing results. According to Fétis of the *Revue Musicale* it didn't come off well because of the "heavy orchestration combined with the rather weak tone Chopin elicits from the piano."[35] Ironically, the work had made more of an impression three months earlier when he played it at the Salle Pleyel *without* an orchestra.

Although Chopin could now boast of having performed at the Conservatory it wasn't in one of those hallowed affairs sponsored by the Société des Concerts. Its august members had turned down his application to play with them that season, and it was to be several years before they saw fit to include him on one of their programs.

• CHAPTER SEVEN •

Paris
1833

THREE DAYS AFTER the Prince de la Moskowa's concert the *Journal des Débats* reported that "the cholera is retreating more and more each day."[1] In its wake, however, the terrible pestilence left 20,000 dead. It also left much of France in a state of poverty and starvation. Such misery demanded a scapegoat and Louis-Philippe was quickly targeted for the role. While the cholera ravaged Paris he had thought only of his own safety. Soon he and his inept administration found themselves blamed for all the woes that now befell the nation.

The poor king, who was never a very regal figure at best, tried unsuccessfully to identify himself with his subjects by dressing and acting like an ordinary citizen. He wore the plain dark frock coat and trousers of a businessman and carried a tightly furled umbrella which ultimately became the symbol of his reign—a sorry substitute for the gilded scepter of his Bourbon predecessors.

Few were fooled by these affectations, and the riots that flared up all over Paris that summer only served to compound the havoc already created by the cholera. The National Guard was called out to suppress the disruptions, and its fierce retaliation simply inflamed the situation all the more.

For Chopin these twin scourges of disease and violence were devastating. They drove away the few pupils he had collected and stripped him of his meager income. Another concert was out of the question since the only music popular during the Parisian summer was that of the dance orchestras in the outdoor cafés along the Champs Elysées. To fill his spare time he added to the pile of musical manuscripts that lay about his apartment gathering dust. Times were too unsettled for publishers to gamble on works by an unknown.

Often during this difficult summer Fryderyk grew homesick and longed to be back in Warsaw. He realized, of course, that life in Poland was no longer the way he remembered it. As bad as things might be in Paris they had to be worse in Warsaw. Surely it would be foolish to return home and exchange the gloved hand of Louis-Philippe for the iron-clad fist of Czar Nicholas.

At times he wondered if he wouldn't do well to take advantage of his passport to London and go there after all. Certainly the political climate was more stable in England than in Paris. But then, as Schumann pointed out, the European public in general had had its fill of virtuosos.[2] America, on the other hand, cried out for musicians, and Chopin toyed briefly with the idea of settling in the United States. There, on the opposite side of the ocean, was a vast young nation with an almost sycophantic adoration of European talent. It's unlikely, though, that a person of his extreme sensitivity could have adjusted well to life among the rough-edged pragmatists of that new democracy. Fortunately he stayed in Paris.

The reason usually given is the unsubstantiated story that one day, while strolling down a street in Paris, Chopin happened to run into Prince Walenty Radziwiłł,[3] who invited him to a soirée at the home of Baron James de Rothschild. There he was asked to play and impressed the baron's wife so much that she begged to become his pupil. After that it was virtually *de rigueur* for all ladies of society to take lessons from the elegant young pianist on the Boulevard Poissonnière.

This new source of income was soon increased by the sale of several of his compositions to the music publisher Maurice Schlesinger. Originally from Berlin (and originally Moritz rather than Maurice), Schlesinger had come to Paris around 1819 as a book publisher. Four years later the frustrations of having to conform to government censorship drove him into the less restricted field of music publishing. Among the first of Chopin's works which he brought out in 1833 were the Études of opus 10 and the E minor Concerto. Their immense popularity marked the beginning of a long and profitable relationship between the two men which lasted until Schlesinger retired from the publishing business in 1846.

The musical success that Chopin began to enjoy during his second year in Paris went hand in hand with the social recognition he acquired then. As the winter season of 1832–33 got under way he suddenly found himself on all the best guest lists in town. Every evening he darted from one great house to the next, treating the city's *haut monde* to impromptu after-dinner performances. Overnight the shy young man became a dashing gay blade. On occasion he was noted to sway tipsily at the piano, while his parlor flirtations provoked rumors of an impending marriage to one aristocratic siren or another.

Nobody was more surprised by this unexpected turn of events than Chopin himself. "I have been introduced all around the highest circles!" he wrote excitedly. "I hobnob with ambassadors, princes, and ministers. I can't imagine what miracle is responsible for all this since I really haven't done anything to bring it about."[4]

In a sense it was just that: a miracle. Rarely did society at that time show such favors to a professional musician. Even superstars of the concert stage like Liszt still entered by side doors, performed, and departed without savoring the delights of the banquet table. In London artists like La Malibran and Luigi Lablache were literally roped off at one end of the drawing room like so many cattle in a corral. No wonder Fryderyk could hardly believe his good luck.

More and more that winter he became preoccupied with the "great world" he had entered and the figure he was cutting in it. Surrounded by the rich and titled he began to affect their habits only to find that fashionable living was a terribly expensive business. Things that once seemed like the height of luxury now became necessities to him, and he could barely pay his bills even with the extra money from his new pupils and his recent publications. "You must think I'm making a fortune," he confided to an old friend, "but don't kid yourself. My carriage and white gloves alone cost more than I earn."[5]

Somehow, in spite of his high living, Chopin managed to stay solvent. As long as he had a few francs in his pocket he avoided the ordeal of giving another concert. The life of a salon pianist was much easier. It didn't require haggling with theater directors, hawking tickets, pleading with singers, or rehearsing orchestras. For nearly a year he stayed away from the concert stage. Not until 1833 did he eventually return to it and then only at the insistence of Ferdinand Hiller, who needed help in performing Bach's three-piano concerto on a program scheduled for March 23.

The twenty-two-year-old Hiller was an erudite musician who had studied with Hummel, played for Goethe, and attended Beethoven on his deathbed. His dedication to the cause of good music led him to champion the works of deserving composers in an age that preferred banal medleys and tinseled variations. In November of 1829, for example, he gave the first Paris performance of Beethoven's *Emperor* Concerto. His own compositions were so "full of poetry, fire, and spirit"[6] that Chopin often assigned them to his students.[7]

The third pianist in the Bach concerto was to be Franz Liszt, who had attended and praised Chopin's debut in Paris the year before. Hiller's concert marked the first of many occasions when the two of them would play together in public, but the brash Hungarian proved a difficult person for Chopin to get along with, and their relationship was often scarred by jealousy and resentment.

Far more to Chopin's liking was the cellist Auguste Franchomme, whom Hiller also invited to take part in his concert. A pupil of Louis Norblin, Franchomme later became a professor at the Conservatory and court soloist to Louis-Philippe. The first time he heard Chopin play he felt an immediate rapport with him which grew into a lifelong friendship. Already they had collaborated on a Grand Duo Concertante for piano and cello which Schlesinger was to publish before the year was out.[8]

Along with Franchomme, Hiller included another string player on the program, the Moravian violinist Heinrich Wilhelm Ernst. He had studied at the Vienna Conservatory under Böhm and later trailed Paganini around Europe trying to fathom the secrets of his fantastic technique. Some critics claim he all but equaled the diabolical Italian, while others say he played even more sensitively.

Hiller arranged for his concert to be held on a Saturday evening in the Wauxhall d'Été, an outlying amusement center near the east end of the Boulevard Saint-Martin. In front of it was a sanded courtyard with flower gardens and fountains shaded by larch trees in painted wooden boxes. A "pretty rotunda" surmounted the main building where dances were held three times a week. For the additional pleasure of its patrons the Wauxhall offered gaming facilities, reading and smoking rooms, a puppet theater, and a concert hall. It was built in 1785 as a "feeble imitation of the London Ranelagh [Gardens],"[9] but unlike its English counterpart, the Wauxhall d'Été catered to a rather raffish clientele. According to the *Revue Musicale,* the setting was "more appropriate for a ball or a fencing match than a concert."[10] This attitude on the part of the *Revue* may explain why none of its staff bothered to travel out to hear Hiller's concert. For those willing to make the trip, however, the paper provided an advance copy of the program.

1. New Symphony for grand orchestra,
   composed by M. Ferdinand Hiller (performed for the first time)
2. Duet, sung by Mlle. Marinoni and M. Richelmi
3. Violin solo, performed by M. Ernst
4. Grand Concerto for piano (in E flat) with orchestra,
   composed by Beethoven and
   performed by M. Hiller (by request)[11]
5. Allegro from the Concerto for three pianos,
   composed by Sebastian Bach and
   performed by MM. Chopin, Litsz [sic], and Hiller
6. Aria sung by Mlle. Marinoni
7. Études and Caprices for the piano (unpublished),
   composed and played by M. Hiller
8. Cello solo composed and performed by M. Franchomme
9. Duet sung by Mlle. Marinoni and M. Richelmi
10. Duet for two pianos, composed by M. Hiller and
    performed by M. Litsz and the composer
11. Overture for grand orchestra, composed by M. Hiller
    (performed for the first time)

Price of tickets: 3 to 10 francs[12]

Shortly after assisting Hiller, Chopin was talked into helping out several other friends who were also giving concerts that spring. One of these, Jean-Amédée le Froid de Méreaux, was a young pianist and composer about seven years older than Chopin. He was born in Paris to a musical family. His grandfather had been a composer with a number of oratorios, cantatas, and operas to his credit, while his father was also a composer as well as organist at the Protestant Oratory next to the Louvre. Jean-Amédée himself began composing at an early age and saw his first works published when he was only fourteen. This changed the course of his life. Instead of being sent to law school as his parents had planned, he was allowed to study with Clementi and Reicha, who turned him into a polished musician. Although he wasn't endowed with Chopin's genius he satisfied his fellow countrymen enough to be made a chevalier of the Légion d'honneur before he died.

In 1830 Méreaux moved to London briefly but returned the following year to Paris where he charmed Mme. Recamier and gained entrée into the city's most cultivated salons. Around this time he met Chopin, with whom he established a cordial relationship. As musicians, though, they had conflicting tastes. Méreaux was a classical purist who played in the "brilliant and correct" fashion of the German school of pianists.[13] He had little love for the romantics and probably didn't care much for Chopin's music, although he did write a Grande Fantaisie on one of his mazurkas in 1839.

Regardless of their differences the two pianists often enjoyed playing four-hand music together, one of their favorite pieces being a duo by Méreaux based on a theme from Hérold's immensely popular opera, *Le Pré aux Clercs*. In 1833 this opera was given nearly 150 performances in Paris alone. Its composer became something of a national hero, and his death at age forty-six that January merely served to heighten the enthusiasm for his music.

When Méreaux decided to give a concert a few months later on March 30, he chose to include his duo from *Le Pré aux Clercs* and asked Chopin to perform it with him.[14] By March 16 Fétis was already announcing the event in his *Revue Musicale* even though Méreaux still hadn't found any singers to appear on the program. Of those he finally engaged, two were among the finest in all Paris: Mme. Laure Cinti-Damoreau and Nicholas Levasseur.

At age thirty-two, Mme. Damoreau was already a veteran trouper, having been admitted to the Paris Conservatory when she was only seven. Until her debut at the Théâtre-Italien she was known simply as Laure-Cinthie Montalant. At that time the theater's director, Mme. Catalani,[15] decided to rechristen her "Mlle. Cinti" in the firm conviction that an Italian name was the key to operatic success. A brilliant soprano like Laure-Cinthie, however, would undoubtedly have succeeded with whatever name she chose. As Chopin remarked when he first heard her, "No one sings better, not even La Malibran."[16]

In spite of her magnificent voice, Mlle. Cinti's career was a checkered one due to frequent conflicts with the managers of the houses where she sang. Her marriage to a tenor named Damoreau merely added to the conflicts in her life, and in 1834 they were divorced. Subsequently she retained his name as a Gallic foil to her pseudo-Italianate Cinti.

The other singer, Nicholas Levasseur, inaugurated the role of Bertram in Meyerbeer's *Robert le Diable,* one of the first operas Chopin saw in Paris. The production, which boggled audiences with its technical gimmickry, was equally memorable for its superb cast. Levasseur, according to his contemporaries, was not only "a thorough musician . . . of rare perfection" but "a good actor" as well.[17]

The third singer on the program, a thirty-three-year-old tenor named Marcelin Lafont, was not as distinguished as either Levasseur or Mme. Damoreau. A customs official until the age of twenty-three, he entered the Paris Conservatory and made his debut at the Paris Opéra all in the same year. From then until his sudden death in 1838 he sang in Lille, Brussels, and lesser cities with sporadic engagements at the Paris Opéra where his performances (often as a stand-in for Nourrit) were greeted with approval by the *Revue et Gazette Musicale* and deplored by the *Revue de Paris*. In its irreverent fashion *Le Charivari* implied that the corpulent tenor offered his public far more to look at than to listen to:

> The Opéra's M. Lafont would certainly be
> A tenor of the highest worth,
> If he'd only been granted by divine decree,
> A voice that could equal his girth.[18]

As it happened, Lafont and his wife lived at No. 18 rue de Rivoli which is where Méreaux's concert took place—probably in their apartment. This was located between the rue de L'Echelle and the rue des Pyramides in one of those buildings that form a long row of arcades extending eastward from the Place de la Concorde.[19] When the Lafonts moved there the rue de Rivoli was a relatively new street, carved by Napoléon through the gardens of an old convent and the former stable yards of the Bourbon kings. The houses on the western end of the street overlooked the formal paths and neatly bordered parterres of the Tuileries gardens, while those on the eastern half (including the Lafont residence) faced the massive stone facade of the Louvre.

Chopin was apparently familiar with the building at No. 18 rue de Rivoli since part of it was occupied by Polish émigrés. Only five days before Méreaux's concert, members of the Polish colony gathered there to hear Lafayette commemorate events of the recent Warsaw uprising.

The crowd who attended the concert in the Lafonts' apartment at eight o'clock on a Saturday evening had to be small. Admission was probably by invitation only. Besides the vocal numbers and the Chopin-Méreaux duo the little group also heard a grand concerto by Weber with orchestral accompaniment and another of Méreaux's works, a duet for piano and horn performed by the composer and a M. Mengal.[20]

The press seems to have been absent. Fétis, whose *Revue Musicale* was about the only music journal of any significance in Paris then, simply couldn't cover everything that went on in the city's three opera houses, half-dozen concert halls, and numerous musical theaters. Besides, he was involved in many other activities above and beyond his editorial duties. In addition to his obligations at the *Revue Musicale,* he composed, organized concerts of neglected "historical" works, and wrote books on harmony, counterpoint, and the lives of famous musicians. Not long after Méreaux's concert King Leopold I of the Belgians appointed him director of the Brussels Conservatory, which meant he would be able to leave Paris and the harassment of his many creditors.[21]

Two years later Méreaux also left Paris, for Rouen, where he spent the rest of his life as a teacher and journalist.

On the same day that Chopin played in the rue de Rivoli, Paris' *Moniteur Universel* announced a benefit performance to be given for Mlle. Harriet Smithson at the Théâtre-Italien on April 2. Its program promised a very full evening for those who wished to attend:

1. *Rabelais,* a vaudeville in one act,
   performed by M. Samson of the Théâtre Français and artists
   from the Théâtre du Palais Royal
2. *Chacun de Son Coté,* a three-act comedy by Mazères,
   performed by MM. Desmousseaux, Armand, Menjaud, Monrose,
   and Mlles. Mars and Dupont

3. Scene from *Atalie* by Racine, performed by Mlle. Duchenois
4. *Cabinets Particuliers,* a vaudeville performed by artists from the Théâtre du Vaudeville

During the entr'actes the audience was to be entertained by a spectacular array of musical artists including such singers as Rubini, Tamburini, and the Grisi sisters (Giulia and Giuditta), the violinist Théodore Hauman, the violist Chrétien Urhan, and the guitarist Francisco Huerta. In addition, it was announced that Chopin and Liszt would be there to offer a piano duo. Paganini had also been asked to play but refused.

This colossal affair was being organized by Hector Berlioz, then madly in love with Harriet Smithson. His infatuation with the thirty-three-year-old Irish actress had begun somewhat like Chopin's love for Konstancja Gładkowska, that is, he worshiped her from afar as one of those unapproachable Romantic "ideals." The first time he saw her she was playing Ophelia in a production of *Hamlet* at the Odéon on September 11, 1827. That, he claimed, was the beginning of "the supreme drama of my life."[22] Nobody on the French stage "ever touched and excited the public as she did."[23] It was nearly five years, however, before he got up the courage to speak to her.

Actually Harriet's talents were sadly mediocre despite some early successes in Paris. The reason she came to France in the first place was to escape the ridicule she suffered in London because of her strong Irish brogue. Since Berlioz couldn't understand English, though, he was hardly dismayed by the quality of her accent.[24]

In time Harriet returned to England while Berlioz went off to study in Italy after winning the French Institute's coveted Prix de Rome. By coincidence both of them came back to Paris in the fall of 1832. Shortly afterward Berlioz sent Harriet tickets to a concert he was giving at the Conservatory on December 9. There, in the presence of Chopin, Liszt, and Hiller, she listened to Berlioz's new work, the monodrama *Lélio, or The Return to Life.* In it the composer eulogized her as the artist's inspiration, and from then on he made no secret of his long-suppressed passion for her.

On March 1, 1833, poor Harriet (whose life was to be an endless series of tragedies) fell and broke her leg getting out of a carriage.

Under any circumstances it would have been a stroke of bad luck, but for Harriet, at that particular moment, it was nothing short of catastrophic. The troupe of Shakespearean actors she had brought to Paris the previous fall had foundered and fallen into bankruptcy, leaving her at the mercy of a horde of creditors. On top of all this she was burdened by a shrewish mother and a hunchbacked sister who relied on her for support. When Berlioz came with an offer of money her indignant mother showed him the door and threatened never to let Harriet see him again. It was then that the indomitable suitor decided to stage a benefit for his beloved in hopes that its profits (not being directly out of his own pocket) would be considered acceptable.

If Berlioz had one characteristic that stood out above all others it was his absolute horror of doing anything in a small way, and nowhere was this more evident than in his efforts to organize the benefit for Harriet Smithson that spring. Such a large undertaking in the vast Théâtre-Italien before a throng of 1,500 people was the very antithesis of the small drawing room evenings Chopin adored so much. Only someone with Berlioz's incredible dynamism could have finagled him into being a part of it.

On the Tuesday evening of this grand affair a large crowd of artists gathered backstage. Some like Liszt and Urhan were familiar to Chopin, but many, especially those from the theatrical world, were not. Among the latter was the famous actress Mlle. Mars (née Anne Françoise Hippolyte Boutet). She was the illegitimate daughter of an actor and actress who pushed her on the stage when she was still a mere infant. In her long career she specialized in comic portrayals of the young ingénue, a role she continued to play up to the time of her retirement at age sixty-two. In 1830 she took part in the tumultuous debut of Victor Hugo's *Hernani,* which ushered in the Romantic era of French theater. Because of her jealous nature Mlle. Mars had difficulty getting along with many of her colleagues, although Harriet Smithson seems to have been an exception. According to Berlioz, Mlle. Mars always behaved splendidly toward her and even assisted in an earlier benefit for her at the Opéra in 1828. Now during the girl's latest misfortunes she "gave money, rallied her friends and did everything in her power to help."[25]

One of the friends she rallied for Harriet's sake that spring was a fifty-six-year-old retired *grande dame* of the theater, Mlle. Duchenois.[26] Like Mlle. Mars, she too began life in deprived circumstances. Her mother ran an inn of questionable repute while her father roamed the countryside selling horses. At an early age she worked in tavern kitchens and brothels before finding her way into the theater. When the great actress Mlle. George seduced Napoléon, the Empress Josephine befriended Mlle. Duchenois out of spite and thrust her into the limelight. Considering the extraordinarily equine contour of her face, it must have been talent rather than beauty that sustained Mlle. Duchenois' popularity over the following decades. To her credit, however, she did possess an excellent figure, not to mention a heart that overflowed with kindness. When Berlioz's benefit failed to raise the needed money, Mlle. Duchenois organized a second one for Harriet which took in an additional 6,000 francs. Two years later the reward for her remarkable generosity was to die penniless and forgotten.

Much younger than the aging mesdemoiselles was the actor Joseph-Isadore Samson, whom Berlioz lured away from the Théâtre Français for the evening. He was a handsome chap with a distinguished profile, crowned by a thick crop of curly hair. In his youth he had studied with the famous actor Talma and later taught the incomparable Rachel.

The four singers on Berlioz's program were all members of Rossini's Italian company and so much in demand that three of them, Rubini, Tamburini, and Giulia Grisi, also sang in one of Fétis' "Concerts historiques" the same night as the Smithson benefit. Chopin had heard them previously and admired their voices. Rubini especially impressed him with his amazing technique. This glib tenor had no regard for the printed page and was forever indulging in the most stunning improvisations which kept his audiences too mesmerized to notice his pockmarked face and pot-bellied figure. Offstage, however, his crude behavior and slovenly attire offered little to admire.

Among the other musicians Chopin encountered that night at the Théâtre-Italien was the twenty-five-year-old Théodore Hauman, a Belgian-Jewish solicitor who had recently given up his legal career to become a professional violinist. Also there was the colorful Spanish guitarist Francisco Huerta. "I am the genius of the guitar," he once bragged. "You haven't heard the fandango if you haven't heard me."[27]

In view of the fact that Berlioz and Paganini were also accomplished guitarists, this was pretty big talk. On the other hand, he may have been right, since the *Revue et Gazette Musicale* called him "a veritable orchestra in miniature,"[28] and dubbed him a second "Christopher Columbus" for having discovered a whole new world of music.[29]

The happy result of this grand conglomeration of dramatic and musical talents was to reap Harriet Smithson the sizable sum of 6,500 francs, which paid off her most pressing debts. Two further benefit performances, however, were necessary before her last creditor was satisfied.

The following October, with barely 300 francs between them,[30] Berlioz and Harriet were married in the chapel of the British embassy in Paris. Only a few friends attended. One of them was Liszt, who acted as a legal witness to the ceremony. Afterward the newlyweds drove up to the modest little home they had rented on the heights of Montmartre. There Chopin occasionally visited them during the sunnier moments of their early married life.

Unfortunately they had few years of marital bliss. Harriet's career never recovered and she gradually turned into a bitter shrew who gave Berlioz no peace. "Poor Ophelia," he commented sadly in his *Memoirs*, "her star was setting."[31] In time she took to drink and later suffered several strokes which left her paralyzed and scarcely able to speak. Even then she continued to torment her husband to such an extent he finally divorced her and later remarried. In spite of all this he retained a great affection for his former love, visited her regularly, and saw that she was well provided for until her death in 1854.

Because of the great gulf between their personalities, Chopin and Berlioz gradually drifted apart as the years went by. While Chopin found it difficult to comprehend the massive scope and radical innovations of his friend's music, Berlioz, with his broader outlook, always retained a certain appreciation of Chopin's talents and never forgot the favor this "Trilby of the piano"[32] had done for Harriet in 1833.

Only twenty-four hours after the Smithson gala Chopin was back on stage again. The celebrated virtuoso and musical entrepreneur Henri Herz had just written an eight-hand piano arrangement of a theme from Meyerbeer's opera *Il Crociato in Egitto,* and needed three extra pianists to help him perform it. Such fantasias on operatic fragments were all the vogue then, and according to the contemporary critic Léon Escudier, Herz himself was their originator.

This minor addition to the piano repertory was but one of Herz's many contributions to the musical life of his era. A versatile genius who was a veritable jack-of-all-trades, Herz made a name for himself not only as a composer and pianist but also as an inventor, piano manufacturer, impressario, publisher, and showman. Born Heinrich Herz in Vienna in 1803, he wasted little time exhibiting his precocious abilities. By the age of eight he was already performing in public, and at twelve he had entered the Paris Conservatory where he walked off with the first prize in piano during his third year. Later, at the peak of his career, he was so swamped by pupils he had to start his lessons at five o'clock in the morning in order to accommodate them all. Still fresh at the end of the day, he often dashed off a few compositions or gave a concert in the evening.[33] Nothing, it seemed, could exhaust his ferocious energy, which eventually drove him to open a piano factory in the 1830s and after that a concert hall. The pianos he produced were equipped with a repetition mechanism of his own invention which allowed the pianist to perform passages with greater velocity than ever before. In general his instruments sold well, but every now and then he encountered some finicky virtuoso who agreed to play in his concert hall only on the condition that he didn't have to use a Herz piano.

Journalism was yet another field that attracted this multifaceted man. In 1837 he financed the journal *La France Musicale,* which exerted considerable influence over the musical tastes of its time.[34]

The apotheosis of Herz's career came in 1849 when he toured the United States at the height of the gold rush. There he dashed from one end of the continent to the other, filling the New World with his fantasias on "Yankee Doodle," "Hail Columbia," and other suitably patriotic tunes. His gargantuan concerts sported up to eight pianos at a time,[35] their shiny lids sparkling in the glow of a "thousand candles"—or so the advertisements ran. On several occasions he featured military bands from the local towns and interspersed the music with lectures on "The Genius of the American People" or "The Rights of Women." It's not surprising that Herz's flair soon caught the eye of that all-time showman, P. T. Barnum. The shrewd circus owner admired the pianist's freewheeling style and hoped to capitalize on it by managing his tour. Herz, though, turned down his lucrative offer when he found he would have to take second billing to Jenny Lind, who was Barnum's main attraction that season.

Such was the flamboyant figure Herz cut in later years. Back in 1833 his tastes were more subdued, and for his April concert that year he was content to use only two pianos with Liszt and himself at one and his older brother, Jacques-Simon Herz, and Chopin at the other.

The elder Herz, who was far more retiring than his sibling, also studied at the Paris Conservatory and later became a professor there. He too was a composer, having written several sonatas, a quintet, and a famous waltz that held Victorian ladies in thrall for many decades.

Liszt, of course, needs no comment other than whatever Henri Herz could do, Liszt could do better. If Herz stunned his public by the marvels he extracted from the keyboard, Liszt would whirl onto a stage with three pianos and triple his accomplishments. If Herz elicited deafening applause from his audiences, Liszt generated frenzied screams, tears, and a barrage of flowers wrapped in lace handkerchiefs. If Herz taught masses of pupils, Liszt (were he still alive today) could boast of being the pedagogical grandfather—or great-grandfather—of most contemporary virtuosos.

Originally Herz planned to give his concert at the Théâtre-Italien on March 29 and asked Chopin to come for a rehearsal at his home one Sunday between four and five o'clock in the afternoon. For some reason, though, the concert had to be delayed until April 3.[36] Presumably the Théâtre-Italien wasn't available then and Herz had to settle for the smaller, less convenient Wauxhall d'Été. Although several popular theaters, including the Ambigu and the Gaité, weren't far from the Wauxhall the neighborhood was derisively labeled the "Indies" by de Musset and other fashionable boulevardiers who considered anything east of the Boulevard des Italiens as quite beyond the pale.

Not all Paris, however, was that snobbish, and *L'Europe Littéraire* reported that an unusually elegant crowd drove across town to the remote Wauxhall on the night of Herz's concert. The gleaming lanterns of their coaches lit up the deserted streets leading to the pleasure park. In the shadow of the graceful rotunda the guests stepped out into the cool spring air. The ladies, it was noted by the journalist, "were conspicuous for their charm and exquisite dress."[37] One of the carriages discharged a frail, ghostlike man who appeared bent and emaciated. In the darkness few recognized the slender silhouette of Paganini.

While the audience was settling into its seats the artists assembled backstage. There Chopin again ran into Liszt and Hauman (with whom he had just performed the night before). A cornetist named Gambati was also there as were several singers, including MM. Bordogni[38] and Géraldi[39] and Mmes. Vigano, Boucaulx,[40] and Tadolini. By far the most outstanding of these singers was Eugenia Tadolini, who had recently married her voice teacher, Giovanni Tadolini. She made her Paris debut in 1830 at the Théâtre-Italien where her husband served as conductor. Verdi, who delighted in the "soft, tender and impassioned" beauty of her voice,[41] later sought her out for many of his operas.

The program Herz had arranged for the evening was composed largely of operatic arias, either sung or transformed into the instrumental fantasias for which he was famous.[42] This obviously pleased Castil-Blaze, the critic of *L'Europe Littéraire,* who also liked to write operatic transcriptions. "It was marvelous to hear the rapid passages burst forth under the fingers of Henri Herz and Liszt," he commented. "MM. Jacques Herz and Chopin played the second piano and provided a worthy counterpart to the first-rate performance of their formidable partners. Within the first eight measures they established a complete rapport and then continued to perform together with a unity difficult to achieve on keyboard instruments."[43]

These few lines, though complimentary enough, were all he had to say about Chopin's performance. At least he spelled his name right. The *Revue de Paris* came close with "Choppin," while the best *Le Charivari* could do was "Riopin." But then Liszt fared no better with contemporary journalists, who usually referred to him as "List," "Listz," "Lizst," or "Litz."

Chopin's failure to make more of an impression on the Parisian public was basically his own fault. In the perfumed sanctuaries of the rich he was smothered with so much attention he no longer craved the favor of those outside it. Not since his Paris debut had he bothered to organize another concert for himself. In his subsequent public appearances he had been content to serve in the minor role of a supporting artist. This brought him little if any money. Then, and for the rest of his life, most of his income was to be derived from teaching.

Out of regard for the many affluent young ladies who now studied with him Chopin moved from his fifth-floor apartment on the Boulevard Poissonnière to another, only one flight up, in the Cité Bergère. After all, it was too much to expect Mme. de Rothschild and her friends to keep struggling up those stairs.

His new apartment was located in a cozy mews-like setting just around the corner from the Conservatory. By the following summer, though, he found the narrow little Cité Bergère hot and airless. Its small dark rooms were stifling, and he began looking for something larger and nearer to the fashionable areas where his pupils lived. In June he found just what he wanted. Through Hiller and Mendelssohn he met a German scientist named Dr. Hermann Franck who planned to spend several months abroad and hoped to sublet his apartment while he was away. He lived at No. 5 rue de la Chaussée d'Antin not far from the aristocratic faubourg Saint-Honoré and only a few doors north of the elegant Boulevard des Italiens. The latter at that time was one of society's most popular parade grounds. Day and night, along its crowded sidewalks, strutted the puffed-up dandies of Paris with their rouged cheeks, powdered eyes, and shaved eyebrows.

There, only a stone's throw from Chopin's new apartment, was the expensive Café de Paris where the city's *jeunesse dorée* gathered around six o'clock every evening on their way from the Bois de Boulogne to the Opéra or the theater. A block east of it stood the famous Café Tortoni,[44] noted for its marvelous ices and a favorite haunt of crowds after the opera. Across the boulevard was the so-called Café Anglais. Although there was little about it that was truly English, its name reflected the intense Anglo-mania prevalent in Paris during the 1820s and 1830s. Also nearby were two other modish restaurants, the Café Riche and the Café Hardy. As Cambacérès once quipped, "You have to be quite hardy to eat at Riche and quite rich to eat at Hardy."[45]

The rue da la Chaussée d'Antin itself was an enclave of rich bankers and successful businessmen in Chopin's time.[46] While its inhabitants were too well established to be considered *nouveaux riches,* they were certainly not as exalted as their titled neighbors in the faubourgs Saint-Germain and Saint-Honoré.

During the summer, life in Paris tended to slow down, and Chopin took advantage of this to spend more time on his compositions. The Nocturne in G minor, op. 15, no. 3, which he wrote then was dedicated to his good friend and concert companion Ferdinand Hiller. Other works in progress that summer included some études which he later inscribed to a confidante of Hiller's, the Countess Marie d'Agoult. This bright and beautiful young lady (married to a kindly but dull man, twenty years her senior), longed for a more stimulating life. Although she had already begun a flirtation with Franz Liszt she now took a fancy to Chopin. The situation was obviously a delicate one, and when she invited Chopin to escape the summer heat at her country estate near Croissy-en-Brie he refused.

That fall Dr. Franck decided to give up his apartment for good and Fryderyk stayed on. To help pay the rent he took in an old acquaintance from Warsaw, Dr. Alexander Hoffmann, whom he affectionately nicknamed "Fatty." It wasn't long, though, before this arrangement broke up, ostensibly because Chopin couldn't stand his friend's cigars. The truth is, he probably found Fatty incompatible for other reasons since he later tolerated nearly a decade of George Sand's cigars without complaining.[47]

Although he wasn't to meet Mme. Sand for another three years, Chopin had surely heard of her by 1833 when her notorious novel *Lélia* first appeared. Her previous novels, *Indiana* and *Valentine,* had been best-sellers, but *Lélia,* with its heretofore unwritten—indeed unmentionable—expressions of women's sexual feelings, was a real shocker. Chopin never spoke of the book and may never have read it. Even if he did, it wasn't the sort of thing one talked about in polite society.

Now that he had become a part of "polite society" Fryderyk paid little attention to what was going on in the musical world that fall. Many of his colleagues like Liszt, Hiller, and Berlioz were busy organizing concerts, but Chopin showed no inclination to do the same for himself. From his point of view there was something disagreeable, not to say vulgar, in courting a public whose tastes he regarded as plebeian.

In November Berlioz, who was forever struggling to get out of debt, gave another gigantic theatrical and musical marathon at the Théâtre-Italien. Liszt and the actress Marie Dorval were two of the principal attractions, but the interminable program was poorly planned and turned into a fiasco. Around midnight members of the orchestra began to drift away, while Liszt didn't even sit down at the piano until nearly one o'clock in the morning. By then the audience was too tired to care and the concert broke up in shambles.

To redeem his fortunes Berlioz started work on another concert for December. According to the *Revue de Paris,* Chopin was supposed to take part in it but apparently he didn't.

That same month Hiller decided to repeat the Bach three-piano concerto he had given with Liszt and Chopin in the spring. This time, instead of the remote and tawdry Wauxhall, he obtained the Conservatory's exquisite red and gold Salle des Concerts. While the Conservatory itself dated back to 1784, its concert hall had been reconstructed in 1811, more with an eye for beauty than for comfort. The accoustics of the new hall, though, were excellent, while its seating capacity of just over 1,000 made it larger than the Wauxhall without losing the intimacy appropriate to a baroque work like the Bach concerto.

In addition to Chopin and Liszt, Hiller invited two other musicians to fill out the program, the cellist Franchomme and a young contralto named Francilla Pixis. The seventeen-year-old girl, whose real name was Göhringer, had been adopted by Johann Peter Pixis, a pianist and composer from Bohemia whom Chopin met briefly in Stuttgart in 1831. The middle-aged man hoped to marry his young charge and was so jealous of anyone who came near her he initially suspected Chopin of trying to seduce her.[48] Once this misunderstanding was cleared up, the two men became friends,[49] and it was through the good graces of Pixis that Chopin first met his Paris publisher, Maurice Schlesinger.

On December 9, 1833, the *Revue Musicale* announced: "M. Ferdinand Hiller, the young pianist and composer of unusual merit, will give a concert on Sunday, December 15, in the Conservatory. Several of his unpublished compositions will be heard in the following program":

PART I

1. Alla Marcia and Finale from the First Symphony, composed by M. Hiller

2. Concerto for piano and orchestra (in C minor) by Mozart, performed by M. Hiller
3. Aria by Mercadante, sung by Mlle. Pixis[50]
4. Second Symphony, composed by M. Hiller (performed for the first time)

PART II

1. Allegro from the Concerto for three pianos by J. S. Bach, performed by MM. Chopin, Listz [sic], and Hiller
2. Solo for violoncello by M. Franchomme[51]
3. German Romance with orchestral accompaniment composed by Gläser and sung by Mlle. Pixis[52]
4. Duo for two pianos, composed by M. Hiller and performed by M. Listz [sic] and the composer

"One concerto by Bach is worth far more than an air and variations by Herz!" exclaimed Edouard Fétis in the *Revue Musicale*. "The fragment for three pianos played by MM. Hiller, Liszt, and Chopin afforded us a rare pleasure: these three artists performed this piece, we can assure you, with an understanding of its character and a perfect delicacy."[53]

Considering that Bach and Mozart were Chopin's two favorite composers, it's no wonder the critic was pleased with his performance. Fryderyk had probably warmed up before the concert as usual by playing excerpts from Bach's *Well-Tempered Clavier.*

• CHAPTER EIGHT •

PARIS
1834–1835

NOT ONCE IN 1833 did Chopin play a solo work in public. Every time he appeared onstage it was in a piano duet, trio, or quartet—and always in the company of Franz Liszt, who seemed to be everywhere on the Paris musical scene. Chopin was beginning to find his constant presence annoying. He disliked Liszt's exaggerated bravado and detected a hint of condescension in his cordiality. In all probability he also envied the enormous success which Liszt (who was a year his junior) had already achieved. In one respect, though, Chopin clearly had an edge over his Hungarian colleague: he possessed a superior education and an innate refinement that made him at home in the discriminating world of the Parisian salons where Liszt's abrasive self-confidence and undisguised flamboyance weren't always welcome. There Chopin found a comfortable retreat, and for the next twelve months he wasn't heard outside the precincts of this elite domain.

At twenty-four Fryderyk was considerably more sophisticated than the youth who had first come to Paris only a few years earlier. No longer the bashful teenager Konstancja had known, he now moved with assurance among bejeweled matrons who fluttered their fans coquettishly at his urbane witticisms and artful flattery. If their husbands viewed him with a jealous eye they had no real cause for alarm. Fryderyk's flirtations were fleeting and soon forgotten. His impeccable sense of propriety kept them from turning into serious affairs. In view of the exhausting efforts it later cost an experienced seductress like George Sand to conquer his sexual inhibitions, it seems unlikely that any boudoir exploits climaxed those sparkling soirées he now attended.

On the contrary, he probably rode home alone through the dimly lit streets to the quiet comfort of his Chaussée d'Antin apartment.

Since his roommate, Dr. Hoffman, had moved out Chopin was left to shoulder all the expenses of his new quarters by himself. To impress his rich pupils he filled it with expensive furniture which cost much more than he could afford. As Liszt wrote the Countess d'Agoult, "That's enough to put him out of sorts for a whole month. Poor boy!"[1]

Luckily the extravagant young man could count several prominent bankers among his new acquaintances. Besides James de Rothschild there were Auguste Léo and the Baron d'Eichthal, each of whom could be depended on to help him out whenever necessary. In gratitude he often dedicated his compositions to them or their families.[2]

So far all Chopin's works in Paris had been published by Maurice Schlesinger. In general their relationship seemed to be working out satisfactorily even though Schlesinger was a hot-headed person and not always easy to get along with. In April 1834 he and the pianist Henri Herz got into a feud which ended in a duel between the publisher and one of Herz's pupils. A lawsuit followed and Chopin was cited as a witness on Schlesinger's behalf. Nothing could have been more distasteful to him than to be caught up in such a public squabble. As it turned out, Schlesinger lost the suit and had to pay damages while Chopin lost an influential friend. Later, when Herz became the financial backer of *La France Musicale,* the journal pointedly ignored Chopin for several years except to print an occasional "venomous" and "sneering" review of his music.

Herz wasn't the only one to criticize Chopin's new compositions. In Berlin there was an even harsher critic, a retired Prussian army officer named Ludwig Rellstab, who attacked them in the most incredibly vicious manner. It was dangerous to play anything by Chopin, he warned, unless you had a surgeon in attendance! The best thing to do with such difficult and discordant pieces was to tear them up and fling them at the composer's feet. For Chopin there may have been some consolation in knowing that he was just one of Rellstab's many victims. Spontini, for example, lost his post at the Berlin Opera because of the critic's vilifications. When Rellstab tried to malign Henrietta Sontag, however, the angry singer turned on him, sued him, and had him thrown in jail for three months. Many years later Chopin enjoyed the satisfaction of seeing a repentant Rellstab take back his insults and grovel for an introduction to him.

One of the first compositions Chopin failed to give Schlesinger was his Waltz in E-flat, opus 18, which he sold to Pleyel in the summer of 1834.[3] The 500 francs he received for this went toward the expenses of a trip to Aachen (Aix-la-Chapelle) where he attended the Music Festival of the Lower Rhineland with Hiller and Mendelssohn.[4] His father had suggested that he raise the money by giving a concert, but that idea didn't appeal to him.

At the festival Mendelssohn found his Paris friends a bit foppish, but the three of them had such a good time together he invited them to visit him in Düsseldorf on their way home.

Later in the summer Mme. Wodzińska, whose three sons boarded with the Chopins during their student days, asked Fryderyk to visit them in Geneva where they had settled after the Warsaw uprising of 1830. With her invitation she enclosed the manuscript of a theme and variations by her daughter Maria, who once took some piano lessons from him. Because he was low on funds Chopin couldn't afford any more trips that year. However, in appreciation of Maria's gift he sent her a copy of the E-flat waltz he had just sold.

Before long his financial situation improved when he found someone to share his apartment. The new tenant, an old classmate from Warsaw, was Jan Matuszyński, a twenty-five-year-old doctor who had just accepted a post at the École de Medicine in Paris. Then by the fall of 1834 a fresh influx of pupils combined with the sale of several more compositions enabled Chopin to return to his old profligate ways.

Less fortunate than Chopin was Berlioz, who found himself in worse straits than ever that year. In August Harriet had given birth to a baby boy which meant another mouth to feed. To meet his new financial obligations Berlioz gave two concerts at the beginning of the season, but his mounting debts forced him into organizing two more before the year was out. For the first of these, to be given on December 7 at the Conservatory, he asked Chopin's participation. While announcements of it appeared in *Le National* and *Le Ménestrel,* Schlesinger (who was Berlioz's publisher as well as Chopin's) gave it a special plug in his *Gazette Musicale.*[5] "We have no doubt that the concert hall at the Conservatory will fill up quickly with avid music lovers who are bound to listen in religious silence to the music of this young and already famous composer."[6]

The principal piece on the program, Berlioz's *Harold in Italy* symphony, had been performed only two weeks earlier on November 23, but the conductor miscued the orchestra then and took the work at a tempo that annoyed the composer. As a result he decided to give the piece a second hearing in the following program:

1. Overture to *Les Francs-Juges* by M. Berlioz
2. *Les Ciseleurs de Florence,* trio with chorus and orchestra by M. Berlioz (performed for the first time)
3. Andante from the F minor Concerto for piano, composed and performed by M. Chopin
4. Aria sung by Mlle. Heinefetter
5. Overture to *King Lear* by M. Berlioz
6. *Ballade du Pêcheur* by M. Berlioz, performed by M. Ernest Boulanger
7. *Harold,* a symphony in four parts, by M. Berlioz (the viola part will be played by M. Urhan)
   The first part: Harold in the mountains, scenes of sadness happiness, and joy
   The second part: March of the pilgrims singing an evening prayer
   The third part: Serenade of an Abbruzzi mountaineer to his mistress
   The fourth part: Orgy of brigands[7]

Although around 500 people attended the event Berlioz made little money out of it after paying the orchestra, the rent on the hall, and other expenses.

Edouard Fétis at the *Revue Musicale* refused to write up the concert since his father had been conducting a vendetta with Berlioz for several years. The rival *Gazette Musicale,* on the other hand, gave it an excellent review beginning with a lengthy blast at Berlioz's detractors (i.e., the Fétises, father and son). Chopin was extolled as a "sublime composer and inimitable pianist."[8] The Andante (i.e., Larghetto) from his F minor concerto, it observed, was "very well-constructed and extremely rich in delicate nuances, which contrast sharply with the colossal weight of M. Berlioz's orchestral productions."[9]

In spite of such praise Chopin was unhappy. He felt overshadowed by Berlioz's loud music and thought he had been given a chilly reception.

This was the last time the two men would ever join together in any musical effort. Their divergent tastes inevitably led them down separate paths. Years later Berlioz remarked in his *Memoirs* that "Chopin simply could not play in strict time."[10] With equal candor Chopin confided to Delacroix that Berlioz's idea of writing music was to pick out a bunch of chords and fill "in the intervals as best he can."[11]

While Berlioz gradually faded out of Chopin's life, Liszt continued to buzz in and out of it like a bothersome gadfly. For a good part of 1834 the Countess d'Agoult engaged her new lover's attention to such an extent he and Chopin saw little of each other. However, toward the end of the year the two men were drawn together again at a Christmas musicale in the drab little schoolroom of a local music teacher named Franz David Christoph Stoepel.

This obscure individual was a Prussian-born schemer whose frustrated aspirations eventually led him to Paris where he opened a music school at No. 6 rue Monsigny. By coincidence this building, called the Hôtel de Gèvres, happened to serve for some time as headquarters for the Saint-Simonists, a group of idealists intent on making society conform to the tenets of "true Christianity" as perceived by their founder, Claude Henri, Count de Saint-Simon.[12] His egalitarian philosophy with its utopian overtones appealed for a while to Liszt, who sometimes slipped into meetings on the rue Monsigny and occasionally even played for them. Berlioz as well as the tenor Adolphe Nourrit also became attracted to the Saint-Simonists and appeared now and then at their headquarters.

Chopin's introduction to Stoepel probably came through Maurice Schlesinger, who invited the Prussian to be an editor on his new *Gazette Musicale*. Stoepel was hardly a novice to this field, having already managed his own musical journals in Frankfurt-am-Main and Munich. His "impetuous and essentially independent character,"[13] however, kept him from sticking to anything for very long. In his youth he took sporadic lessons on the piano and the violin before dabbling in theory and music history. With these superficial accomplishments he set out on a quixotic career that carried him from Berlin to Potsdam and on to London. Later he returned to Germany where he lived briefly in Erfurt, Gotha, Meiningen, Darmstadt, Frankfurt, and Munich before settling in Paris around 1829. The abruptness of his departure from many of these cities suggests he may well have been run out of town. Fétis described him as a man "devoured by ambition,"[14] while the *Revue et Gazette Musicale* considered him a capricious person whose "feverish fantasies . . . showed him imaginary Eldorados wherever he turned.[15]

While in London Stoepel adopted Logier's method of piano teaching, a form of mass instruction supplemented by various mechanical devices called finger guides, wrist guides, and position frames. In his classes Logier would teach 20 pupils at a time by seating them in pairs at ten pianos. Over the course of a week he could accommodate 240 students or more in this fashion. Logier academies sprang up all over Europe, America, and even in India. Kalkbrenner himself opened one in London, and many prominent pianists like Cramer and Clementi endorsed the method. Others, however, considered Logier merely a shrewd opportunist.

While Stoepel remained a disciple of Logier for some time, he eventually wrote his own *Method for Piano and Voice* which he advertised in the *Revue de Paris* at a "moderate price." The part for voice claimed to "give everyone access to the art," while the piano part boasted "views as original as they are profound."[16] His *Method of Singing* became so popular the French government authorized its use in normal schools throughout the country.

Once a month Stoepel's pupils gave a recital in the little auditorium of his school. The rest of the time it was available for hire. A born hustler like Stoepel, though, didn't just sit back and wait for renters. As often as possible he would organize concerts himself to fill up his hall—not to mention his wallet. In December of 1834 he asked Chopin and Liszt to play on a program he was planning for Christmas Day.

It was advertised to start at two o'clock in the afternoon and offered the usual mixed bag of performers with a special exhibition of the recently developed harmonium. This new instrument was to be demonstrated by Louise Geneviève de La Hye, whose "great taste" and "well-grounded knowledge of music"[17] were often linked—by some unclear connection—to the fact that she was a great-niece of Jean-Jacques Rousseau.

The harmonium had a keyboard like that of a piano but it sounded more like an accordian. Its tones were produced by forcing air through metal reeds with a pair of bellows operated by two foot pedals. In America the instrument was known as the melodeon and became quite popular in rural parlors and small churches which couldn't afford a bona fide organ. A complicated version of it, manufactured by Mason and Hamlin in Boston, was called a "Liszt organ" although there is no indication that Liszt had anything to do with it. Certainly at M. Stoepel's concert the Hungarian seems to have preferred the tried-and-true virtues of the piano, leaving Mme. de La Hye to do what she could with the harmonium.

The program, published in the *Gazette Musicale* on December 21, is given below:

1. Grand Duo for two pianos, composed by M. Fr. Listz [*sic*] and performed by M. Chopin and the composer[18]
2. Two Romances: "Le Pécheur Napolitain," music by M. Thys, and "Ma Normandie," words and music by M. Bérat, sung by M. Richelmi
3. Violin solo, composed and perfomed by M. Ernest [*sic*][19]
4. Aria from *Niobe* by Pacini, sung by Mlle. Heinefetter
5. Improvisation on the harmonium by Mme. de La Hye
6. An Italian aria sung by Mme. Degli-Antoni
7. Piano Duet for four hands by Moscheles, performed by MM. Chopin and Listz [*sic*]
8. An Italian aria, sung by Mme. Degli-Antony
9. Improvisation on the harmonium, by Mme. de La Hye
10. Variations on the aria from *Le Garçon Suisse,* sung by Mlle. Heinefetter

In a review of the concert the following week, the *Gazette Musicale's* critic made it clear that he hadn't enjoyed his assignment. "The system of afternoon musicales hardly fits into our idea of art or the way it should be cultivated," he began haughtily. Nevertheless, he had to admit that the "distinguished artists" on the program did merit some consideration, and he lauded the "brilliant manner" in which Liszt and Chopin opened the program. "It would be impossible to hope for anything more than this talented collaboration of two artists equally sublime and equally endowed with such a profound sensitivity of their art."[20] Their second number, he added, "electrified" the audience.

Regardless of such praise, the concert was hardly a success from M. Stoepel's point of view. Because of the small size of his auditorium and the cheap price of admission (five francs a ticket) he earned little from it. That December he was on the brink of financial disaster, and shortly afterward he had to close his music school for lack of funds. Two years later a "maladie de langueur" brought an early end to his unsettled life. At the time of his death he was only 42.

The artistic commercialism of a man like Stoepel with his slick "system" of teaching and assembly-line production of pupils offended Chopin, who continued to grow more and more disenchanted with the musical life of Paris. Besides Stoepel others like Henri Herz were just as adept at exploiting the public for a profit. Even Liszt and Berlioz often indulged in ostentatious displays of their talent for the sole purpose of making money.

By contrast Chopin had such a horror of anything mercenary that he always insisted on having his pupils leave their payment on the mantel rather than hand it to him directly. In this way he avoided the appearance of conducting a business transaction. His art was not a commodity to be bought or sold. Such an attitude made him equally loath to "sell" himself on the concert stage. As a result his rare performances in Paris had been limited mostly to brief appearances for the sake of friends and not for his own benefit. It must have astonished many a Parisian therefore to read in the *Gazette Musicale* of December 28 that this seldom-heard artist was considered one of "the two greatest piano virtuosos of our era."[21]

In spite of himself Chopin was becoming a musical as well as social celebrity, but the fame he once craved now seemed to annoy him. As his reputation grew so did his desire to keep out of the public eye. In January of 1835 he submitted his resignation to the Chantereine Hall

Music Society, which gave an annual series of concerts similar to those of the Conservatory's Concert Society.[22] By doing this he deliberately forfeited an excellent opportunity to perform on the society's many fine programs each year.

Clearly Chopin had begun to turn his back on a virtuoso career which could have provided him with a much better income than he was making as a teacher. So far what he had earned from his compositions was rather meager. This, he claimed angrily, was due to Schlesinger and his German publishers, who were always taking advantage of him.[23] As Nicholas Chopin pointed out, however, the fault was really his own. If he wouldn't live in such a hand-to-mouth fashion he could afford to hold out for a better price on his works instead of letting them go cheaply for the sake of quick cash. Typically, the son ignored his father and refused to curtail his life-style as long as he had enough rich pupils to support it.

While it was easy to shrug off the advice of a parent hundreds of miles away it was harder to ignore the pleas of a friend at hand. In February Hiller, who was about to move back to Germany, asked Chopin to perform a piano duo with him at one of his last concerts in Paris. It was to be held in the Salle Érard at No. 14 rue du Mail, just across the street from a house occupied for many years by Mme. Recamier.

The small hall with a seating capacity of less than 400 people was owned by the Érard family, whose main interest was the manufacture of pianos. In 1768 Sebastian Erhard, a native of Strasbourg, first came to Paris where he soon changed his name from Erhard to Érard and his business from harpsichords to pianos. During the French Revolution, when he saw his instruments being chopped up for firewood, he fled to England and opened a new shop. There he busied himself trying to perfect an instrument that would combine the sonority of English pianos with the rapid action and light touch of continental ones. Before long he had accomplished this through the use of iron frames and the invention of a device called a "double escapement action." The latter allowed the hammers of the piano to bounce back into position so quickly a pianist could repeat any note within split seconds after having played it.[24] With such pianos, virtuosos were soon performing runs and trills at a previously unheard-of speed and creating dazzling effects impossible on earlier instruments.

The entrance of Sebastian's son Pierre into the family business (now back in Paris again) led to even greater successes. By 1834 the company employed 150 men and made 400 pianos a year. With the profits from all this Pierre was able to buy the luxurious Château de la Muette in 1835. There he installed a large art collection comprising paintings "of every school,"[25] many of which found their way onto the walls of the Salle Érard for the enjoyment of its audiences.

Hiller's concert in which Chopin had agreed to play was another of those afternoon affairs so deplored by the reviewer of the *Gazette Musicale*. In fact the critics disdain for such enterprises probably explains why the *Gazette* failed to write it up. However, from Fétis' *Revue Musicale* of March 8, 1835, we can pretty well reconstruct the program, which consisted entirely of works by Hiller.

> Trio, performed by MM. Baillot, Franchomme, and the composer
> Quartet, performed by MM. Baillot, Vidal, Franchomme, and Sauzay
> Études, performed by the composer
> Duo for two pianos, performed by MM. Chopin and the composer
> "Le Songe", "La Fiancée du Pêcheur" sung by Mme. Dorus-Gras
> "Vanitas, Vanitatum, Vanitas!" "La Chanson Suisse," "La Chanson à Boire," sung by the German chorus of the Opéra-Comique

All the soloists on the program were well known to Chopin. With the exception of Mme. Dorus-Gras[26] and the French violinist, Charles Eugène Sauzay, he had already performed with them in previous concerts. Since Sauzay was Baillot's son-in-law (and later a member of his quartet) he and Chopin could hardly have been strangers to one another. As for Mme. Dorus-Gras, Chopin had often enjoyed her exceptional voice at the Opéra. She made her debut there in 1831 and for the next fifteen years remained one of the house's brightest sopranos and dullest actresses.

SALLE ÉRARD, PARIS

MLLE. DUCHENOIS

HENRI HERZ

HECTOR BERLIOZ

WAUXHALL D'ÉTÉ, PARIS

SALLE FAVART (THÉÂTRE ITALIEN), PARIS

While the *Revue Musicale* voiced some reservations about Hiller's compositions it found the performers uniformly good apart from the off-key singing of the German chorus. The duo in which Chopin participated was described as "sparkling."[27]

If he had wanted to, Chopin himself could have given a similar concert of his own works in 1835. Besides his compositions for the piano (several of which were supported by orchestral accompaniments), he had already written a number of songs and several chamber works with parts for cello, violin, and flute. Not until the last year of his life, however, when he was in desperate financial straits, was he ever motivated to do so.[28] Prior to that only the rich in the princely splendor of their grand *hôtels particuliers* had the privilege of hearing an all-Chopin recital.

Toward the end of February Chopin came down with an attack of "influenza" and coughed up blood for several days. On March 1 he passed his 25th birthday at home under the care of his roommate, Dr. Matuszyński. Two weeks later he was well enough to appear onstage again in the concert debut of one of Kalkbrenner's pupils, Camille Stamaty. He felt particularly obliged to take part in this concert since Stamaty had been good enough to help him out at his own Paris debut three years earlier.

Stamaty seems to have been a special favorite of his teacher, who treated him more like a son than a pupil. He was even invited to live in the Kalkbrenner home while taking lessons there. For someone who had never played the piano until he was sixteen it is remarkable that Stamaty could be ready to make his formal debut at age twenty-four. This, Kalkbrenner decided, was to take place on Sunday, March 15, at 8:00 P.M. in the Salle Pleyel.

By 1835 Pleyel's hall was already in its sixth season. Situated on the narrow rue Cadet, toward the northern perimeter of fashionable Paris, it still lay within the boundaries considered acceptable by society, which flocked there regularly to hear the finest musicians of the era. When the hall opened on January 1, 1830, Kalkbrenner was one of the soloists, partly because of his outstanding virtuosity and partly because of his business connections with the hall's owner, Camille Pleyel.

The firm of Pleyel et Cie. had been founded in 1809 by Camille's father, Ignace, who was—*mirabile dictu*— the 24th of 38 children! As a youth Ignace studied with Josef Haydn and created a favorable impression on Mozart. In his lifetime he was regarded as a composer and pianist of considerable importance. For well over a decade he supervised his company's piano factory until the 1820s when he turned it over to his oldest son, Camille. As far as Chopin was concerned, nobody in all Europe made pianos like Pleyel's. They "are the absolute pinnacle of perfection," he exclaimed when he first tried them out in 1831.[29]

Camille Pleyel, like his father, was an incredibly versatile individual. He played the piano beautifully and might well have become a great virtuoso if he hadn't been saddled with the family business. Under his management the company branched out into the publishing field. In 1829 he took in Kalkbrenner as a partner, and the following year he opened the Salle Pleyel. The only real failure in Camille's life was his marriage to the bewitching Belgian pianist, Marie Moke, whom he seduced away from Berlioz.[30] Soon he discovered that almost anyone who wanted to could seduce the beautiful young lady. Her many affairs (with Hiller, Fétis, and Liszt among others) became notorious, and after five years of marriage he left her.

In making the arrangements for Stamaty's debut, Kalkbrenner, with his typical egocentricity, couldn't resist turning the concert into a vehicle for his own glory. His Variations on Rossini's "Di Tanti Palpiti" and his Grand (piano) Duo figured prominently on the program while the extraordinary collection of six pianists assembled for the occasion suggests that he also added his musical behemoth, the Grand Polonaise to it. Besides Kalkbrenner, Stamaty, and Chopin, the other members of the sextet were Hiller, Osborne, and Henri Herz—the same team that tackled the work at Chopin's debut except for Herz, whose "brutal pounding"[31] replaced the loud thumping of Sowiński.

Since Stamaty after all was the star of the show, Kalkbrenner allowed him to play one of his own compositions, the Concerto for piano and orchestra, opus 2. For this (as well as Kalkbrenner's Rossini Variations) a conductor was needed, and the one chosen seems to have been Anton Reicha.[32] A Czech by birth, Reicha served for years as professor of composition, counterpoint, and theory at the Paris Conservatory where he eventually came to teach just about everyone of any musical importance in nineteenth-century France. He had little success, though, with his own compositions, which were poorly received in their day and seldom performed since. Elsner once recommended that Chopin study with Reicha, but this never came to pass. "Reicha doesn't really like music," Chopin claimed. "He doesn't even want to talk about it. When he teaches he spends the whole time watching the clock."[33]

The rest of Stamaty's program consisted of some Variations for cello by August Franchomme and several vocal numbers. One of these, a Gluck aria, was sung in an "admirable" fashion by Mlle. Leroy.[34] Mlle. Antonia Lambert, another of the vocalists that afternoon, enjoyed a considerable vogue in such distinguished salons as those of Mme. Sophie Gay and Mme. de Girardin,[35] although her voice was said to be "uneven" and her intonation "imperfect."[36] The two other singers, Giulio Marco Bordogni and Jean-Frédéric-August Ponchard, could hardly have been very exciting. Both were well past their prime and had come out of retirement for the occasion. Bordogni was a thin-sounding tenor whose operatic career had been extraordinarily lackluster, while the plain-looking Ponchard was a former violinist who once managed to extract a certain expressive quality out of an otherwise mediocre voice.

Stamaty himself never went on to become a great pianist even though the critics of both the *Gazette Musicale* and the *Revue Musicale* predicted a bright future for him. After his debut at the Salle Pleyel he studied composition with Schumann and Mendelssohn and is best remembered today as the teacher of Louis Moreau Gottschalk and Camille Saint-Saëns.

More musical obligations awaited Chopin in April. The first of these involved an old friend from Warsaw, the Princess Anna Czartoryska. She was the daughter of Prince Sapieha, whose distinguished family could trace its ancestry to Poland's fourteenth-century Jagiełłonian rulers. Sometime in 1834 Mme. Czartoryska and several of her Polish friends formed a society to raise money for the benefit of their fellow exiles in Paris. The result was the Benevolent Association of Polish Ladies.

When the society decided to give a concert on April 4, the princess asked Chopin's help, although by then she should have known he was not a very effective organizer. After nearly four years in Paris he had barely been able to put together one concert on his own—and then only after numerous delays. Now in 1835 he was to run into the same problem that frustrated him in 1831: there simply weren't any available singers in the city. A week before the benefit, *Le National* assured its readers that "the leading artists of the capital will be on the program,"[37] but it didn't give any specific names. The truth was, so Jules Janin of the *Journal des Débats* reported,

> this concert, which started out looking so auspicious, wound up in serious trouble. At first everyone made all sorts of promises only to break them later. Things reached such a pass it began to look as if the noble president of the concert, Princess Czartoryska, for lack of any singers, would have to send for the drummers of the 11th Legion at the last minute and proclaim to her audience with a loud flourish of drums: "*Gentlemen, this is the best the granddaughter of the Jaggiellons could muster up in all Paris to help out her poor comrades.*"[38]

Janin, however, had underestimated Mme. Czartoryska, who didn't give up that easily. Before the week was out she came up with two of the brightest operatic stars in the Parisian firmament: the soprano Marie-Cornélie Falcon and the tenor Adolphe Nourrit. Mlle. Falcon had made her debut in Meyerbeer's unforgettable extravaganza *Robert le Diable*.[39] Her voice was "strong and of great extent," while her acting was "animated and expressive."[40] Unfortuntaely, in 1839 when she was only twenty-six her voice failed from overexertion and she was forced to retire.

Nourrit too had sung in *Robert le Diable*. In fact, Meyerbeer actually conceived the tenor role expressly for him.[41] His father, who was an earlier tenor at the Paris Opéra, originally planned for young Adolphe to become a diamond merchant, but when he discovered that his son's voice was far more valuable than any gem he could peddle he sent him off to study with the noted voice teacher Manuel Garcia.[42] Because Nourrit got a late start in his career he never achieved as much technical dexterity as some of his contemporaries, but the great sensitivity of his musical and dramatic interpretations made up for this. Despite his Pickwickian proportions, Nourrit lacked the phlegmatic personality often associated with obesity. On the contrary, he had an alert and clever mind with a range of interests extending well beyond the field of music.

The other performers who responded to the Polish Ladies' appeal that spring were equally esteemed musicians whose names appear over and over again in the Paris newspapers of the period: the violinist Heinrich Wilhelm Ernst, the flutist M. Dorus (a brother of Mme. Dorus-Gras), and the ubiquitous Liszt and Hiller. Habeneck from the Conservatory conducted the orchestra.

Gambling on a big turnout, Princess Czartoryska engaged the spacious Théâtre-Italien. This large structure not far from Chopin's apartment was tucked away in a cramped little cavity just off the Boulevard des Italiens.[43] Its peculiar location was due to the fact that the Duke of Choiseul who built it in 1782 reserved the boulevard frontage of his property for expensive shops and apartments that would bring him high rents. Both the theater and the neighboring boulevard derived their names from the Comédie-Italienne, which first inhabited the building. For many years the theater was also known as the Salle Favart in honor of the eighteenth-century dramatist and librettist Charles-Simon Favart, who was its first manager.[44]

On Saturday evening, April 4, Princess Czartoryska proudly presented the following program:

Aria from *The Siege of Corinth* sung by Mlle. Falcon
Duet from *William Tell*,
sung by M. Nourrit and Mlle. Falcon
Schubert lieder, sung by M. Nourrit,
accompanied by the orchestra
Concerto in E minor,
composed and performed by M. Chopin
Duo for two pianos by Hiller,
performed by the composer and M. Liszt
Violin solo, composed and performed by M. Ernst
Schubert lieder, sung by M. Nourrit,
accompanied by M. Liszt at the piano
Flute solo, by M. Dorus
Overtures from *Oberon* and *William Tell*,
by the orchestra under the direction of Habeneck[45]

That night the Polish ladies garnered a handsome sum from their charitable endeavor. On the whole everything went well, although the size of the hall created problems for some of the performers. As the *Gazette Musicale* pointed out, several numbers on the program didn't carry adequately across the huge interior, and yet for once Chopin escaped the usual complaint that he played too softly. His concerto was considered "an enormous success"[46] by the paper's critic who, oddly enough, regarded concertos in general as a "worn-out" and "monotonous" form of music.

Actually Chopin seemed rather tired of them himself and never bothered to finish his third concerto, which he had started some time earlier. After letting it languish for another six years he finally pieced together fragments of it into an Allegro de Concert which he published in 1841.

As an expression of gratitude to those who made their benefit a success the Benevolent Association of Polish Ladies gave Liszt and Hiller each a diamond ring, Habeneck a snuff box, Nourrit a tiepin, and Mlle. Falcon a bracelet. Chopin apparently received nothing—probably because he refused to accept any reward for what he considered a moral obligation to his fellow countrymen.

The concert for Polish exiles may have been indirectly responsible for Chopin's next public appearance on April 26. It too was a benefit, this time for Habeneck, to whom he was indebted for conducting the orchestral score of his concerto on April 4.

The fifty-four-year-old François-Antoine Habeneck was one of the most respected musical figures in Paris then, even though Berlioz dismissed him as an "able but limited and unreliable conductor."[47] On the contrary, his career was highly distinguished and his abilities quite out of the ordinary. The son of a violinist and military band conductor, he studied violin at an early age and later took lessons from Baillot. Eventually he became director of the Opéra's orchestra, a post he held for twenty-five years. Unlike Berlioz, who loved the new vogue of conducting with a baton (which allowed him to gyrate ostentatiously on a podium in the middle of the stage), Habeneck preferred to conduct quietly with his bow from the first violinist's seat. Once the tempo was established, he often leaned back, took a pinch of snuff, and let the orchestra carry on by itself.

It was Habeneck who, in 1828, founded the famous Concert Society of the Conservatory in an effort to bring the public neglected works of many great composers. The first of its concerts, given on March 9 of that year, featured Beethoven's *Eroica* Symphony, and for many decades to come the society remained a worthy cultural tradition in Paris. It was considered a great privilege to perform with the society, and Chopin, who had hoped for such a favor back in March of 1832, was now pleased when Habeneck finally offered him that opportunity in 1835. The concert in which he participated was the last of the seven given by the society that year and took place on April 26. Sharing the honors with Chopin once again were Marie-Cornélie Falcon and Adolphe Nourrit. Habeneck's intense admiration for Beethoven's music is evident in the program given below:

1. Symphony No. 6 (*Pastoral*) by Beethoven
2. "The Erl King," by Schubert, sung by M. Nourrit[48]
3. Scherzo from the Symphony No. 9 by Beethoven
4. Grande Polonaise, preceded by the Andante Spianato composed and played by M. Chopin
5. Scena by Beethoven ("Ah! Perfido"), sung by Mlle. Falcon
6. Finale from the Symphony No. 5 by Beethoven

In announcing the event the *Gazette Musicale* printed Chopin's name in capital letters and promised those who planned to attend enough music "to fill the church of the Invalides."[49] After making this extravagant claim, however, it then proceeded to overlook the occasion completely. Only the *Revue Musicale* of May 3 bothered to mention the concert and then chiefly to complain about the society's programs (too much Beethoven).

For his Grande Polonaise and Andante Spianato Chopin was given a standing ovation. This sort of reception at one of the Concert Society's performances was the dream of every young virtuoso in Paris, but for Chopin it had come too late to arouse much enthusiasm. Now, at the end of his fourth musical season in Paris, the life of a concert artist no longer appealed to him as it once had. To be a successful virtuoso, one needed an insatiable hunger for public acclaim and the competitive drive to achieve it—qualities typical of Liszt, for example, but painfully lacking in Chopin.

This significant disparity between Liszt and himself was particularly evident in the way the two of them reacted to the arrival of Sigismond Thalberg for his Paris debut in 1835. The dandified young Viennese pianist possessed a technique so fantastic he seemed almost superhuman. Some said he played with three hands instead of two, while the sculptor Dantan created a caricature of him showing ten fingers on each hand. To Liszt this newcomer posed such a challenge he spent the next two years jousting with him in a running keyboard contest that divided all Paris into opposing camps. Chopin, by contrast, sat on the sidelines, avoiding the fray and scorning the vulgarity of open rivalry. In the long run the price he paid for his patronizing passivity was to see Liszt and Thalberg grow rich while he himself had to struggle along on a teacher's pay and the scanty royalties doled out by his publishers.

Even Habeneck, whom few remember today, found his talents better rewarded than Chopin's. Only two days after the Conservatory concert still another benefit was given for him in the Hôtel Laffitte.

• CHAPTER NINE •

PARIS 1836

THE SUMMER OF 1835 began quietly for Chopin. Short of money, he remained in or near Paris until August when he learned that his parents were leaving for Bohemia to take the waters in Karlsbad.[1] This provided an unexpected chance to see them without returning to Poland where he might be detained. It was an opportunity too great to miss, and with little regard for the cost of the trip, he rushed off to join them.

In those days the fastest—if least comfortable—means of travel was the mail coach, which brought him to Karlsbad late on August 15 several hours before his parents' arrival. Near dawn of the next day the three exhausted Chopins fell into each other's arms for their first reunion in nearly five years.

Over the following month they remained in Karlsbad enjoying what would be their last visit together. Around the second week in September Nicholas and Justyna Chopin set out for Warsaw while their son headed back to Paris at a leisurely pace. In Dresden he stopped to see the Wodziński family, who had been urging him to visit them for over a year. During the two weeks he was there he found himself quite attracted to their sixteen-year-old daughter, Maria. Since he had last seen her years earlier in Warsaw she had blossomed into a remarkable young beauty.

From Dresden he journeyed on to Leipzig where Mendelssohn introduced him to Robert Schumann and the pianist Clara Wieck. Next, he stopped in Heidelberg to look up the family of his pupil Adolf Gutmann. Here he was delayed for some time by a severe bout of bronchitis. When he finally got back to Paris it was late October.

In November he had still another attack of bronchitis, much worse than before. This time he coughed up blood and ran such a high fever he became confused and suffered from hallucinations. In Poland rumors of his death compelled the *Kurjer Warszawski* to reassure its readers that these reports were themselves nothing but hallucinations. All the same, Chopin was quite shaken up by the experience. While the streets outside his windows rang with noisy celebrations in honor of the newly completed Arc de Triomphe, he sat down and wrote out a will for the first time in his life.

By Christmas he was feeling well enough to go next door and play at Princess Czartoryska's annual bazaar for Polish refugees. This affair, which ran from December 21 to 24, was held in quarters provided by M. Meurice at No. 3 rue de la Chaussée d'Antin.[2] Every day the doors opened at noon but Chopin wasn't expected until eight o'clock, when he took his place at the piano and improvised for two hours to amuse the crowds browsing among Renaissance paintings, illuminated manuscripts, and other luxury items on sale in the princess' expensive little stalls.

Because of his poor health Chopin avoided any other musical commitments until February 1836, when a casual acquaintance, Charles Schunke, asked him to take part in a small concert at the home of Monsieur D. Levi, a history professor in the faubourg Saint-Germain. The thirty-five-year-old Schunke, just recently appointed "pianist to the Queen," had studied with Beethoven's pupil Ferdinand Ries before coming to Paris in 1828. Physically he had the strong, solid frame of an athlete, but temperamentally he was a shy, sensitive creature, afflicted with the same horrible stage fright that Chopin often experienced.

Their personalities made both men better suited to teaching than to concertizing, and both attracted a preponderance of female students. In the case of the young ladies who studied with Schunke, music was only part of a much broader education he provided for them. To accomplish this he collaborated with Professor Levi, the author of several scholarly works entitled *Elements of General History* and *Historical Sketches*. Together they devised a "Systematic Course of Instruction" that included a series of recitals by Schunke and his pupils. Between their musical numbers Professor Levi would sprinkle dramatic recitations of choice passages from the "finest" European literature. According to the *Revue et Gazette Musicale,*[3] this happy melding of the arts made for evenings "at once useful and agreeable."[4] Ordinarily they took place in a house at No. 19 rue de Lille (next door to Professor Levi's own home at No. 17) and were attended mostly by the family and friends of the young ladies for whose uplift they were designed.

Schunke's concert in which Chopin played on February 7, 1836, differed from these lecture-recitals in several ways. First of all it was held in Professor Levi's house itself, and second it was given without any student participation or literary readings. Because of the limited space, admission was by invitation only. In the words of Sophie Gay,[5] who wrote up the occasion for the *Revue et Gazette Musicale,* it was a "brilliant soirée."[6] M. Schunke, who evidently felt relaxed in the small rue de Lille salon, showed no signs of the nervousness that usually affected him, and the "flood of joyful notes" he poured out filled Mme. Gay with "wonder and amazement." Altogether he played several solos and participated in two duets, once with Chopin in a four-hand sonata by Moscheles[7] ("You can doubtless imagine the effect of this superb piece when played by two such magnificent artists"),[8] and again with the violinist Ernst in a work based on a theme from Weber's *Oberon.*

Mme. Gay was struck with Ernst's "capable and powerful abilities" but marveled even more at the "unheard-of-effects" produced by "M. Lewi and his horn."[9] Taking into account the careless spelling of journalists in those days, M. Lewi was probably the same Josef Lewy with whom Chopin once performed in Vienna.[10] Later he became the principal horn player in the royal Saxon chapel at Dresden. Prior to that, however, he traveled extensively during the mid-1830s and served for a while as director of music to His Royal Highness the Prince of Sweden and Norway. At that time he was known to have visited Paris where he played in a number of concerts.

The other artists that night failed to elicit any special comment from Mme. Gay. The cellist Alexandre Batta, who had just come from Brussels, was not yet well known in Paris although his glittering technique soon made him a great favorite in the city's salons. Basically, however, he was a person of superficial tastes. Even less distinguished were the two singers on Schunke's program, Ernest Boulanger and Joseph Lanza. While Boulanger achieved some success in Paris, Lanza didn't and subsequently moved on from the rue de Lille to the city of

Lille itself. There he fared no better, and in 1841 he set out across the Atlantic, hoping to find an appreciative audience in America.

Far worse was the fate that waited poor Schunke. Early in 1838 when he was just thirty-seven years old a stroke left him badly crippled and unable to speak. For some time he vegetated in a sanatorium where he eventually grew so despondent he dragged himself to a window and jumped to his death on December 16, 1839.

Beyond Professor Levi's little realm lay another faubourg Saint-Germain, the aristocratic world depicted by Stendahl and Balzac, the world of great houses with secluded gardens and cobblestoned "courts of honor," a world of cool marble floors warmed by soft Savonnerie carpets, of tapestried walls reflected in the patina of marquetried tables, and gilded boiserie glistening in the glow of crystal chandeliers. In this fashionable domain lived many of Chopin's new friends whom he often visited, including the Maréchale de Lannes and her son the Duke of Montebello, the Austrian ambassador Count Apponyi, and a number of other venerable aristocrats, descended from the *ancien régime* of prerevolutionary France. On the Quai Malaquai was the home of the Count and Countess d'Agoult, where Chopin had been a frequent guest until the previous summer when the countess ran off to live with Franz Liszt in Switzerland. Already she had given birth to a child by him, a baby girl born in December 1835.

For some time after the concert at Professor Levi's Chopin was seldom seen by his friends in the faubourg Saint-Germain or elsewhere. The winter was a harsh one with long spells of subfreezing temperatures which kept him from getting out much. Often he was sick and had to turn his pupils away, which took its toll on his income. Luckily his compositions were selling well. In 1836 Schlesinger bought up a number of polonaises, nocturnes, and mazurkas and saw to it that they got plenty of publicity. To every new subscriber of his *Revue et Gazette Musicale* that season he offered a free copy of the four Mazurkas, opus 24.

While Chopin remained shut in a good part of that winter the kaleidoscopic pageant of Paris continued on around him. Gaslights illuminated the rue Saint-Honoré for the first time in February, and at the Hôtel de L'Europe the famous Siamese twins were on view from one to four o'clock every afternoon for only two francs, fifty centimes. February also saw the execution of Fieschi and his accomplices who tried to assassinate Louis-Philippe with their "infernal machine," a deadly device composed of twenty-five rifles that fired simultaneously.

By spring, crowds were gathering daily at the Left Bank's Luxembourg Palace to witness the so-called "Monster Trial" of those arrested in Lyons and Paris during the republican uprisings of 1834.[11] At that time such trials were delegated to the Court of Peers headed by a *grand référendaire* (or chief justice) who, in 1836, happened to be a friend of Chopin, the Duke Decazes. Only a few months earlier his wife had tended one of the stalls at Princess Czartoryska's Christmas bazaar in the Chaussée d'Antin. As the trials got under way many Parisians became critical of the way they were being run. The *Revue de Paris,* for example, scored the "old-time politicians, those tired, flabby creatures who sit on the benches of the peerage," and recommended that M. Decazes step down.[12] "He belongs to an epoque that has passed," it claimed.[13]

Actually the duke was only fifty-five years old then and just in his prime. Politically he was a moderate who had been skillful enough to maintain his influence through four successive reigns. In his youth he served under Napoleon's brother King Louis of Holland and acted as secretary to the Bonapartes' mother, "Madame Mère." During the Restoration Louis XVIII made him a duke, while Charles X sent him to England as ambassador to the Court of St. James's. Now under Louis-Philippe he had been appointed *grand référendaire* of the Court of Peers. Even the critical *Revue de Paris* readily admitted that he was a conscientious, hardworking man.

The easy adaptability that the duke displayed in his political life was reflected in the great diversity of people he and the duchess invited to their salon. A typical crowd there consisted of "an amusing potpourri of individuals representing every belief, every mood, and every level of society."[14] To entertain their many friends the couple often held concerts in the spacious apartments provided for them by the government in the Petit Luxembourg Palace. Set in its own private garden to the west of the newer main palace, the Petit Luxembourg had its origins in the sixteenth century. Marie de Medicis, wife of Henri IV, bought it in 1612 and gave it to Cardinal Richelieu. Later it descended to members of the Bourbon-Condé family, housed the Austrian ambassador to Louis XVI's court, and served for a while as home to Napoleon and his empress, Josephine.

The musical soirée given by the Duke and Duchess Decazes on April 21, 1836, was predominantly a vocal concert with Chopin being the only instrumentalist. None of the four singers invited to perform was particularly outstanding. Only two of them, in fact, were professional artists: Ernest Boulanger, who had recently sung at Professor Levi's, and a young man named Géraldi who eventually joined the faculty of the Brussels Conservatory after Cherubini refused to waste the Paris Conservatory's money on him.

The other two singers that night were Baron Christophe, an aristocratic dilettante, and Adele Meneghini Crescini, an amateur Venetian contralto. The latter's husband, Jacapo, had just written the libretto for Mercadante's new opera, *I Briganti,* which premiered at the Théâtre-Italien on March 22.[15] Although Mme. Crescini wasn't part of the cast, she performed privately in many of the city's salons where she created quite a stir. Shortly after her arrival she appeared at the home of Countess Merlin (the "undisputed queen" of musical society in Paris then)[16] and later sang before the royal family in the Tuileries "with great success."[17]

At the Duke and Duchess Decazes' she performed a cantata entitled *Eloisa nel Chiostro,* "an extremely sensitive and melodious work"[18] written specially for her by the Italian composer M. Alary. In the opinion of the *Revue et Gazette Musicale* she walked off with the "honors of the evening,"[19] surpassing all the other performers including Chopin, who had played one of his waltzes with that "delicacy for which he is famous."[20]

Such success encouraged Mme. Crescini to reserve the Théâtre-Italien for a concert of her own shortly afterward, but the boldness of this venture soon frightened her and she fled to London without being heard in Paris again. *Sic transit* Adele Crescini, who in her brief moment of glory eclipsed even Chopin himself.

• CHAPTER TEN •

Paris and Rouen 1837–1838

With the return of good weather Chopin ventured out of Paris several times in the spring of 1836. At the popular spa of Enghien-les-Bains he visited Countess Delfina Potocka, a Polish siren with a divine voice and a dreadful husband. Nearby at Saint-Gratien was the country estate of the cultivated Astolphe de Custine, a forty-six-year-old marquis who traveled, wrote, and dabbled in the arts. Both the voluptuous countess and the dilettantish marquis were noted for their romantic escapades: both had flagrant reputations for seducing men. Whether the countess ever had an affair with Chopin is still the subject of much dispute; that the marquis certainly wanted to seems less controversial. He flattered the musician with constant attentions, hovered over him in the salons, invited him to dinner in Paris, and asked him for weekends in the country.

The chances that Chopin succumbed to either of his new admirers is slim, since he had secretly devoted himself to a new "ideal" over the past year: the demure and childlike Maria Wodzińska he had visited the previous summer in Dresden. When word reached him in May 1836 that the Wodzińskis were considering a trip to Marienbad he put aside all other plans (including a visit to Mendelssohn in Düsseldorf) in order to go there.

With his health and finances in unusually good shape he arrived at Marienbad in July to find his lovely Maria more captivating than ever. One evening at twilight he proposed to her and she accepted. Mme. Wodzińska appeared delighted but whether Maria's father would feel the same way was another matter, which prompted the couple to keep their engagement a secret until they had his consent.

Early in September the happy fiancé left for Paris, stopping briefly in Leipzig to call on Schumann and Clara Wieck, another young couple in love. His visit with them was pleasant enough even though Schumann had lost some of his initial enthusiasm for Chopin's compositions and now regarded Clara as a much better pianist.

Back in Paris, the prospect of supporting a bride and a future family did nothing to curb Chopin's habitual extravagance. By October he and Matuszyński had moved up the street to a more expensive apartment at No. 38 rue de la Chaussée d'Antin. He seldom felt homesick or thought of leaving Paris anymore. After all, what other city could possibly equal it for beauty and excitement? Now that the new Arc de Triomphe crowned the hill at the west end of the Champs Élysées, work had begun on the fountains in the Place de la Concorde at the other end of the avenue. In October crowds gathered there to watch the raising of the obelisk of Luxor, a feat that took three hours of ticklish maneuvering.

That same month Liszt and the Countess d'Agoult returned from Switzerland and took rooms at the Hôtel de France in the rue Laffitte where they were soon joined by George Sand and her two children, Maurice, aged thirteen, and Solange, aged eight. Although Mme. Sand owned a small chateau in the village of Nohant, about 150 miles south of Paris, she had come to spend more and more time in the city since leaving her husband, the Baron Dudevant, in 1831. Her early novels had made her a celebrity and she now knew almost everybody of importance in Paris with one significant exception: Fryderyk Chopin. Often that fall she badgered Liszt for an introduction to him. But this was no easy task since Chopin wanted nothing to do with the trouser-clad, cigar-puffing female who displayed such a tasteless obsession with sex in her books. Only through the clever wiles of Mme. d'Agoult was Liszt finally able to lure Chopin to the Hôtel de France for his fateful encounter with George Sand.

The brazen amazon he had pictured turned out to be a petite, olive-skinned brunette who hardly opened her mouth all evening. If she wasn't as offensive as he had imagined, he still didn't find her particularly attractive. On the contrary, when he left the Hôtel de France that night he had a distinctly disagreeable impression of her.

Nevertheless, there was something about this quiet little baroness that intrigued him, and in December he invited her to his apartment for a small evening musicale. Instead of her famous pants she wore a striking red and white Turkish outfit and sat quietly throughout the performance. Afterward she sipped tea and sampled the flavored ices Chopin served his guests while her lover, Charles Didier, waited impatiently for her back in the Hôtel de France. When she returned toward midnight Didier found her restless and moody. Their relationship was never the same again.

For Chopin, the thirty-two-year-old novelist was nothing more than a fascinating curiosity. Six years his senior, she had none of the girlish charm of Maria Wodzińska, who was now writing him regularly in the form of little notes added to her mother's letters. As the months went by, this correspondence began to taper off without any mention of the long-awaited approval by Maria's father. From Warsaw word came that the Wodzińskis had visited Chopin's family to inquire about his health. People were saying he was sick again. This time the rumors were true.

All through the winter of 1836–37 Fryderyk was plagued by attacks of "influenza" which kept him away from the concert stage most of that season. If anything he welcomed this, since the rivalry between Liszt and Thalberg was rapidly building to a climax that now absorbed the attention of all Paris. By spring the spectacle-hungry public was calling for a face-to-face confrontation between the two pianists.

In response to this demand the Princess Belgiojoso organized a three-day charity bazaar which was to culminate in a concert featuring Liszt and Thalberg together on Friday, March 31, 1837. The uninhibited princess was a lady of florid eccentricities who habitually dressed in black velvet and wore water lilies pinned to her hair. Once a week she reigned over her exclusive Thursday salon, crowded with such prized *literati* as Heinrich Heine, Victor Hugo, and the elder Dumas. The witty repartee that flashed back and forth between her guests kept them far too occupied ever to suspect that upstairs in a secret closet their hostess kept the mummified body of her dead lover, dressed in evening clothes—or so gossip had it. Such stories didn't seem to bother *la Belgiojoso* or affect her standing in Paris society. The bazaar she planned drew support from the highest quarters. The ladies of the royal household, for example, donated a collection of tapestries, while Meyerbeer gave her one of his unpublished songs and artists like Delacroix, Delaroche, Lehmann, and Ary Scheffer sent over some of their paintings.

One of the prizes to be auctioned off at the bazaar was a new set of variations for piano based on the march from Bellini's *I Puritani*. A different composer was responsible for each variation; these included Liszt, Thalberg, J. P. Pixis, Czerny, Henri Herz, and Chopin. Because of its six authors the work was christened *Hexameron*. Unfortunately Liszt, who coordinated the effort, was too busy to finish it in time. Three months later the princess was still heckling him for it.

His failure to have the *Hexameron* ready thwarted Mme. Belgiojoso's plans to have it performed at her concert with each of the composers playing his particular variation. Without them only Liszt and Thalberg remained on the program—which may have been Liszt's intention all along. Certainly this spectacular pair of pianists was capable of providing excitement enough for the lucky concertgoer who could afford the forty francs to get past the little Moor at the entrance to the princess' salon. In the end the competition between these two rivals seems to have been a draw. According to the *Revue et Gazette Musicale,* there was "neither victory nor defeat . . . the applause was equally divided between both of the artists."[1]

This colossal publicity stunt didn't improve Chopin's opinion of either pianist. He had never cared for Thalberg since their first encounter in Vienna, and he was finding Liszt's grandiloquent airs more and more irksome. Regardless of this he still accepted Liszt's invitation to take part in his so-called "farewell" concert scheduled for April 9 at the Salle Érard. Now that the battle with Thalberg had ended in a truce, Mme. d'Agoult was able to persuade her lover to retire to a secluded spot in northern Italy where he could compose. In Paris she felt uncomfortable under the disapproving eyes of her husband and his stuffy Saint-Germain friends. Besides, she thought Franz was wasting his talents at the keyboard and had visions of herself as the muse that would lead him to his true calling: the creation of immortal music for posterity.

In the wake of the Princess Belgiojoso's sensational spectacle anything was bound to seem anticlimactic, and Liszt's farewell concert received little attention even though he brought together no less than fourteen artists for it. What they performed is recorded in the following program, which took place at 1:30 on a Sunday afternoon in spring.[2]

PART I

1. Grand Septuor, executed by Liszt, Urhan, Mathieu, Dorus, Brod, Pierret, and Lee[3]
   by Hummel
2. Duet, sung by Mme. Taccani and M. Géraldy [sic]
   by Rossini
3. [Violin] Solo, executed by M. Massart
4. Aria from *Crociato in Egitto,* sung by Mme. Taccani
   by Meyerbeer
5. Scene from *Les Huguenots* (fourth act),
   performed on the trumpet by M. Pierret
6. Reminiscences from *Les Huguenots,* a grand fantasy,
   composed and performed by M. Liszt

PART II

7. Grand Quintet, performed by MM. Liszt,
   Brod, Clauset, and the Pierret brothers
   by Beethoven
8. Aria from *The Magic Flute,* sung by M. Géraldy
   by Mozart
9. [Harp] Fantasy on themes from *Robert le Diable,*
   performed by Mlle. Bertucat
   [by Meyerbeer]
10. Cavatina from *Norma,* sung by Mme. Taccani
    by Bellini
11. Études by Chopin (unpublished),
    performed by M. Liszt
12. Grande Valse for four hands,
    performed by MM. Chopin and Liszt[4]

Among the performers that afternoon was the twenty-six-year-old Belgian violinist Joseph Lambert Massart, for whom Liszt must have felt a special bond of sympathy. Cherubini, who succeeded in barring Liszt's admission to the Paris Conservatory (on the grounds that he wasn't French-born) had tried to do the same to Lambert. Thanks, however, to the intercession of the latter's teacher, Kreutzer, and his patron, the King of the Belgians, Cherubini finally agreed to accept him. In 1843 Lambert rose to the rank of professor at the Conservatory where he taught Wieniawski and Fritz Kreisler.

For Chopin the high point of this concert was surely Liszt's interpretation of his études. Listening to him play them "drives me out of my mind," he once told Hiller. "How I would love to rob him of his knack of playing my own études."[5] Already he had dedicated his first set of Études (opus 10) to Liszt in 1833, while the ones performed that April (from his second set, opus 25) he inscribed to the countess d'Agoult on their publication only a few months later.

Having bade "farewell" to Paris Liszt left for Italy by way of Nohant where he and his countess were the guests of George Sand until July. Chopin had been invited to Nohant also and wrote one of the Wodziński brothers that he might go. Instead, though, he lingered on in Paris, waiting for some news about his engagement to Maria. She and her family were spending some time in Poland that spring and so far her father had remained ominously silent.

Meanwhile the Marquis de Custine renewed his attentions and urged Chopin to come back to Saint-Gratien. The baths there, he insisted, would do wonders for his health. He even offered to lend him money and got his Polish lover, Ignacy Gurowski, to join in his pleas. "Don't feel obliged in any way except to love me," he went on boldly even though he knew that this was "exactly where the problem lies."[6] To his surprise Chopin accepted and returned for a few days' visit.

The end of June found the Wodzińskis still in Poland. Apparently they intended to stay there indefinitely, which meant Chopin would have no chance of seeing Maria that summer. Furthermore the evasive tone of Mme. Wodzińska's letters indicated that the family was anxious to drop the whole matter of the pretended "engagement."

At this point the discouraged young lover decided to take up Camille Pleyel's invitation to spend a week with him in London that July. The two made excellent traveling companions since Pleyel had recently separated from his wife and readily understood the difficulties of coping with the opposite sex. The trip, however, failed to cheer Chopin up. Under the gray English skies he grew even more depressed than before. The British annoyed him and no amount of sightseeing could distract him from his misery. Most of the time he stayed to himself and refused to see anyone—not even Mendelssohn or Moscheles, who were both in London then.

One of the few people Pleyel got him to visit was the piano manufacturer James Shudi Broadwood, who had a handsome brick town house in Bryanston Square, an area known to Londoners then as "Millionaires' Square." Broadwood's pianos were considered by many to be the equal of Pleyel's, but Chopin always preferred the more delicate tone and lighter touch of the latter.

Toward the end of his visit Fryderyk received an upsetting letter from Mme. Wodzińska. Its exact contents are unknown but for Chopin its meaning was perfectly clear: he and Maria would never be married.

A few days later he was back in Paris where he remained morose and irritable for the rest of the summer. In October when George Sand returned to the city for a few weeks she called on him and was astonished at the reception she got. Suddenly Chopin, who had regarded her as a masculine hussy the previous fall, now found her a tantalizing temptress, sensitive and sympathetic—in short, an irresistible *femme fatale*. "I was overcome," he wrote in his journal that month. "My heart was conquered. . . . She understood me. . . . She loves me."[7]

The turning point in their relationship had come, but one serious obstacle blocked its fulfillment: George already had a lover. After Didier she had taken up with a young playwright named Félicien Mallefille who was now living with her at Nohant under the guise of tutor to her children. Because of this she couldn't linger long in Paris and soon left for the country where she and Mallefille settled down for the winter together.

In the months that followed, Chopin returned to his teaching and composing. Schlesinger ran advertisements of his new works regularly in the *Revue et Gazette Musicale,* often alongside those for Johann Strauss' waltzes, which his firm also published. The popular waltz king, whose music Chopin scorned in Vienna, had now come to Paris where he was giving a series of concerts. Crowds flocked to hear him, and in all probability Schlesinger made far more off Strauss waltzes than he did from Chopin mazurkas. Be that as it may, for some people Chopin was by far the better composer. He "hails from the land of Mozart, Raphael, and Goethe," Heinrich Heine claimed. "His true home is in the realm of Poetry."[8]

An even greater tribute came from Count Pozzo di Borgo, the Czar's ambassador in Paris, who proposed that Chopin be nominated for the post of court pianist in St. Petersburg. The job carried with it a lifetime pension that would free him forever from financial worries. Of course, Chopin wouldn't have accepted such a position under any circumstances, although he could scarcely help but relish the triumph of seeing his nation's oppressors bow before his genius.

In February 1838 he received still another royal honor when Louis-Philippe invited him to play at the Tuileries. Perhaps the French king was curious to hear this extraordinary pianist whom the Russian court was trying to steal away from him.

Approximately once a month the royal family held a musicale either in its private apartments or in the palace's sumptuous Salle de Spectacles. To Louis-Philippe, who didn't have much of an ear for music, these occasions were more of an obligation than a pleasure. Bored with the music, he would take advantage of the time to "write and sign documents and chat with various individuals he had invited."[9] Every now and then, when he heard some familiar strain that pleased him, he would stop and sing along. The rest of his family weren't much more attentive. "Throughout the music the Queen and her daughters-in-law" ordinarily sat "around a large table knitting, sewing, or making paper flowers."[10]

On Friday evening, February 16, Chopin's carriage (which was not allowed to enter the courtyard of the Tuileries) discharged him at the palace gate. In those days the royal residence was "surrounded by mud,"[11] which created quite a problem for guests arriving in bad weather. As one of the Paris dailies noted, it was a pathetic sight to see National Guardsman in their "white pants, officers in polished boots, and distinguished members of the peerage with white-plumed hats" dashing across the soggy courtyard to arrive in the king's presence, moments later, rain-drenched and mud-splattered.[12]

Except for Czar Alexander I Chopin had not performed for any other reigning monarch. What he selected to play was a portion of one of his concertos. Two days ahead of time he tried it out at the home of Louis-Philippe's godson the Baron de Trémont,[13] who knew as well as anyone what the king was capable of appreciating. On the night of the concert, though, it proved to be his improvisations on a theme proposed by the king's sister, Mme. Adélaïde, that pleased the royal family most. For once the court ladies put down their work baskets and listened in amazement. Chopin's playing "created the greatest effect on his audience," the *Journal des Débats* reported, "and the gifted artist was repeatedly congratulated by the Queen and the princesses."[14]

Sharing in the compliments that night was Mlle. Bazin, "a young singer endowed with a most beautiful voice," who sang several French romances.[15]

Shortly afterward a silver tea service embellished in gold and inscribed "Louis-Philippe, Roi des Français à Frédéric Chopin" was delivered to the pianist's apartment in the rue de la Chaussée d'Antin.

Two weeks later, on Saturday evening, March 3, Chopin found himself seated in front of another audience only a few blocks north of the Tuileries in the less majestic setting of M. Henri Pape's concert hall at No. 19 rue des Bons Enfans.[16]

Johann Heinrich Pape (to use his true baptismal name) was a forty-nine-year-old German who began his career working in Ignace Pleyel's piano factory. Before long he rose to become manager of the plant, and in 1818 he opened his own piano factory. Pape was a mechanical genius whose active brain churned with useful ideas. During his lifetime he was said to have taken out between 120 and 140 different patents on inventions which ranged from player pianos to the use of compressed felt for covering piano hammerheads. One of his most brilliant innovations was the cross-stringing of piano wires, which allowed the production of small, space-saving instruments like our present-day spinets.

Certainly no one can deny that M. Pape was blessed with an abundance of originality. Many of his ideas, though, were less than practical. His eight-octave piano had a brief vogue but his oval, circular, and hexagonal instruments never really caught on. In 1838 he designed a most remarkable "piano-oven" with a concealed heating unit under the keyboard that enabled the owner to cook and play at the same time. Among the delectable products of this musical bakery, according to a leading Paris journal, were "excellent pastries including rice cakes, baba au rhums, meringues, etc."[17]

Like Pleyel and Érard, Pape was quick to see the advantages of having his own concert hall as a source of extra income and a convenient display case for his instruments. His "salon de concerts," however, never achieved the prestige or popularity of his competitors'.[18]

If M. Pape was an unusual man, Charles Henri Valentin Alkan, who organized the March 3 concert, was even more so. Three years younger than Chopin, he came of an orthodox Jewish family named Morhange. ("Alkan" was his father's first name, which he adopted for professional purposes). Since childhood he had been obsessed with religion and remained forever torn between the callings of a rabbinical scholar and a musician. For years he labored on a translation of the Bible—both the Old and the New Testaments—and met a bizarre end at the age of seventy-five when he accidentally knocked over a shelf of Hebrew religious texts which crushed him to death.[19]

As a pianist Alkan was outstanding although, like Chopin, he had an aversion to playing in public. His technique must have been phenomenal judging from the enormous complexities of his compositions. Their incredible difficulty and interminable length led his contemporaries to nickname him the "Berlioz of the piano."

In later life Alkan grew misanthropic and withdrawn. For nearly twenty-five years he lived like a virtual recluse, preferring the company of his pets to that of people. When his parrot died in 1859 he wrote a funeral march for it, scored for three oboes, bassoon, and mixed voices.

On his own death in 1888, *Le Ménestrel* reported, "Charles-Valentin Alkan has just died. His demise was necessary for us to suspect his existence."[20] At his interment in the Montmartre Cemetery on a bleak Easter Sunday afternoon, only four mourners showed up.

In the 1830s and 1840s, however, Chopin found Alkan an interesting and congenial person. For some time the two men lived next door to each other and became quite good friends.[21] Later, in his will, Chopin left Alkan the fragments of his unfinished *Piano Method* in hopes he might complete it.[22]

Often in the course of their friendship Chopin and Alkan got together to play duets and other ensemble numbers. Alkan's teacher, Pierre Joseph Guillaume Zimmerman, gave evening musicales every Thursday at his home in the Square d'Orléans, and it was probably there that Chopin and Alkan first tried out an eight-hand piano version of Beethoven's Seventh Symphony with Zimmerman and Johann Peter Pixis. Subsequently, as Alkan was preparing for his concert in the Salle Pape, he decided to include this work on the program. When Pixis proved unavailable, one of Chopin's students, Adolf Gutmann, took his place, turning the performance into a joint teacher-pupil exhibition.

Except for Chopin, few people seemed to think Gutmann had much talent. According to von Lenz, the hefty young man had a fist like a prizefighter and played like a porter. Why "Chopin took so much trouble to try and carve a toothpick out of this log" amazed him.[23]

Quite the opposite of the big and oafish Gutmann was the brilliant and elegant Zimmerman. Once a pupil of Cherubini, the fifty-three-year-old Zimmerman now headed the piano department at the Paris Conservatory where he taught such musical greats as Gounod, Bizet, César Franck, and Ambroise Thomas. The American Louis Moreau Gottschalk might also have been on this distinguished list had Zimmerman not been such an arrogant chauvinist. When Gottschalk appeared at the Paris Conservatory for an audition, he refused to hear him. Instead he advised him to go back home and become a mechanic since it was impossible to make a decent pianist out of anyone from such an uncivilized part of the world!

Besides the Beethoven transcription Alkan's program was to include nine other selections as noted below:[24]

1. Second Trio of Mayseder,
   performed by Ernst, Batta, and Alkan
2. Duo Italien, sung by M. Dérivis[25] and Mme. Marix
3. Third Concerto *da camera,*
   composed and played for the first time by M. Alkan
   (second piano accompaniment by Alkan, the younger)
4. Aria, sung by Mlle. d'Hennin
5. Two Études by Alkan, No. 1, "The Wind," and
   No. 2 in C-sharp major
6. "Le Moine," sung by M. Dérivis
7. New Fantasia, composed and played by Batta
8. Duo Français, sung by M. . . . and Mlle. . . .
9. Fragments [Andante and Finale] from the Symphony in A
   by Beethoven for two pianos,
   by MM. Alkan, Chopin, Guttmann [*sic*], and Zimmerman
10. Chansonnettes sung by M. Levassor

Among the cast were two of Alkan's relatives, his twelve-year-old brother, Napoléon, and his older sister, Celeste Marix, a piano and voice teacher who dashed about Paris in her spare time giving home demonstrations of the harmoniums manufactured by her husband.

As for the other performers, M. Levassor, the leading tenor at the Palais Royale Theater, sang some comical "chansonnettes" which were his habitual stock-in-trade. To Henri Blanchard of the *Revue et Gazette Musicale* the result was "highly amusing" if "not terribly musical."[26] The bass Alizard, who stood in for Nourrit's pupil Prosper Dérivis, was an undisciplined singer whose performances were never predictable. Sometimes, as one critic sniped, they shouldn't even be "called singing at all."[27] To make matters worse Alizard annoyed his audiences by fidgeting nervously on stage and left many people with the impression he was deformed because of his abnormally squat, muscular frame. The remaining singer on the program, Mlle. d'Hennin, was a competent but colorless creature, never known for anything particularly distinctive in either her voice or her appearance.

All in all, the *Revue et Gazette Musicale* found Alkan's concert generally pleasant. In his write-up of it Henri Blanchard had few criticisms to make, but his compliments tended to be restrained. Only one thing really aroused his wrath, and that was the Beethoven piano transcription which he considered a "sacrilege."[28] Even though it was ably performed, he bristled at the thought of tampering with the monumental works of Beethoven. Purists today would agree, but in 1838 this was the only way some people ever got to hear a Beethoven symphony.

Whether Chopin concurred with Blanchard or not, he certainly didn't like it when other people meddled with his compositions. Back in Warsaw he once got very irate at Antoni Orłowski for incorporating various themes from his F minor concerto into a series of little salon pieces. That was in 1830. A few months later Orłowski left Warsaw during the November uprising and settled in Paris. By the time Chopin arrived there the following year, his anger had cooled and the two men renewed their friendship.

Orłowski, as it turned out, didn't stay in Paris long. Although he was a person of diverse accomplishments (he could play the piano, the violin, and several percussion instruments as well as sing, conduct, and compose) he didn't seem to excel in any of them. As a result he fared poorly in a city like Paris where there was an overabundance of artistic excellence. In 1835, therefore, when he heard the post of Philharmonic director at the Théâtre des Arts in Rouen was empty he snapped it up.

As a provincial conductor he was assured a small but steady salary which didn't exactly afford him a luxurious life. To better his lot he followed the example of many of his contemporaries and planned a benefit concert for himself to be held on March 11, 1838. After three years in Rouen he had come to understand the local mentality enough to know that nothing could ensure the success of his venture like a "big name" from the city. And what brighter celebrity could he get than Chopin who, as he put it, was "à la mode" in Paris then?[29]

In spite of their past altercations and the prospect of a 250-mile round-trip, Chopin accepted Orłowski's invitation. Thanks to his presence, approximately 500 people showed up that Sunday for the concert given in the auditorium of the Rouen Town Hall. While this was exactly what Orłowski hoped for, the price he paid for it was the humiliation of being completely outshone at his own gala.

Ernest Legouvé, whom Schlesinger sent out to cover the affair, wrote one of the most glowing reviews in the annals of musical criticism. "Chopin, who can never be forgotten once he had been heard," left his audience "stunned, moved, and intoxicated. . . . Throughout the entire performance the hall quivered with electricity and rippled with murmurs of ecstasy and astonishment."[30] In his excitement the critic all but forgot that the focal point of the concert was supposed to have been Orłowski, whom he mentioned in passing as simply "a Polish professor."

In a final salvo Legouvé closed his exuberant remarks with this booming exhortation: "On, Chopin! On! May this triumph convince you not to be selfish any longer. Spread your wonderful talent on the winds. Admit that you are who you are. Stop this great debate which is dividing the artistic world. Henceforth when the question is asked, 'Who is the foremost pianist in Europe, Liszt or Thalberg?' let all the world be able to reply, like those who have heard you, 'It is Chopin!'"[31]

Under different circumstances such acclaim might have fired Chopin with a renewed enthusiasm for the concert stage. But events soon followed that were to take him out of the public eye for quite some time. In April of 1838 George Sand returned to Paris from Nohant.

• CHAPTER ELEVEN •

PARIS
1839–1842

THE MAIN PURPOSE of Mme. Sand's trip to Paris in the spring of 1838 was to consult lawyers about the terms of her separation from the Baron Dudevant. Also on her agenda was an important rendezvous with Chopin. Already her prolific mind was sketching the outlines of a new plot—this time not for some novel but a real-life drama in which she and the young musician were to play the leading roles.

To her chagrin Fryderyk greeted her rather coolly, with none of the previous fall's ardor. As yet she didn't know him well enough to understand his behavior around women. In the drawing room he could be disarmingly debonair, but in private he shied away from any intimacy with them. Puzzled by his diffidence, she wondered if he were still in love with Maria Wodzińska and pestered several of his friends to find out. Once she learned the true state of affairs she launched a determined assault on her flustered victim. By the end of the summer she and Chopin were lovers.

The first ecstasies of their new love were soon marred by the Sand children's tutor, Mallefille, who was not as adept at giving up mistresses as George was in taking on lovers. Armed with a pistol, he stalked the sidewalk in front of Chopin's apartment, awaiting his moment of revenge. One day after George had barely escaped his bullets, she and Chopin began making plans to flee Paris. For the impeccably proper musician it wasn't so much a matter of saving his life as his reputation. At the end of several weeks of harried debate the two finally selected the island of Majorca off the coast of Spain as the ideal haven, far away from Mallefille's fury and well out of reach of his gun.

Because of the complications of travel in those days it wasn't until late October that the couple were able to leave for their island paradise in the remote waters of the Mediterranean. Accompanied by George's two children and a maid, the lovers reached Majorca in a few weeks' time only to find that the paradise they sought had somehow eluded them.

Everything about the little ménage from Paris seemed to offend the Majorcans. First of all, the couple weren't married, which made their relationship an unholy alliance in the eyes of the Catholic islanders. Furthermore Mme. Sand wrote books, smoked cigars, and drank coffee—all dreadfully unladylike by provincial Spanish standards. Still worse, she dressed her daughter in boy's clothing, which was a flagrant sin against nature. All this was further compounded by the fact that the two lovers never went to church on Sunday and liked to roam around graveyards in the moonlight.

Quite apart from their religious scruples the Majorcans were loath to accept the newcomers because they recognized that Chopin suffered from tuberculosis, a fact that had gone undetected by the sophisticated Parisian doctors who repeatedly misdiagnosed his illness as "bronchitis," "laryngitis," or, at the worst, "influenza."

From the beginning, life on the island was an ordeal. During their first week in Palma the travelers lived in cramped, noisy quarters over a barrelmaker's shop. As soon as possible they escaped to the country where they settled into a picturesque little villa on a rocky, pine-covered hillside. A few weeks later howling winds and drenching downpours heralded the onset of the rainy season and left them shivering on the muddy slopes of their rural retreat. Chopin became sick and the landlord evicted him. In desperation George sought refuge for her homeless brood in an abandoned monastery on the edge of a village called Valldemosa. There they set up camp in three dark, drafty cells once occupied by a Carthusian monk. As best she could, George tried to make their Spartan quarters livable with a motley assortment of trunks, boxes, and secondhand furniture including an old upright piano that was battered but playable. Outside one of the cells she and the maid put together a primitive kitchen in the open air where the charcoal fumes from the stove wouldn't irritate Chopin's throat.

For three months they survived this crude existence until one grim day in February when George decided she had been chilled, soaked, and ostracized long enough. It was time to head back to France. By then Chopin was so debilitated she feared for his life and booked the first available passage to the mainland. This, unfortunately, turned out to be a tiny, stench-filled cabin in the depths of a packet boat with a cargo of squealing pigs. In the course of their trip Chopin hemorrhaged profusely. After a brief rest in Barcelona George took him on to Marseilles where they stayed several months while he recuperated.

In Marseilles news reached the couple of the death of their friend Adolphe Nourrit, who had committed suicide in Naples. For the past several years he had been overshadowed by a new tenor in Paris named Duprez. Because of this he resigned from the Opéra and went to Italy on a concert tour. While there he succumbed to a fit of depression and killed himself by jumping out a window.

Shortly afterward as his widow and children were accompanying the body back to Paris, they stopped in Marseilles where a memorial service was held for the late singer at the church of Notre-Dame-du-Mont. Chopin, who was now much stronger, attended and played an organ transcription of Schubert's "Die Gestirne" while George hid in the choir loft and watched. Among the mourners were a host of curiosity seekers who came only to hear the famous Chopin play. According to Mme. Sand, his performance was incredibly moving despite the church's decrepit organ. However, it was far from the smashing tour de force expected by many who felt cheated out of the fifty-centimes donation they had left at the front door.

In May the Chopin-Sand household left Marseilles for George's chateau at Nohant. In the fresh country air Chopin recovered rapidly, but the monotony of rural life began to bore him. Most days he amused himself at the piano George had bought two years earlier when Liszt and the Countess d'Agoult came to visit her. Free from the distractions of Paris and the discomforts of Majorca, he was able to sit down and compose for hours at a time. Over the next seven years he would pass all but one summer in this fashion.

When it came time to return to Paris that October, both George and Fryderyk were hard-pressed for money. Their Majorcan adventure had cost them much more than they expected. For Chopin the year away from Paris meant the loss of at least 13,000 francs he could have earned in teaching. He also lost his grand apartment on the Chaussée d'Antin. The new one he found that fall at No. 5 rue Tronchet just behind the Church of the Madeleine never really suited him very well.

For the sake of appearances George and her family lived apart from Chopin in two small pavilions on a little courtyard off the rue Pigalle. They had been carefully chosen to give George maximum privacy. Her bedroom was well separated from the children's and had its own door to the outside. Such an arrangement would indicate that Chopin's rue Tronchet apartment served merely as a daytime studio for his pupils.

Only a few weeks after getting back to Paris Chopin was again invited to play for the court, this time at the Palace of Saint-Cloud, just west of the city. In the nine years of Louis-Philippe's reign this palace, with its terraced gardens, fountains, and waterfalls, had become one of the royal family's favorite residences. Originally it was a small sixteenth-century chateau which one of the king's ancestors, Philippe d'Orléans, purchased in 1658. Over a century later it had been enlarged to a palace and sold to Marie Antoinette. After the Revolution it passed through the hands of Napoléon and the last of the Bourbon kings before being returned once more to the Orléans family in 1830.[1]

Chopin's invitation to Saint-Cloud came from the director of the king's music, Count Perthuis, whose wife was one of his pupils. Besides Chopin the count invited another pianist, Ignaz Moscheles. Famous all over Europe, the forty-five-year-old Moscheles was born in Prague and studied with Salieri in Vienna. Since 1826 he had been living in London where he was a director and conductor of the Philharmonic Society. As a musician he was skilled and sensitive but, having been trained in the Clementi tradition, he was considered "old-fashioned" by 1839. Although he made serious efforts to "update" himself he was never able to compete in popularity with the new school of piano virtuosos represented by Liszt, Thalberg, and Herz.

In England Moscheles had become acquainted with Chopin's compositions, which he found clumsy, awkward, and impossible to play. It was therefore a revelation to him in October 1839 when he first heard them exquisitely transformed by the fluid artistry of their composer. After that Moscheles' aversion turned to admiration. However, Chopin, who had played Moscheles' compositions since he was a teenager, didn't reciprocate these feelings and always regarded the older musician with a certain disdain.

The day of the performance, Tuesday, October 29, found the king and queen in Paris, where they had entertained the British ambassador, Lord Grenville, and his wife the night before. That evening they were expecting the United States minister to dine with them at Saint-Cloud and left the Tuileries at five in the afternoon to receive him. The minister, Lewis Cass, was a heavyset, humorless man of fifty-six who had achieved the rank of brigadier general during the War of 1812 and later served as Andrew Jackson's Secretary of War and governor of the state of Michigan. He was an ardent Francophile and prided himself on his unusually friendly rapport with the king. Following dinner the Princess de Wagram and the Countess de Bondy were to join the royal family for the evening's music.

At nine o'clock a torrential thunderstorm struck Paris just as the Count and Countess Perthuis came by to pick up Chopin and Moscheles for the drive out to Saint-Cloud. When they reached the palace they were escorted through a series of rooms to the *salon carré* where the royal family and their guests awaited them. Seated around a large table with their sewing baskets at their sides, the queen and princesses appeared the picture of quiet domesticity. The entrance of the two pianists disrupted this placid scene as the royal ladies made a great fuss over their guests, inquiring how the instruments suited them and whether the piano stools needed adjusting.

What happened next was described in detail by Moscheles.

> First of all Chopin played a "melange of Nocturnes and Etudes" and was extolled and admired as an old court favorite. I followed with some old and new "Studies" and was honored with similar applause. We then sat down together at the instrument, he again playing the bass, a thing he always insists on. The small audience now listened intently to my "E-flat Major Sonata" which was interrupted by such exclamations as "divin!, delicieux!." After the Andante the Queen whispered to one of her suite: "Ne serait-il pas indiscret de leur redemander?" which was tantamount to a command; so we played it again with increased *abandon* and in the finale gave ourselves up to a "musical delirium." Chopin's enthusiasm throughout the whole performance of the piece must, I think, have kindled that of his hearers who overwhelmed us with compliments equally divided.[2]

After a short break Chopin returned to improvise on excerpts from Grisar's *La Folle,* and Moscheles performed variations on themes from a Mozart opera.[3] At the close of the evening refreshments were served, and the pianists "left the palace at 11:30, this time under only a shower of compliments, for the rain had ceased."[4] The ride back to Paris was starlit and serene.

To express his thanks the king presented Chopin with a Sèvres vase trimmed in ormolu and Moscheles with a leather traveling case. The latter, Chopin observed caustically, was a hint for the Czech pianist to get out of town. Far more cutting were the remarks about Moscheles which appeared in *La France Musicale* a few days later. "M. Moscheles," its correspondent wrote, "is a third-rate pianist—no more, no less. He bangs away at the piano with a heavy touch which must have come as a considerable surprise to Her Majesty, the Queen of the French."[5]

Of course, Henri Herz, who owned *La France Musicale,* was notoriously conceited and not very tolerant of competition. His barbs often fell indiscriminately on the good and bad alike as Chopin well knew.

Throughout the rest of the fall and the following winter Chopin and Mme. Sand struggled to repair the financial ravages of their Majorcan trip. With the resumption of his income from teaching and the 1,500 francs Pleyel paid him for finishing the Preludes,[6] Chopin was soon able to repay the money he had borrowed the previous year. For George the situation was more difficult. Up to now her literary success had been based on the writing of novels, but books like that required a lot of time, so she tried her hand at plays which could be turned out much faster. By the spring of 1840 her first drama, *Cosima,* was finished and opened at the Théâtre Français in April. The result was a fiasco. The production hadn't been adequately rehearsed, the actors missed their cues, the audiences booed, the crowds dwindled, and after a week the show closed.

For lack of money George was forced to spend the summer of 1840 in Paris. To open Nohant would have cost too much. In lieu of the country she went riding along the wooded trails of the Bois de Boulogne and basked in the sun beside its lakes. Once in a while Chopin accompanied her, but he didn't care much for outdoor life and stayed in his apartment most of the time. He had never really regained his strength since Majorca and weighed only ninety-seven pounds that year. All day he dabbed his forehead with cooling applications of eau de cologne and sipped gum water flavored with opium drops to ease his cough. Many of his pupils were away that summer, allowing him more time to compose, but in the evenings he was almost always out.

On December 15, 1840, Napoleon's ashes were brought back to Paris by Louis-Philippe's son, the Prince of Joinville, and placed in the crypt at the Invalides. That day the entire house of Orléans showed up to pay homage to the Corsican upstart who was now treated with all the honor due a beloved emperor. The archbishop of Paris presided over the service in the black-draped church, packed with high-ranking clergy, military officers, peers of the realm, government officials, and other important personages, all dressed in mourning.

A choir and orchestra of 300 musicians were present, and Chopin came to hear his good friends Pauline Viardot, Louis Lablache, and Alexis Dupont sing the solo parts of Mozart's *Requiem*. Every fifteen minutes the music was punctuated by thunderous blasts of cannon lined up along the quai below the church. Nine years later the *Requiem* would be heard again in Paris with the same soloists at Chopin's own funeral in the Church of the Madeleine.

Early in the new year Fryderyk learned that Maria Wodzińska had been married—and to, of all people, his godfather's son Józef Skarbek. At the time he seemed unaffected by it but after his death a bundle of Maria's letters were found in his apartment, neatly tied up with ribbon. Across them he had scrawled the bitter words, "Moja bieda"—my sorrow.

February marked the second anniversary of George and Fryderyk's return from Majorca. By then Chopin had resumed a fairly normal life, but his long convalescence had brought about a subtle change in their relationship. For the past two years his onetime mistress had come to hover over him like a mother hen. She saw that he was bundled up whenever he went out and gave his valet stern instructions on what to feed him in her absence. She even took to calling him her "second son."

During this period Chopin avoided playing in public and George, forever protective of his health, made no effort to force him. How long he might have stayed in retirement is hard to say if Liszt hadn't returned to Paris in March 1841.

The presence of this formidable pianist was invariably a seismic event that sent tremors far and wide. Two years earlier he had shocked Rome with a series of concerts given entirely by himself—unaided by any other musicians.[7] At first he called them "musical soliloquies" but the London press, a year later, dubbed them "recitals," an expression that persisted despite its unmusical connotations. In the spring of 1841 he decided to try out his daring innovation on the Parisians, a decision deplored by the *Revue et Gazette Musicale*,[8] which urged him to give a "concert in the usual style, surrounded by artists worthy of him."[9] Liszt, however, ignored this advice and forged ahead with his usual self-confidence. Not only did he intend to be the only artist on stage, his compositions were to be the only ones on the program.

Just as in Rome and London, his recital proved a tremendous success. All Paris roared its approval and the *Revue et Gazette Musicale* had to admit that "the artist walked away victorious."[10] The only sour note came from Liszt's rival Henry Herz, whose journal, *La France Musicale,* ridiculed his theatrical gyrations and labeled him "The Weeping Willow" because of his long hair. "It's clear," the paper carped, "the artist spared nothing to exploit his reputation and his compositions."[11]

While Chopin had no desire to give a solo recital himself he could hardly disregard Liszt's spectacular feat that spring. Judging from the comments in *Les Guêpes* his performance must have been quite a spectacle indeed. "M. Listz [*sic*] leaves a slaughtered piano behind at every concert," it wrote. "The last time he played standing up. The next time he will play lying down."[12]

Before the season was out Chopin announced he would appear in public again. What's more, he was going to organize the concert on his own, something he hadn't done since his Paris debut in February 1832. As Marie d'Agoult saw it this idea wasn't really Chopin's but Mme. Sand's. George, she claimed, was so jealous of Liszt's triumph she wanted to "resuscitate" her own lover and push him back into the limelight once more.

For some time now there had been considerable tension between the Liszt-d'Agoult and Chopin-Sand households. It began in 1838 when George whispered some confidences about Franz and Marie to Balzac, who incoporated them into a novel called *Béatrix, or The Galley Slaves of Love*. Later, on discovering George's duplicity, Mme. d'Agoult became incensed. She had never been particularly fond of Mme. Sand

and always envied her literary fame. She too aspired to be an authoress but so far had made little progress toward her goal.[13] Chopin's success as a composer also galled her. Only a few years earlier she had dragged Liszt away from his glittering virtuoso life so he would have time to write serious music. In her willful and possessive fashion she forced him to endure months of isolation in the north of Italy only to find that he wasn't one to be tied down. Soon his restive nature pulled him back into the concert circuit, and from then on their relationship began to wane.

More and more Marie found herself alone. During one of Liszt's frequent absences she wrote him of her disenchantment with George over the Balzac incident. Naturally he was irritated too. However, he knew how to control himself better than his vindictive mistress, and for the time being he advised her to keep up a friendly facade until the right moment came their way. "The best thing in this sort of situation," he told her, "is to smile until one can plunge the knife in deeply. Just be patient. I'll handle things."[14] Reluctantly Mme. d'Agoult bided her time.[15]

Then in April 1841 the opportunity she and Liszt were waiting for came when Chopin announced he would give a concert at Pleyel's on the twenty sixth of that month. Liszt planned to attend as critic for the *Revue et Gazette Musicale*, and afterward he and Marie would write up the concert together. That was to be their revenge.

While Chopin's decision to come out of retirement was prompted in part by Liszt's return to Paris, there were other reasons behind it, many of which had no connection with Liszt at all. Among them was the continued improvement of his health under George's care. Besides that, his nine years in Paris now gave him the experience to arrange a concert there without the difficulty he encountered in 1832. Pleyel was eager to have him try out his new concert hall (which had just opened in December 1839), while Schlesinger promised to advertise the concert in his journal and sell tickets for it at his offices on the rue Richelieu.

Pleyel's new hall at No. 22 rue Rochechouart was larger and more elegant than its predecessor in the rue Cadet. From its foyer on the street level a double stairway, covered in plush, led up through two small antechambers to the main auditorium on the floor above. There the visitor was confronted by the opulent sight of crystal chandeliers and gilded mirrors that sent light dancing across the oblong room into the curved recesses of the stage and ceiling. For the inauguration of the new building, as for the earlier one, Pleyel had entrusted the program to his business partner, Frédéric Kalkbrenner. Under his direction the first-night audience heard an imposing array of fantasies, études, and other morsels culminating in one of his giant concatenations for eight pianos and thirty-two hands.

This second Salle Pleyel, which came into existence on the eve of a new decade, would see a wave of younger musicians emerge to challenge the established artists of the day. By 1841 Chopin was no longer really part of the musical avant-garde. In Paris the public was already besieged by a wealth of fresh talent including men like Jacques Offenbach, César Franck, Charles Hallé, and Anton Rubinstein.[16] The presence of this challenge may also have played a role in bringing Chopin back to the concert stage.

Whatever his reasons, George was clearly delighted. "A great—absolutely the greatest—news is that little Chip-Chip [Chopin] is going to give a grrrrrrrrand concert," she wrote Pauline Viardot. "Three-quarters of the tickets [at fifteen to twenty francs apiece] were snapped up before the concert was even announced."[17]

With his chronic horror of playing in public Chopin soon regretted his decision. The whole thing, as George put it, was a "nightmare" for him. "He doesn't want any notices posted or any programs printed. The very thought of a crowd scares him to death and it's almost impossible to get him to discuss the matter at all. In fact, everything about it upsets him so much I have suggested that he play alone in the dark on a dummy keyboard."[18]

For Delacroix the event was such an occasion he deliberately stayed in bed for two days, nursing a sore throat, so he would be well enough to attend. On the night of the concert he came by the rue Tronchet in his carriage and drove Chopin over to Pleyel's.

Since the new hall hadn't been provided with a separate portico for vehicles, there was quite a snarl of traffic outside the main entrance. Those arriving by foot had to dodge oncoming horses, while the carriages found little room to discharge their passengers for the throng of pedestrians and onlookers blocking the narrow sidewalk in front of the building.

Inside, Pleyel's rooms were "magnificantly lit up" and "perfumed with flowers," according to Liszt. Through the foyer and up the stairs streamed a procession of "the most elegant ladies, the most fashionable young men, the most celebrated artists, the richest financiers, the most illustrious peers, indeed all the elite of society, all the aristocracy of birth, fortune, talent, and beauty."[19] Their arrival soon filled up the grand salon. When extra chairs were placed on the stage near the piano crowds of people rushed forward to grab them.

The program planned by Chopin was in keeping with the era's traditional pattern of concerts. He had neither the temerity nor the stamina to give a Lisztian "recital." To assist him he called on two old friends, Mme. Cinti-Damoreau and Heinrich Wilhelm Ernst. "A greater trinity of artists cannot be imagined," exclaimed *La France Musicale*.[20]

Surrounded by the crowd, both onstage and off, Chopin played a selection of his own works, most of them recent compositions.[21] Among these the Ballade in F major (opus 38) and a group of études generated such applause they had to be repeated.

The rest of the concert consisted of two arias from Adam's new opera, *La Rose de Perrone,*[22] sung "in a ravishing manner"[23] by Mme. Damoreau and Ernst's performance of an "elegy" written by himself. "If you want to hear a violin weep," Léon Escudier wrote in *La France Musicale,* "listen to M. Ernst." On this occasion, though, he felt Ernst overdid it "with a little too much melancholy."[24]

When Chopin rose to take his final bow, Liszt (who loved to feign exhaustion and drop lifeless across the keyboard at the end of his own concerts) rushed up and flung his arms around the frail-looking pianist as if to keep him from collapsing. This theatrical gesture, according to the satirical journal *Les Guêpes,* arose out of his need "to play some role" that evening since he hadn't been allowed "to play the piano."[25]

Liszt's scene-stealing attempt, however, failed to diminish Chopin's glory. In the words of Léon Escudier, the Polish virtuoso was "a pianist of feeling par excellence . . . who cannot be compared with any other."[26] The critic for *Le Ménestrel,* on the other hand, wasn't above making comparisons and stated that Chopin was definitely better than Liszt—at least as a composer if not as a pianist.[27]

The most effusive and yet the most offensive of all the reviews was the one written by Liszt himself (along with the Countess d'Agoult) in the *Revue et Gazette Musicale.* Under a veil of flattery Chopin could feel its subtle sarcasm. What irritated him most was Liszt's seemingly complimentary reference to him as the "king of the evening's entertainment."[28] "Yes," he retorted angrily, "he made me a king, but a king within *his* empire." In return Chopin sneered that even if Liszt were to become the "king of Abyssinia or the Congo" he still wouldn't possess the power to write any decent music. All his works, he predicted, were destined to become as "outdated and forgotten as last year's newspapers."[29]

Except for the aggravation of Liszt's review the concert at Pleyel's left Chopin unusually pleased with himself. Along with the praise it brought him, he also received 6,000 francs, a sum it would normally take him three months to earn from teaching. A friend of his, the poet Witwicki, couldn't help but be envious. Reciting verses for the same amount of time, he observed, would hardly be as profitable.

As George Sand quipped, the concert at Pleyel's had earned Chopin so much money he could afford to loaf away the whole summer. Since her finances were also in much better shape than the year before, the two of them left for Nohant around the middle of June. There they found the weather cool and drizzly. In the dank gloom of Mme. Sand's old chateau Chopin longed for Paris and all the little amenities he enjoyed there. He wrote friends to send him newspapers, eau de cologne, and hot water bottles. Most of all he wanted someone to talk to. The local folk were such provincial bores! George's half-brother, Hippolyte Chatiron, could be amusing enough when he wasn't drunk, but his mousy wife, Emilie, was a drab little thing who generally went to sleep in the middle of a conversation.[30]

A brief visit from Pauline Viardot and her husband brought a welcome relief from the tedium of country life. Both Chopin and Mme. Sand adored Pauline, a young singer with a magical voice, great intelligence, and a soul as gentle as it was generous. She was the daughter of the noted Spanish voice teacher Manuel Garcia and the younger sister of the famous mezzo-soprano La Malibran. Only the year before, she had married Louis Viardot, the new director of the Théâtre-Italien who later took over the management of her career.

After two weeks of hiking, picnicking, and music making the Viardots left, and the rest of the summer found Chopin and Mme. Sand bickering frequently over petty household matters. These squabbles were triggered by the basic differences in their tastes and interests. At the end of three years together the two lovers were finally having to face up to the vast psychological gulf that separated their personalities. George was expansive and volatile; Chopin, reserved and formal. George enjoyed the rugged pleasures of outdoor living; Chopin preferred the subtle refinements of urban society. George was egalitarian at heart and active in many socialist causes; Chopin clung to the familiar patterns of a social structure handed down from the past. Although George came from royalty on her father's side,[31] she surrounded herself with people of peasant or working-class backgrounds whom Chopin considered coarse and disagreeable. In Paris he could escape them by fleeing into the bastions of the affluent, but at Nohant there was no place to go.

Out of frustration he retreated into himself and spent most of his days alone at the piano. George, who usually worked through the night, often slept well into the afternoon and seldom disturbed his solitude. This allowed Chopin hours of unbroken concentration which resulted in the creation of some of his finest compositions.

One of the works from that year, the Prelude in C-sharp minor, he donated to an album entitled *Keepsake des Pianistes,* which was being sold to raise money for a monument to Beethoven in Bonn. Liszt, it so happened, was the moving spirit behind this project and had already given large sums of money to it. By comparison, Chopin's contribution seemed minor. Once again he felt himself enmeshed within his rival's empire.

George, like Chopin, still remained piqued at Liszt and his countess. Many nights during the summer of 1841, while her lover lay asleep in his bedroom next to her study, she churned out a new novel, called *Horace.* In it she took some nasty broadsides at Marie d'Agoult, whom she depicted as the Viscountess de Chailly, a lady of such utter artificiality that everything about her (including her teeth, her bosom, her heart, and even her aristocratic title) was a fake. When Liszt read the novel he couldn't help but recognize the painful similarities between the viscountess and Mme. d'Agoult. This time he made no effort to retaliate. By then he too had begun to lose patience with his exasperating mistress.

Early in November Chopin and Mme. Sand left Nohant for Paris. To George, who loved the country, the city was a cold, gray prison where she felt confined and depressed. If it didn't cost so much to run Nohant she would gladly have stayed there all year round.

Chopin, by contrast, was thrilled to be back in Paris. Nowhere else was he so content. In 1841 the city already had a population of nearly one million people. Its boulevards and quais throbbed with activity by day and glimmered with gaslight by night. No city in all Europe had more beautiful monuments and parks, more palatial homes, or a richer cultural life. But what Chopin especially looked forward to, on returning to Paris, were his pupils and his parties.

That year some of the most brilliant soirées of the season were the musicales given by the king's oldest son, the Duke of Orléans, and his new wife, the former Princess Hélène of Mecklemburg-Schwerin. The duchess, in spite of being a German and a Protestant, was quickly adopted by the French, who referred to her lovingly as "the adorable Hélène."

In 1837, just after their marriage, the royal couple moved into the Pavillon de Marsan on the north side of the Tuileries. Their apartment had been a "new" addition to the palace during the reign of Louis XIV. In the early nineteenth century it was occupied by the ill-fated Duke of Berry, the Bourbon heir-apparent until his assassination at the Opéra in 1820. A similar tragedy later befell the Duke of Orléans when he was killed in a carriage accident en route from Paris to Saint-Cloud in 1842.

During his brief five years in the Pavillon de Marsan the Duke of Orléans turned it into a sumptuous museum which could be viewed by the public with special permission whenever the inhabitants were away. The ducal apartments, according to a contemporary account, were "exceedingly splendid and fitted up with the greatest taste."[32] Under the watchful eyes of liveried footmen in velvet and red braid, guests could gaze on such treasures as the desk at which Louis XVI worked during his last days before the Revolution. Not even Louis-Philippe's own quarters (which were said to have been maintained in a lax, often disorderly fashion) could match the impeccably run household of his son.

In describing one of the musical soirées at the Pavillon de Marsan the *Revue et Gazette Musicale* emphasized the stringent etiquette demanded in royal circles. "Concerts at court differ markedly from ordinary concerts," it reported. "To begin with, one never expresses one's admiration with noisy gestures; applause is not considered proper and one rarely talks. The illustrious audience indicates its pleasure merely by a nod of the head."[33]

It was for one of these formal galas that Chopin received an invitation to play on Wednesday evening, December 1, 1841. Five hundred guests were expected, including the Prussian, Swedish, and Saxon ministers, Louis-Philippe's former premier, Adolphe Thiers,[34] the poet Alfred de Musset,[35] and the painters Delacroix, Delaroche, and Ary Scheffer.[36] Half an hour before the music was to begin the king and queen arrived with three of their children, the Duke of Montpensier, the Duke of Aumale, Princess Clementine, and their daughter-in-law, the Duchess of Nemours. Also with the royal family was the exiled Queen Maria Cristina of Spain, who had recently been forced to resign as regent for her ten-year-old daughter, Isabella II.

At nine o'clock Jacques Halévy, director of music for the Duke of Orléans, appeared and opened the following program:

1. Trio des Masques from *Don Giovanni*,
   sung by Mmes. Grisi and Persiani and [M.] Mario
2. The cavatina from *Lucrezia Borgia* by Donizetti,
   sung by Mme. Grisi
3. Ballade [the third, in A-flat major, opus 47],
   composed and performed on the piano by M. Chopin
4. Quartet from *Nina* by Païsiello,
   sung by Mmes. Grisi and Dotti, [Mm.] Mario and Lablache
5. Romance from the *Illustri Rivali* by Mercadante,
   sung by [M.] Mario
6. Duet from *Turco in Italia*, sung by Mme. Persiani
7. Piano improvisation by M. Chopin
8. Cavatina from *Adele de Lusignano* by Carafa,
   sung by Mme. Persiani
9. Duet from *Nozze di Figaro*,
   sung by Mmes. Grisi and Persiani
10. Neapolitan songs, by M. Lablache[37]

Apart from Chopin the only other instrumentalist that evening was Giovanni Tadolini, who provided piano accompaniments for some of the vocal numbers. Since 1811 he had been connected with the Théâtre-Italien in various capacities from chorus master to musical director.[38] His wife and pupil, Eugenia Tadolini, had known Chopin since his early days in Paris.

Giulia Grisi had also known him for quite some time, at least since 1833 when she and her sister Giuditta appeared with him at Berlioz's benefit for Harriet Smithson in the Salle Favart. Not long after that, Giuditta married and retired,[39] but Giulia went on to follow in the footsteps of Pasta and La Malibran with her "magnificent displays of vocal and dramatic power."[40] In 1841 she had just turned thirty and was considered a great beauty. Her behavior, however, was far from attractive. Vicious and scheming, she maneuvered behind the scenes to take roles away from her rivals at the Opéra. After her liaison with the tenor Mario,[41] she refused to let him sing in any productions with Pauline Viardot, whom she especially disliked.

At the time of the Tuileries concert Mario was a relative newcomer to Paris, having just made his debut there in 1839. He had little vocal training but an incomparable voice that led him from the career of an army officer to that of an opera singer. His full name was Giovanni Matteo Mario, cavaliere di Candia, but because his father, the governor general of Genoa and Nice, objected so violently to his singing, he dropped the family name and became known simply as Mario.

The other two singers on the program were also from Italy although the bass, Luigi Lablache, actually had an Irish mother and a French father. His exceptionally fine voice impressed Chopin greatly. "You can't imagine what he is like!" he exclaimed the first time he heard Lablache.[42]

Of comparable ability was Fanny Persiani (née Tachinardi), a pale, wispy creature with lovely flaxen hair. Her voice, like her figure, was small and delicate but of such purity and perfection Donizetti wrote the title role of *Lucia di Lammermoor* for her. At age eighteen she married an opera composer, Persiani, who managed London's Covent Garden for a time. She herself later served—briefly and disastrously—as director of the Théâtre-Italien in Paris.

Out of the many splendid performers at the Pavillon de Marsan that night it was Chopin who seemed to please the royal family most.

The *Revue et Gazette Musicale* spoke of his "maginficent talent" and "the extraordinary charm of his performance,"[43] while *La France Musicale* was overwhelmed by his "absolutely incredible genius" and the "grace, elegance, and ease" with which he improvised. After he finished, Queen Marie Amélie walked over to the piano and "paid him the most flattering compliments."[44]

Strangely enough Chopin didn't seem at all pleased by such regal attentions. In a letter to her brother, George Sand commented, "Chip-Chip [Chopin] played at court in white tie the day before yesterday but isn't very happy about it."[45]

To his own family Chopin gave the same impression. "You mention that you attended the court soirée but weren't in a good mood," Nicholas Chopin wrote him on December 30.[46] What could the trouble be, he wondered. Everywhere in Warsaw people were saying his son was in "such great favor with the queen."[47] Ludwika even heard that he had been given a magnificent china service for his performance while all the other artists received money. "They wouldn't have dared [offer you money]," she told her brother. "They knew you wouldn't have accepted it. Some people say, though, that you would have agreed to be paid, provided the money were sent to your father. I could hardly keep from laughing. . . . Isn't it nice that people think you can express your wishes at court and expect them to be granted!"[48]

All this amused Ludwika but not her brother. Something upset him that night at the Tuileries, and he never again played for the royal family.

Winters in Paris were always the worst time of the year for Chopin. Because of this he finally left his apartment in the rue Tronchet, which had a northern exposure that made it damp and chilly. In the fall of 1841 he moved into one of the two little pavilions George had rented at No. 16 rue Pigalle. Still conscious of appearances he took rooms in the building occupied by Maurice while George and Solange shared the other. Such precautions were hardly necessary since all Paris now knew about the couple's liaison and accepted it as a matter of fact. Far from being ostracized, Chopin was more lionized than ever. His social obligations, in fact, consumed so much of his time, Berlioz complained he was never seen in the theaters or concert halls anymore. Other artists who had befriended him on his arrival in Paris were also miffed that Chopin now seemed too busy to keep in touch with them. In the *Journal des Débats* Berlioz publicly chided him for his aloofness, commenting sarcastically that he seemed to have become "afraid of music and musicians."[49]

Chopin's preoccupation with the exigencies of society made him feel that his move to the rue Pigalle had been a mistake. It was too far away from the city's fashionable districts. What if his pupils objected to traveling such a distance? Over and over George assured him this wasn't about to happen. After all, he was so well established then that any young lady too squeamish to venture up the rue Pigalle would gladly pay for the privilege of having him come to her for a lesson.

His recent concert at the Salle Pleyel had particularly bolstered his reputation. Scarcely a month afterward the sale of his ballades, mazurkas, and polonaises soared, which prompted *La France Musicale* to observe that "they are quite *en vogue* these days."[50]

By the beginning of 1842 the temptation to repeat the success of that concert goaded Chopin into considering another one. This time he wouldn't have to worry about some snide review by Liszt, who was far away on a concert tour of Berlin, Warsaw, and St. Petersburg.

Pauline Viardot's presence in Paris that winter was a further inducement for him to give another concert. The year before, he had asked her to assist him, but she was too heavily booked. Already she was considered one of the finest mezzo-sopranos on the European continent. What's more, she could act as well as sing, which enhanced her appeal to operatic directors everywhere. In time her exquisite voice would inspire Meyerbeer, Gounod, and Saint-Saëns to write operas and Brahms his Alto Rhapsody for her.[51]

Pauline's vocal artistry represented merely the brightest of her many musical facets. At one time she studied both the piano and organ and gave public performances on each. In addition she composed several operettas which were said to sparkle with charm. Less lustrous were her attempts to write lyrics for Chopin's mazurkas and change the words of the "Marseillaise."

With all her brilliance and versatility Pauline was unfortunately not beautiful. Her large nose, receding chin, and bulging eyes often obscured the lovely, thoughtful person behind them. George Sand treated her like a daughter and portrayed her affectionately as the heroine of her novel *Consuelo*. Men adored her. She bewitched George Sand's son, Maurice, elicited a proposal from the poet Alfred de Musset, and won the long-standing devotion of the Russian novelist Ivan Turgenev.

The other performer Chopin wanted on his program was the cellist Auguste-Joseph Franchomme. Over the years he had proved to be a loyal friend whose patience and humility often led Chopin to take advantage of him. During the previous summer—and for many summers to come—he imposed on the good-natured Franchomme to look after his apartment, copy out his manuscripts, and run endless errands for him when he was away at Nohant.

The preparations for this concert were as painful for Chopin as those of earlier ones. With his aversion to publicity he tried to carry out the arrangements for it as quietly as possible. On February 13, though, the *Revue et Gazette Musicale* let all Paris know about it. "What is being whispered around we are going to say out loud," it announced. "In two weeks' time [actually eight days] Chopin, the pianist par excellence, will give a concert. Everyone in Parisian society as well as the artistic world is reveling in the news. This delightful evening will take place in the tasteful rooms of M. Pleyel."[52]

The following day the *Journal des Débats* also advertised the concert, and the next week it announced the program which was scheduled for Monday, February 21, at 8:30 P.M.

1. Andante Spianato, followed by the third Ballade by Chopin
2. "Felice Donzella," aria by Dessauer, sung by Mme. Viardot-Garcia
3. Series of Nocturnes,[53] Preludes,[54] and Études[55] by Chopin
4. Various fragments by Handel, sung by Mme. Viardot-Garcia
5. Solo for violoncello, by Franchomme
6. Nocturne, Preludes, Mazurkas,[56] and Impromptu[57] by Chopin
7. "Le Chêne et le Roseau," sung by Mme. Viardot-Garcia, accompanied by Chopin[58]

On the evening of the performance an audience of nearly 400 wended its way up the graceful double staircase at Pleyel's. From the bare shoulders and slender necks of the ladies radiated the soft glow of pearls and the sparkle of precious stones while their perfumed hair fluttered with "golden ribbons" and "delicate blue veils." Here and there above the brilliant assemblage towered the military plumage of an officer or one of "those awful black hats"[59] shaped like a stove-pipe which men of fashion had taken to wearing then.

When George Sand appeared with Solange and her young cousin Augustine Brault, a sudden hush fell over the hall. Scores of curious eyes turned to stare at them. Unruffled, Mme. Sand acknowledged their gaze with a slight nod of her head and guided the girls quietly to their seats. "What must it feel like to be such a literary celebrity?" one observer sighed.[60]

At the opening ripple of the Andante Spianato everyone's attention was riveted on Chopin. He seemed "to have an infinite number of fingers," the critic for *La France Musicale* exuded. In his fanciful imagination Chopin's music conjured up "the faint voices of fairies sighing under silver bells" and "showers of pearls falling on crystal tables." The total effect, he vowed, was nothing less than "pure poetry."[61]

Without the aid of such flowery metaphors the *Revue des Deux Mondes* said simply that Chopin's performance was one of "pristine elegance . . . magnificent and exquisite but of extreme delicacy."[62] For some, this delicacy bordered on preciousness, and the *Revue et Gazette Musicale* complained of his tendency to strive for "too much refinement" which sometimes made his playing "a little mannered."[63]

Comparisons with Liszt, of course, were inevitable. Maurice Bourges found Chopin "more subdued" and "less fiery" than the Hungarian but, on the whole, "more profound" and "more substantial."[64] Quite the opposite of Liszt, Léon Escudier pointed out, Chopin "has no desire to dazzle you with tricks of speed . . . nor does he try to generate hysteria or make you faint on the spot. . . . His aim is to speak to the heart and not to the eyes. He wants to caress his audience and not devour it."[65]

Franchomme's "extremely pure and polished talent"[66] made his cello solo one of the highlights of the evening. "He remains almost invisible when he plays, as if he were part of the instrument," *La France Musicale* observed.[67]

The concert closed with "the thrilling voice of Mme. Viardot-Garcia"[68] and the resounding ring of 5,000 francs in Chopin's pockets.

From Warsaw, Nicholas Chopin sent his son a letter of congratulation, garnished with his usual admonitions. He worried that the critics' comments about Liszt might stir up trouble and warned Fryderyk to avoid getting caught in such a trap.

Also from Warsaw came the sad news that Wojciech Żywny, Chopin's childhood piano teacher, had died on February 21, the very day of his famous pupil's concert in the Salle Pleyel.

A month later Cherubini, who had finally resigned as head of the Paris Conservatory, also died. His last years served as an epilogue to the Classical era. Now, on his death, the age of Chopin's beloved Mozart was gone forever,[69] leaving Romanticism with its "furious and frenzied face" to reign unchallenged over the whole of Europe. In the decades that followed, the world was to change dramatically. Hand in hand with the Romantic movement came an era of greater social equality and expanding scientific horizons which inevitably led to an increased mechanization and depersonalization of life. Ironically, Chopin, whose music was the quintessence of Romanticism, would have preferred to turn back the clock to the smaller, more intimate world which had passed.

• CHAPTER TWELVE •

PARIS
1843–1848

ALTHOUGH CHOPIN ONCE studied Cherubini's *Treatise on Counterpoint* and respected the man's musicianship, he always found him cold and remote as a person. Even when the two first met in 1831, the elderly Italian already seemed like someone who had outlived his time, a "dried up chrysalis" who "just babbles on about cholera and revolutions."[1]

Following a funeral mass at the Church of St. Roch on March 19, Cherubini's body was taken to the Cemetery of Père La Chaise and buried only a few feet from the site where Chopin himself would one day lie. Strangely enough, these two dissimilar individuals were to become closer in death than they had ever been in life.

The day after Cherubini's interment Chopin performed at a soirée given by Prince and Princess Adam Czartoryski in their house at No. 25 rue Faubourg du Roule.[2] He had often been a guest there and probably never left without repaying the family's hospitality with some impromptu musical offering. This time a formal program had been planned in advance with several other Polish musicians as well as some of the leads from the Opéra.[3] Considering the Czartoryskis' wealth, their home must have been quite grand. Even so, it isn't likely to have matched the splendor of the Hôtel Lambert on the Île Saint-Louis where they moved the following year.

For the rest of that season society saw little of Chopin. Almost every day after he finished teaching he returned to his old apartment in the rue Tronchet, where Jan Matuszyński was now living. Like Chopin, he too suffered from tuberculosis and had been quite sick all winter. By spring it was apparent that he had little time to live. As his condition worsened George and Fryderyk moved him into the pavilions in the rue Pigalle where they did everything possible to ease his final days. Toward the end of April he died.

For Chopin, Matuszyński's death meant more than just the loss of a close friend. It was like a preview of his own death. He was so devastated by it George feared he would go to pieces if she didn't get him away from the rue Pigalle where he kept reliving the agony of those last moments. As soon as she could wind up her affairs in Paris they left for Nohant.

In the country Chopin's grief gradually abated. His recovery was speeded by a visit from Delacroix, whose company he always enjoyed.[4] Both men were similar in their meticulous and elegant habits. According to gossip, Delacroix was said to be the illegitimate son of Prince Talleyrand. Certainly his demeanor was aristocratic enough to make such stories credible.

At Nohant that summer a studio had been set up in which Delacroix spent part of each day giving art lessons to George's son, Maurice. Once done with this obligation he often went to Chopin's room to hear him play or just to chat. Neither of them had much sympathy with their hostess' growing absorption in socialist issues. For years Mme. Sand had been an ardent disciple of Pierre Leroux, whose philosophy was a nebulous blend of political liberalism and metaphysical fantasy. In her devotion to his ideals she had begun to promote the works of proletarian authors and soon planned to start a leftist journal in collaboration with Leroux and Pauline Viardot's husband, Louis.

Chopin had no taste for such projects and avoided any involvement in them. Instead he preferred to shut himself up in his room and compose. Except for dinner, usually served around five in the afternoon, he and George actually saw little of each other during their summers together at Nohant. If the weather was warm they ate outdoors on the lawn in back of the house. Sometimes after the meal Chopin would play for a while on the little upright piano in the ground floor salon. Other evenings George gathered her friends around the large oval table in the center of the room and read them several chapters from her latest novel. By eight o'clock Chopin was off to bed. Later, after her guests had gone, George would go upstairs, check on her companion, and then sit down at her desk to write for six or eight hours.

By fall Chopin had completed a number of new works, including his Polonaise in A-flat major and the Ballade in F minor. The polonaise was dedicated to the banker Auguste Léo, who had loaned him money for his trip to Majorca, while the dedication of the ballade went to a member of another banking family, Baroness Charlotte de Rothschild. She was the daughter of James, the youngest of the five Rothschild brothers whose financial empire dominated Europe then. Chopin may well have intended the ballade as a wedding present for her since she had just married her English cousin Baron Nathaniel Rothschild that year. The young bride, a dreamy, sad-faced girl, was not only rich and beautiful but talented as well. Like her mother, Betty, she also took piano lessons from Chopin and became one of his favorite pupils.

His most promising student at that time, however, was an eleven-year-old Hungarian boy named Karl Filtsch, who had come to Paris with his older brother, Joseph, in November of 1841. Earlier in Vienna Karl had studied with Franz Liszt's teacher, Karl Czerny, and probably would have continued his studies in Paris with Liszt himself if the latter hadn't been away in Weimar that fall.[5] Although Liszt didn't really have much interest in teaching then (this was his so-called *Glanzperiode,* 1839–1847, in which he devoted himself primarily to concertizing), he was so overwhelmed when he eventually heard Filtsch play that he resolved to have him as a pupil. Consequently the next summer, while Chopin was away at Nohant, he offered Karl free lessons.[6] At first Filtsch hesitated, fearing this would offend Chopin, but in the end he succumbed and studied with Liszt for several months.

In August Chopin returned to Paris briefly, looking for a new apartment. The little pavilions in the rue Pigalle were too cramped for four people. Both he and George wanted more space. After a few days he found some rooms on the ground floor of the Square d'Orléans where a number of his friends—including the Zimmermans, the Kalkbrenners, Alkan, and Mlle. Mars—already lived. From his new quarters he had a delightful view across a quiet, grassy courtyard where prim little gravel paths led up to a central fountain. The setting was charming and the location more convenient than the rue Pigalle. Mme. Sand also relished the beauty and privacy of the square and took a second-floor apartment for herself and the children diagonally across from Chopin's. With this comfortable arrangement the couple remained near each other and continued to take their meals together, either in George's apartment or with a mutual friend, Mme. Charlotte Marliani, who lived with her husband, the Spanish consul, in still another apartment on the square.

When Chopin resumed his lessons with young Filtsch in November he seemed to bear no grudge against Liszt for his tactless interference that summer. The boy, whom he nicknamed his little *gamin*, was a veritable genius and played with such feeling that his brother Joseph more than once saw tears in Chopin's eyes as he listened to him.

Many evenings the two boys were invited to Mme. Sand's for dinner. George received them warmly and fussed over them in her usual motherly fashion. They, in turn, reacted to her like typical teenagers. From their adolescent point of view the thirty-eight-year-old novelist already had one foot in the grave. "She is still interesting," Joseph commented, "and preserves as best she may the remains of her former beauty."[7] Some of his youthful observations were, in fact, quite penetrating. "With all her intelligence," he noted, "she seems to me very touchy and extremely capricious, not easy to live with, and of a teasing disposition."[8]

After dinner Chopin often took Karl out to show him off in the salons of various friends like Count Apponyi, the Duchess of Osmond, and the Kalkbrenners. Wherever they went the boy made such an impression he threatened to outshine his teacher.

One of those who was especially impressed by the remarkable prodigy was the Baroness Betty de Rothschild, who heard him at Chopin's apartment some time in November of 1842. Shortly afterward the baron also met him and insisted that he come play for them in their magnificent mansion at No. 15 rue Laffitte.[9] This invitation pleased Chopin immensely, for he knew from his own experience that recognition by the Rothschilds was a virtual guarantee of success. Their influence was extraordinary, not to say downright incredible, considering how recently the family had come to prominence.

It was only in 1811 that Baron James first set foot in Paris, an ambitious but unpolished neophyte straight from the Frankfurt ghetto.

He was known then simply as Jacob Rothschild. In France he found life easier than in Germany. For twenty years Jews had been allowed the privilege of French citizenship and enjoyed a degree of freedom denied them in most other parts of Europe then. Since Rothschild money played a significant role in defeating Napoleon, young Jacob came into great favor with the restored Bourbon regime from 1814 on. Rothschild aid to the Allies during the Napoleonic Wars also gained him (as well as his four brothers) the title of baron from the grateful emperor of Austria.

Not long after Waterloo Jacob decided to launch himself into "society" by inviting the Duke of Wellington to dinner. It was a calculated risk, but the English hero accepted and all Paris blinked in amazement. Around this time a wave of anglophilia swept France and prompted the new baron to change his name from Jacob to the more voguish "James." Now both rich and titled, Baron James soon became a powerful figure in the Parisian establishment. His elevated station in life, however, burdened him with many social obligations. What he needed was a fine house and a wife to run it for him. In 1818 he found the house, an ornate residence originally built for another banker named Laborde and later owned by Queen Hortense of Holland and Napoleon's minister of police, Fouché. Six years afterward, he married his niece Betty, the daughter of his brother Salomon, who ran the Viennese branch of the family bank.

James' remarkable rise from virtual obscurity to the heights of prestige took barely thirteen years to accomplish. People might gape at his coarse features—he had the profile of an "intelligent monkey" according to one of his contemporaries[10]—or snicker at his harsh German accent. But with assets exceeding those of the Banque de France, he had to be respected.

All this success made James a little arrogant and somewhat ostentatious. He filled his great house with furniture from Marie Antoinette's personal collection at Versailles and paintings by old masters like Rembrandt, Velasquez, and van Ruisdael. Everywhere there was gilt—on the walls, on the ceilings, and on the furniture. Even the upholstery and draperies glittered with the heavy strands of gold thread woven into them. Such opulence was not to be missed. It lured even the haughty scions of Saint-Germain to "the rich Jew's" parties just to see his palatial home.

HÔTEL DE VILLE, ROUEN

SABINE HEINEFETTER

PIERRE JOSEPH GUILLAUME ZIMMERMAN

MME. DORUS-GRAS

SALLE PLEYEL, RUE ROCHECHOUART, PARIS

PALACE OF SAINT-CLOUD

MME. CINTI-DAMOREAU

DUKE OF ORLÉANS

HEINRICH WILHELM ERNST

SALLE DE SPECTACLES, TUILERIES, PARIS

THE RESIDENCE OF
BARON JAMES DE
ROTHSCHILD, PARIS

By the time Chopin came to know the Rothschilds they were in the habit of giving three or four soirées a week. Sixty guests for dinner was a commonplace thing. With such a crowded agenda they weren't able to find a slot for young Filtsch until after the New Year. The evening they finally selected was one in mid-January when they were planning a grand musicale featuring four of Paris' leading opera singers, Giulia Grisi, Pauline Viardot, Luigi Lablache, and Mario. Naturally Chopin was expected and he took part on the program with Karl in a performance of his Piano Concerto in E minor. While the boy played the solo part Chopin provided the orchestral accompaniment on a second piano.

If this affair had been a public rather than a private concert Parisians would have paid top prices to hear such a fantastic program:

1. Cavatina from *Don Pasquale*,[11]
   Mme. Grisi
2. Duet from *Semiramide*,
   Mesdames Grisi and Viardot
3. Serenade from *Don Pasquale*,
   M. Mario
4. Piano concerto by M. Chopin,
   MM. Chopin and Filtsch
5. Aria [by Balfe],
   Mme. Viardot
6. Romance by Schubert,
   M. Mario
7. Duet from *Don Pasquale*,
   Mme. Grisi and M. Lablache
8. Romances,
   Mme. Viardot
9. Quartet from *Bianca e Faliero*,
   Mesdames Grisi and Viardot
   and MM. Mario and Lablache

Accompaniment by M. Tadolini on a Pleyel piano[12]

The following Sunday Léon Escudier of *La France Musicale* called Chopin a "poetical pianist" and his concerto "ravishing."[13] But it was the splendor of the Rothschild mansion that seemed to have dazzled him far more than anything else. "Look at those glass portals, those regal tapestries, those magnificent paintings, those furnishings swathed in gold!" he gasped. "What magical brilliance! How overpowering! It's like an incredible dream. Such fairy-tale luxury belongs only to the realm of kings and princes."[14] By 1843 most people didn't have to be told that Baron James was a part of that realm. Less than a generation out of the Frankfurt ghetto, the Rothschilds were readily acknowledged to be one of Europe's newest and most illustrious dynasties.

The soirée in the rue Laffitte provided the intimate and cultivated setting in which Chopin loved to perform. Such evenings seemed to stimulate rather than tire him as did his public concerts. To hear Karl play in the great salons of Paris brought back all the excitement of his own youthful triumphs in the grand palaces of Warsaw. The boy, who was now thirteen, electrified his audiences just as he himself had done at the same age. Surely an incomparable career lay ahead for the brilliant youngster. Even Liszt confessed he would have to retire the moment Filtsch started giving concerts. Actually that moment was almost at hand. The Rothschild's soirée was, in effect, a dress rehearsal for a concert the boy planned to give that April in the Salle Érard.[15] Unfortunately the promising future Chopin anticipated for his pupil never came about. Two years later Karl was dead of tuberculosis at the age of fifteen.

May 1843 found Chopin and Mme. Sand back at Nohant where a cool rainy spring kept them indoors most of the time. The dreary days were brightened by visits from Delacroix and Pauline Viardot. As before, Chopin took advantage of his enforced leisure to compose. Two of the nocturnes he wrote that summer were dedicated to another of his pupils, a thirty-nine-year-old spinster named Jane Stirling.[16] She doted on her teacher like a shy schoolgirl, and with the right encouragement her adulation might have flowered into love. While Miss Stirling didn't really have the desire or the ability to become a great concert artist, she had enough money to indulge her musical interests in a dilatory fashion abroad. Often in the summer she returned to England and Scotland where she had a large family scattered about in splendid castles and country houses. If it weren't for George Sand, who whisked Chopin off to Nohant every year, she would have been tempted to invite him home with her.

When Chopin returned to Paris in the fall of 1843 he wasn't feeling well. More than once that winter he was forced to bed by illness. George, of course, saw to it that he had the best care possible. Several times each day either she or one of her domestics would scurry across the courtyard between their apartments with warm food, fresh linens, or whatever he happened to need.

One cold day in February he struggled out of bed to attend the graveside services for Camille Pleyel's mother. All bundled up and shivering, he looked pathetic in the stark winter sunlight. His presence at the cemetery touched Pleyel so much he "threw himself in his arms and the two men wept copious tears."[17]

Only a few months later Chopin himself experienced a similar loss. On May 3 his father died in Warsaw, and for days after hearing the news the grief-stricken son remained shut up in his rooms without seeing anyone or eating anything. Eventually George persuaded him to pack his things and go back to Nohant where he slowly pulled himself together again.

In July he went up to Paris to meet his sister Ludwika and her husband Kalasanty Jędrzejewicz, who had come from Warsaw to visit him. During the first part of their stay he showed them around the city, took them to the opera, and gave parties for them. Later he satisfied their curiosity by taking them to Nohant and introducing them to Mme. Sand, whom he referred to simply as "Pani domu," the "lady of the house." She greeted her Polish guests like old friends and charmed them with her gracious manner and her obvious concern for their brother. After the sorrow of the spring the summer of 1844 turned out happily for Chopin, who was once again in good spirits when he and George arrived back in Paris late that fall.

In the sixth year of their relationship the couple had settled into a life that was placid and routine. Physical passion no longer played a part in it, but Chopin seemed perfectly content with his new role as George's "second son." Other members of the family, though, were not. Maurice could accept his mother's lovers but a "second son" provoked feelings of sibling rivalry in him. Solange, on the other hand, welcomed the cessation of intimacy between Chopin and her mother. She had always been something of a coquette and now flirted shamelessly with her mother's companion. Had she been older and more experienced she might well have tried to become his mistress.

As for George, who never found celibacy very agreeable, she sought solace in the arms of Louis Blanc early in 1843. It didn't bring her much satisfaction, however. Blanc, who was a young socialist writer, stimulated her more from an intellectual point of view than a physical one. Three years later, during the revolution of 1848, the onetime lovers found themselves far more compatible as political collaborators than they had ever been as sexual partners.

The musical season of 1844–45 was the third in a row where Chopin failed to appear in public. That winter it was not so much poor health as just plain indifference that made him refuse Alkan's request to repeat the eight-hand piano version of Beethoven's Seventh Symphony in the Salle Érard.

Around the middle of June he and George set out for Nohant once more where a stormy summer awaited them. Devastating floods inundated the countryside. Roads and fields lay under water, bridges were washed out, and everywhere there were scenes of privation and misery. Nohant itself experienced little hardship, but boredom, irritability, and a host of trivial vexations plagued the inhabitants there. The household was slowly dividing into camps with George and Maurice lined up against Chopin and Solange.

In September a young cousin of Mme. Sand's, Augustine Brault, came to live with the family. She had been raised in poverty by coarse, unscrupulous parents from whom George was anxious to rescue her. At Nohant her presence only served to increase the existing tensions and tipped the balance in favor of the mother-son camp, with which she sided.

When the family got back to the Square d'Orléans that fall matters grew worse. "Titine," as the teenaged girl was called, became the all-consuming object of Mme. Sand's compulsive maternalism, while Maurice began to fancy he was in love with her. This left Solange feeling excluded and resentful. Her only ally in the situation was Chopin, whose undisguised distaste for Titine's plebeian background infuriated George. After eight years of putting up with a moody semi-invalid who no longer gave her any gratification—sexual or otherwise—Mme. Sand had reached the saturation point. She wanted out of the relationship.

In January she decided to let Chopin know what an onus he had become to her. She could have told him so directly but preferred to get her point across in a more delicate fashion, through a novel she was writing called *Lucrezia Floriani.* In it she portrayed herself as the fatal victim of a parasitic lover. When Chopin read the book he seemed to miss its message completely. On the surface he treated the story as just another piece of fiction and complimented his mistress on her superb creative skill.[18]

Nevertheless, the summer of 1846 was—as George intended—his last at Nohant. In the fall he went back to Paris while Mme. Sand and her family stayed in the country until well after the New Year. During this time—the first in eight years the couple had ever been separated for so long—Chopin missed George's daily attentions and his health began to suffer from it.

His finances suffered as well that winter. February 1847 marked the fifth anniversary of his last concert at Pleyel's, and he had little if anything left to show for it. The 500 francs he collected weekly from his pupils was a negligible sum compared with what he could have earned by concertizing. That winter his colleague Henri Herz took in the equivalent of 38,000 francs for just four concerts given in New York on his American tour.[19]

If only Chopin had been willing to return to the concert stage an eager audience awaited him. In March 1847 the *Revue et Gazette Musicale* complained of his absence and advised its readers to attend a concert by his pupil Adolf Gutmann as the next best thing to hearing the master himself.[20]

When Mme. Sand finally came back to Paris in February, it wasn't because of Chopin but for Solange, who was about to marry a handsome young squire she had met at Nohant. Suddenly in the middle of the wedding arrangements the fickle girl fell in love with a swaggering, fast-talking sculptor name Clésinger. A whirlwind courtship followed, and on May 19 she married him at Nohant in the little village church just beyond the gates of her mother's house. Chopin wasn't invited. George no longer wanted him involved in her family affairs.

Only a few weeks later she made this unmistakably clear to him. In a stinging letter she excoriated him for loaning his carriage to Solange and her husband against her wishes. From then on she refused to have anything more to do with him.

Chopin was stunned. He couldn't believe she really meant to break off their relationship for good. When he got no invitation back to Nohant that summer he whiled away his time in the country homes of other friends, including the Rothschild's chateau at Ferrières. Under the circumstances he was too upset to compose much. His entire musical output for 1847 consisted of only three waltzes (opus 64) and a song ("Melody," opus 74).

In December George decided to give up her apartment in the Square d'Orléans, a further indication that she now wanted to avoid her former lover altogether. By Christmas Paris lay under a blanket of snow which confined Chopin to his rooms. "All Paris is sick," he wrote Solange.[21] He himself was coughing and wheezing, but worse than that he was bitterly depressed. The year 1847 had been one of the most miserable of his life.

At the beginning of January several of his friends tried to rouse him out of his apathy by suggesting that he give another concert. As an inducement they volunteered to make all the arrangements for him. Pleyel even promised to wrap the stairways of his hall in flowers for the occasion. Finally Chopin gave in. By the time he wrote his sister about it on February 10, the house had been sold out for a week. Actually the tickets were never offered for sale publicly. Instead, they had been circulated privately to an exclusive "guest list" drawn up from Paris' most elite society. As Chopin explained to Ludwika, "There were only 300 tickets at twenty francs apiece.[22] The king has requested ten of them, the queen ten, and the Duke of Montpensier ten also.[23] A subscription has already been taken up for a second concert, but I don't intend to go through with it since this one has already been such an aggravation."[24]

Rather than give another concert Chopin preferred to get away from Paris for a while. His destination, though, was uncertain. "Do you have any idea where he is off to?" George Sand asked her son, who was at the Square d'Orléans, closing down her apartment.[25] In Poland there was speculation that he might go to Holland, Germany, or even Russia. His mother hoped his travel plans would include Warsaw, while

Jane Stirling was pressuring him to come to England now that Mme. Sand was out of the picture.

As always Chopin went through agony the week before his concert. To ease matters for him Pleyel sent over the piano he was to use so he could get the feel of it, but a sudden attack of "influenza" kept him from practicing. This made him fret even more. His playing, he was convinced, had never been so bad. In a state of anxiety he took himself over to Delfina Potocka's apartment a few days before the concert to try out his program before a small group of Polish friends.

On the evening of the concert itself he was so nervous he couldn't make up his mind what to wear. Later, when he finally arrived at the Salle Pleyel in one of his many tailcoats, he found Miss Stirling waiting backstage. She had come early to be sure the hall was adequately heated for her teacher. Also there was the cellist Franchomme, with whom he was to play his new Sonata for piano and cello that night.[26] This work had never really satisfied Chopin in the past two years that he had been writing—and rewriting—it. In rehearsal it didn't sound right and now, only minutes before the concert, he began to have qualms about performing it at all. After a frantic discussion with Franchomme he decided to delete the first movement and go ahead with the rest of it.

Because of this last-minute crisis Chopin found little time to converse with the other artists who were collecting in the Green Room. Among them was Jean-Delfin Alard, the first violinist of the King's Chamber and Baillot's successor at the Conservatory. He was to open the program with Chopin and Franchomme in a reading of the Mozart Trio in E major.

The evening's singers were probably selected by those friends of Chopin's who arranged the concert for him, since neither was a particular favorite of his. The tenor, Gustave Hippolyte Roger, had always struck him as second-rate, even though Jenny Lind liked him well enough to go on a concert tour with him and Meyerbeer chose him for a leading role (John of Leyden) in his opera *Le Prophète*. The other singer, Mlle. Antonia Molina de Mendi, was a young cousin of Pauline Viardot. Both her "enchanting . . . light soprano" voice and her "angelic" figure were of pleasant but diminutive proportions.[27]

At 8:30 Chopin, Franchomme, and Alard stepped out among the baskets of fresh flowers Pleyel had placed around the stage. Chopin, as usual, looked pale but held himself erect. Throughout the first half of the program he played superbly, but the strain of it told on him later when he arrived backstage close to prostration. After a short rest he was able to continue, and by the end of the concert he felt strong enough to repeat one of the waltzes as an encore.[28] When he took his final bow and walked offstage for the last time, few in the audience suspected what an ordeal he had gone through to finish this lengthy program.

FIRST PART

Trio by Mozart for piano, violin, and violoncello,
performed by MM. Chopin, Alard, and Franchomme

Aria sung by Mademoiselle Antonia Molina de Mendi

Nocturne, Barcarolle } composed and performed by M. Chopin

Aria sung by Mademoiselle Antonia Molina de Mendi

Études, La Berceuse } composed and performed by M. Chopin

SECOND PART

Scherzo, Adagio, and Finale from the Sonata
in G minor for piano and violoncello,
composed by M. Chopin and
performed by the composer and M. Franchomme

A new aria from *Robert le Diable,*
composed by M. Meyerbeer and sung by M. Roger

Preludes, Mazurkas, Valses } composed and performed by M. Chopin

Accompanists: MM. Alary and de Garaudé

"The sylph has kept his promise and with what success, what enthusiasm!" the *Revue et Gazette Musicale* announced deliriously. Chopin's performance, it claimed, was an experience that "has no equal in our earthly realm."[29] Certainly most of the audience would never know such an experience again, for that memorable evening at Pleyel's was the last time Paris was to catch the incomparable sylph on the wing.

• CHAPTER THIRTEEN •

London and Manchester 1848

EIGHT DAYS AFTER Chopin's concert the July Monarchy of France collapsed. On Thursday afternoon, February 24, 1848, Louis-Philippe abdicated in favor of his little grandson the Count of Paris.

This turn of events didn't exactly take the nation by surprise. For some months Paris had been suffering from inflation, food shortages, and widespread unemployment which neither the king nor his reactionary minister, Guizot, could control. The population was growing frustrated and angry. Several days before things came to a head mobs roamed the city, causing minor incidents here and there. Then, on the night of February 23, gunfire broke out in front of the Ministry of Foreign Affairs. Moments later fifty-two people lay dead and a revolution had begun.

By morning pavements were torn up and barricades thrown across many of the streets. Before the day was out the Hôtel de Ville had been seized and the Tuileries sacked. Unnoticed in the midst of so much confusion, Louis-Philippe and his family escaped to England. Shortly afterward a provisional government was established and the Second Republic proclaimed. All this happened in the space of a few days, but it would take months before Paris returned to anything resembling order.

Exhausted from his concert, Chopin stayed secluded in his rooms at the Square d'Orléans throughout these turbulent events. A bad case of "neuralgia" made him so miserable he barely knew what was going on. His neighborhood, which lay some blocks north of the disturbances, remained relatively calm.

The cold gray courtyard outside his windows looked unusually bleak to him that February now that George Sand no longer lived there. She and Maurice were spending the winter at Nohant while Solange was off in Guillery awaiting the birth of her first child.[1] For weeks he seldom saw anyone. Many Parisians had left the city for safer parts. Stores were closed and necessities like food and clothing hard to find.

The following month on one of the rare occasions when Chopin ventured away from the Square d'Orléans he was surprised to run into Mme. Sand at a friend's apartment. She had been lured back to Paris by the revolution and was anxious to get involved in the struggle. Soon she found a role for herself as a polemicist for the new government, which she envisioned as the fruition of her socialistic ideals. Her chance encounter with Chopin early that March was awkward and chilly. He was just leaving as she arrived. They passed on a narrow stairway where it was impossible for them to ignore each other. After a few words they parted and never met again.

Spring brought little stability to Paris. The revolution drove the cost of living up so sharply Chopin found the profits from his recent concert dwindling rapidly. He had few pupils left in the city, and of these, most were afraid to brave the violence of the streets for a piano lesson.

At this point Miss Stirling again entreated him to visit England. Now seemed the time to press her case since political unrest all over Europe that spring made the British Isles a unique haven of tranquillity.

Although Miss Stirling had spent much of her life in England and was thoroughly at home in London society, she was actually Scottish by birth. Her father, John, laird of Kippendavie, belonged to a junior branch of the Stirlings of Keir and had made a fortune in West Indian sugar. Like George Sand, she was six years older than Chopin, but apart from that the two women had no other similarities. Jane Stirling was a prim Calvinist of impeccable lineage and the most circumspect behavior.[2] Except for her love of Paris (suspect in the eyes of many Englishmen), she had a reputation of untainted purity. Throughout her life she remained a spinster and probably a virgin as well. Since the age of eleven she had been an inseparable companion of her older sister, Katherine Erskine, a devoutly religious widow thirteen years her senior.

As early as 1832 Miss Stirling—and the omnipresent Mrs. Erskine—started spending a great deal of time in Paris. There they met Chopin, who was sufficiently impressed with the younger sister's talent to accept her as a pupil. In time, Miss Stirling came to idolize her new teacher. However, she was much too proper to exhibit any unladylike emotions, and no matter what she may have felt for him secretly she always behaved with the well-bred reserve of her social class. Had she been able to break through the barriers of propriety she might have acquired a better understanding of him, and their relationship might have developed along a deeper plane. As it was, the two of them communicated on a superficial level, hedged in by an excess of etiquette and hampered by the French language, in which neither was ever entirely at ease.[3]

In her eagerness to entice Chopin to England Miss Stirling assured him that London would provide him with an ample number of pupils and many opportunities to give concerts. After all, he had already gained quite a reputation in England through his compositions, which had been published and played there for well over a decade.

Chopin, of course, wanted to believe this and readily took her word for it. On the evening of April 19, the Wednesday before Easter, he boarded a train for the English Channel. The boat crossing tired him, but after a few hours' rest in Folkstone he proceeded on to reach London by six the following evening. During his first few days in England Chopin found that Miss Stirling—and her sister—had thoughtfully anticipated his every need; every one, that is, except his need to rest.

From the moment he set foot in the city, his hostesses snatched him up and spun him around London's social circuit in an exhausting whirl. "I have countless calls to make," he wrote Adolf Gutmann.[4] Besides meeting his Scots ladies' myriad acquaintances, he had friends of his own to look up. On Good Friday he visited some of Louis-Philippe's entourage who had taken refuge in London and later dined with the deposed King's former minister Guizot.

"This life of dinners and soirées is very hard on me," he complained before long.[5] "I have to go out every day and never get home until late at night."[6] After a few weeks he began to cough up blood and went on a bland diet of ices and lemonade. The damp English weather only made matters worse. For his first ten days in London he never saw the sun once.

As a result of this tiring treadmill Chopin managed to glean a handful of pupils and several invitations to play in fashionable drawing rooms. He welcomed the money but shrank from the servile role England's upper classes imposed on the professional musician. In the salons of Paris he had always been a pampered guest who might improvise at the piano after dinner if he happened to be in the mood. By contrast, in the London drawing rooms he was regarded as a hired entertainer who received twenty guineas to provide background music whether anyone listened or not. The English, he learned, insisted on having music, day and night. It was a social ritual. "There's no such thing as a flower show, a dinner, or a charity bazaar without music . . . it doesn't matter what it's like, nobody cares."[7]

Fortunately by 1848 the once-popular practice of roping musicians off in a corner of the drawing room (to keep them from mingling with the guests) had died out. Still, Chopin was appalled by the general lack of respect shown to musical artists in London. He himself was treated better than most since, as he put it, he wore clean shoes and didn't hand out business cards. As much as he hated having to hire himself out for money, he considered himself lucky whenever he found someone to hire him. Competition in London was stiff that season since the revolutions on the Continent had sent musicians scurrying to England by the hundreds—not just the hacks but many of Europe's best, including Berlioz, Charles Hallé, Liszt, Thalberg, Pauline Viardot, Marietta Alboni, and others. The city had become a veritable "beehive of artists," Berlioz observed.

Chopin's first offer of employment came from Lady Gainsborough, one of Queen Victoria's ladies-in-waiting. As it happened, she was the aunt of Dr. Mallan, a prominent homeopath whom Miss Stirling had called in to look after her ailing teacher.[8] Although Lady Rothschild (the English sister-in-law of Baron James) cautioned him to keep his fees low, Chopin charged twenty guineas to play at Lady Gainsborough's soirée. Later he asked the same for performing at the Marquis of Douglas'.[9] His most prestigious engagement, however, came from the Duchess of Sutherland, who was planning a lavish reception in honor of her daughter's christening on May 15.

The Sutherlands lived in Stafford House, one of the grandest private residences in all of London. It was (and still is) located at the west end of the Mall, only a stone's throw from Buckingham Palace.[10]

The Duke of York, an uncle of Queen Victoria, began the mansion in 1825. However, his death interrupted its progress, and in 1827 the Crown offered a ninety-nine-year lease on the unfinished house to the Marquis of Stafford. A short while later, after having become the first Duke of Sutherland, he too died before the building was completed. Its first inhabitants, therefore, were the second Duke of Sutherland and his duchess, Harriet, who was a confidante of the queen and her Mistress of the Robes.

Once when Queen Victoria came to visit Stafford House she was so impressed with its magnificence she reputedly told the duchess, "I have come from my house to your palace."[11] As if the structure weren't splendid enough, the duke enriched it further with a priceless collection of art which had once belonged to the Duke of Orléans, an ancestor of Louis-Philippe and regent of France during the minority of Louis XV.

Both the Duke and Duchess of Sutherland were closely associated with the colony of Polish exiles living in London then. While the duke served as vice-president of the Literary Association of the Friends of Poland, the duchess aided the city's indigent Poles by holding fund-raising events (frequently musicales) in Stafford House.

Besides organizing these charitable activities and fulfilling her obligations at court, the tireless duchess managed to produce a total of eleven children. In the exclusive clubs along St. James's Street and Pall Mall, Stafford House was jestingly referred to as the "Lying-In Hospital." One year the duchess and her two oldest daughters each gave birth to a child there in the space of a few months.

On May 15 the latest offspring of the Sutherlands, a daughter named Alexandrina, was baptized in the private chapel of Buckingham Palace before Queen Victoria, Prince Albert, and the cream of Burke's Peerage.[12] The queen herself served as one of the godparents and was the guest of honor that evening at a dinner for eighty people given at Stafford House.

According to the press which covered the affair in detail, "Her Majesty arrived . . . at five minutes after eight and on alighting, was received by the Duke and Duchess of Sutherland."[13] On the arm of the duke she passed through the front door into the entrance hall where she was greeted by the assembled guests, including her mother, the Duchess of Kent. All the ladies that night were dressed in white which created a stunning contrast to the hall's red walls and brightly colored murals. In the background a broad marble staircase led up to a spacious landing where it divided before continuing on to a pair of columned galleries along either side of the vast reception area.

After paying their respects to the queen, the guests dispersed and circulated about. Among those who could be seen chatting as they strolled up and down the crowded stairway were the Duke of Wellington and the Prince of Prussia.[14]

At dinner the queen, "sparkling in her diamonds and decorations," was the center of attention.[15] Just before dessert the Duke of Sutherland stood and proposed the health of Her Majesty, to which all the guests rose while the band played "God Save the Queen." A toast was then offered to Prince Albert, following which a kilted Highlander stepped forward and played some Scottish airs on the bagpipes. It was the Duchess of Kent's turn to be honored next, after which the queen herself saluted her new goddaughter and called on those present to drink the health of the "Noble Infant."[16]

After the meal Her Majesty and the ladies of the party retired to the picture gallery where a rich assortment of French and Italian masters hung side by side with family portraits by Romney and other English artists. A group of newly arrived guests, who had been invited for the concert only, were waiting there to be presented to the queen.

A little while later, in the state drawing room, the distinguished audience heard a program featuring the singers Mario, Lablache, and Tamburini along with the pianists Chopin and Jules Benedict.[17] This was one of the few times Chopin ever performed with the great bass-baritone Antonio Tamburini. Far from being a vain, temperamental artist, this modest son of an Italian bandmaster lived such a quiet, ordinary life he has given historians and biographers little to write about. In London during the 1840s, however, he was so popular, people rioted in the streets to hear him.

Chopin's contributions to the evening included several of his mazurkas and waltzes followed by a rendition of Mozart's Variations in G major for two pianos. Jules Benedict, who took the second piano in these variations,[18] was the musical director of the Drury Lane Theater. A German by birth, he had studied with Hummel and Weber and conducted at Vienna's Kärnthnerthor Theater before coming to London in 1837.

During Chopin's solos Prince Albert walked over and stood beside the piano while he played. Afterward the queen chatted with him, not once but twice, in the course of the evening. Such royal attentions, he was told, were a sign of great favor and a guarantee that he would be asked to play for the court, either at Buckingham Palace or Windsor Castle, in the near future. All in all "it was quite a success," Chopin boasted.[19]

Sometime after midnight as the queen and her consort were preparing to leave, the Duchess of Sutherland presented Her Majesty with "a magnificent bouquet . . . of acacias, azalias, roses and lilies of the valley, all of the purest white."[20]

A few days later the *Illustrated London News* claimed that Chopin's playing before the queen "created a great sensation."[21] Actually Victoria hadn't even taken the trouble to remember his name. In her diary she expressed her delight at the wonderful performances of "good Lablache, Mario and Tamburini." Only as an afterthought did she recall that "some pianists" had also been at Stafford House that night.

Chopin, of course, wasn't privy to the queen's diary and always assumed he never got invited to court because he failed to pay a courtesy call on the royal music director.

Not only did Chopin snub the queen's director of music, he turned down an invitation to play with the Royal Philharmonic, which the man conducted. This was an insult not to be forgiven in London. No one had ever spurned an offer from the Philharmonic Society. On the contrary, it was a favor sought after by anyone who hoped to make a reputation in England. Men like Kalkbrenner and Hallé tried in vain to appear with the orchestra that season.

Chopin realized the furor he was causing but refused all the same. He wasn't that impressed with the Philharmonic. Like English roast beef and turtle soup, it seemed to him "heavy and highly touted but that's about all."[22] In 1848 he wasn't entirely wrong. At that time the orchestra had many glaring faults—"bassoons too weak, oboes never in tune [and] horns never seeming to know their parts."[23] For years it had been led by two men at the same time (the first violinist and another musician who directed from a piano). Neither of them, according to

Spohr, knew what he was doing. Even after Sir Michael Costa took over as conductor in 1846, many of the orchestra's members still chose to rely on the first cellist or the bass player for their cues.

In Chopin's opinion the worst thing about the Philharmonic Society was that it allowed only one rehearsal for each performance—hardly enough for programs that often included a couple of overtures, a symphony or two, a concerto, and several chamber works or vocal numbers.

In London as in Paris it was the city's social life more than its musical activities that occupied most of Chopin's time. "Every night," he wrote, "I'm out at some party."[24] Wherever he went he ran into familiar faces. Some, for example, were friends he had met on his first trip to England like Christian Wessel, his English publisher, or Henry Broadwood, the piano manufacturer.[25] Others included Pauline Viardot, who had just arrived for an engagement at Covent Garden, and several of his former pupils (Thomas D.A. Tellefsen and Lindsay Sloper) who were now living in London. Among the new acquaintances he made in his rounds of the London drawing rooms were Jenny Lind, Charles Dickens, Ralph Waldo Emerson (lecturing then at Exeter Hall), and the Thomas Carlyles.

Compared with the French, so many of the English he met seemed dull and humorless. Once after a brief conversation with Lord Byron's widow, he wrote his family, "No wonder she bored Byron!"[26] One of the most tiresome things about the English was their absolute obsession with their ancestry. Over and over again Chopin had to listen to them rattle on about their lineage in endless genealogical recitations. The only way he found to get an Englishman's mind off his pedigree was to talk about money. "Everything here is measured in terms of the pound sterling," he observed. The more expensive something is the more the English love it. "The only reason they appreciate art is because it's considered a luxury."[27]

As much as Chopin carped at the English, he had no intention of going back to France just then. In Paris that spring nobody cared about art, whatever the price. Night after night most seats at the Opéra went begging—even after the cost of tickets had been drastically cut. At the Opéra-Comique the situation was almost as bad, although the tenor Roger could still draw a small crowd on good nights. As for concert halls, only the Conservatory's remained open.

Besides the sixty guineas Chopin made from his drawing room engagements, he also earned a little from teaching, although hardly what he expected.[28] Many young ladies sought him out but few had any real interest in music. Most simply wanted the chance to say they had been his pupils, and after several lessons they quit.

In a city as expensive as London Chopin needed a larger and more predictable income. He had barely settled into spacious new quarters at 48 Dover Street when his landlord (thinking he had a rich celebrity in his house) doubled the rent from twenty-six to fifty-two guineas a month. Whenever he went to hear Pauline Viardot or Jenny Lind at the opera it cost him two and a half guineas. And, of course, like every gentleman of fashion he had to have a valet. Unfortunately the one he hired proved to be even more fastidious than himself and refused to accompany him anywhere unless they rode in a private carriage rather than the more economical cabs.

By mid-June Chopin was so short of money he decided to give a concert. When Mrs. Sartoris, the wife of a rich industrialist and a leading figure in London society, heard this she offered him the use of her house in Belgravia. Chopin had known Mrs. Sartoris for many years, possibly as early as 1832 when she first came to Paris to study singing. In those days she was Miss Adelaide Kemble, a bright, talented, and well-disciplined young lady who could converse fluently in four languages. Her father, Charles Kemble, was a famous name on the London stage and had brought up his children in an exhilarating milieu of actors and writers. His daughter Fanny became a noted actress in her own right, while Adelaide (or "Dot" as she was called by Thackeray and other close friends of the family) preferred a career in music. After finishing her vocal studies in Paris, "Dot" toured the Continent, giving concerts in Germany and Italy, sometimes with Liszt as her accompanist. In 1841 she returned to London where she made her debut in Covent Garden as Norma in an English translation of Bellini's opera.[29] The music critic Chorley found her "a poetical and thoughtful artist."[30] Occasionally, though, he felt her singing got a bit heavy because of her tendency to approach music in too meticulous and intellectual a fashion.

Two years after her London debut Miss Kemble gave up her career to marry Mr. Sartoris, whom she had met in Paris. By 1848 she was the mother of two children, "beautiful as angels" according to Chopin. Although she had become somewhat stouter than before, she still sang "very nicely" and was a delightful hostess of unusual intelligence.[31]

Chopin's concert in the Sartoris home at 99 Eaton Place was an afternoon affair given in the large second-floor drawing room that stretched across the front of the narrow stone town house. On the day before it was to take place all 150 seats (at a guinea apiece) had been sold. As expected, "high society showed up" along with such literary and artistic figures as Thackeray, Jenny Lind, and Mrs. Carlyle.[32]

"It came off very well, Chopin wrote Solange Clésinger several days later.[33] He was especially thrilled with Jenny Lind's presence. Few people in London delighted him like the "Swedish nightingale." He dined with her, went to her performances, and sat up until midnight listening to her sing Swedish folk songs. At one point he thought of asking her to take part in his concert but concluded she was too busy. Only later did he learn how gladly she would have accepted his invitation.

As it was, he asked the tenor Mario to assist him. In London that season the brilliant Italian (reputedly descended from the Borgias) was considered "the fashionable society vocalist par excellence."[34] In the course of the concert he sang three sets of selections,[35] while Chopin appeared four times playing a collection of nocturnes, the ballade in F major, the Andante Spianato, two mazurkas, two waltzes, an impromptu, and the Berceuse.

His performance, the *Illustrated London News* of July 1, 1848, declared, was unrivaled by "any other executant of the present day." He played "with the greatest energy," it claimed while the *Examiner* noted the loudness of his *fortes*.[36] Such remarks indicate what a forceful impression Chopin could create in the intimate setting of a drawing room like Mrs. Sartoris'. The *Athenaeum* described his compositions as "gems" and "pearls"[37] but was less enthusiastic about his playing, which it regarded as "peculiar" yet "charming."[38]

One of London's most influential critics, J. W. Davison, who wrote for the *London Times* and the *Musical World,* didn't attend the concert. This was just as well. He was a devotee of Mendelssohn, by whom he measured all contemporary musicians. Years earlier, without ever hearing Chopin, he decided he disliked him and wrote a number of diatribes against him.[39]

Toward the end of June the musical season in London was almost over. Even though the concert in Eaton Place had brought him over a hundred guineas Chopin still needed more money to stay on in England, and there was little time to earn it. Soon the queen and all society would be leaving for the country. His pupils would be gone, and there would be no more drawing room musicales or concerts until the fall. Another "matinée" like the one at Mrs. Sartoris' was still possible if he acted quickly. This, however, was difficult for the indecisive Chopin, who probably would have done nothing had friends not taken the initiative for him.

Sometime that June, Henry Fowler Broadwood introduced him to George Henry Boscawen, the fifth Viscount and second Earl of Falmouth. The latter, an eccentric old bachelor, had a fine town house at No. 2 St. James's Square, which would be an ideal setting for another concert. The problem was whether he would let Chopin use it. Since Broadwood knew that the earl was a great music lover and an amateur violinist, he thought he might be persuaded. Still, one could never count on the strange fellow's behavior. With all his wealth Lord Falmouth went around so shabbily dressed no one on the street ever suspected who he was. Even in his own home he was more apt to be taken for a servant than the master of the house.

Once in Paris Chopin had met the earl's niece, but he would never have dared to approach her uncle on the basis of such a slight acquaintance. In England he knew that would be considered presumptuous. The British were such a stuffy lot, even worse sticklers for etiquette than the French. "It's difficult to do anything here, there are so many rules to be observed," he once complained.[40] With Broadwood's tactful mediation, though, Lord Falmouth's consent was obtained by the end of June and Chopin began preparing for his second London matinée.

The earl's house, which he inherited in 1842, had been in the Boscawen family for nearly a century. The land it stood on once belonged to the Bennet family, who had the dubious distinction of managing the royal mistresses of Charles II. By 1848 St. James's Square had become an enclave of the wealthy and aristocratic, lined by private homes, several clubs, and the West End branch of the London and Westminster Bank.[41]

Despite Lord Falmouth's personal peculiarities, he ran a well-organized house with a large staff decked out in immaculate liveries.

Considering the location and elegance of the earl's home, Chopin had every reason to expect "high society" would again turn out for his concert. An audience of around 200 could be accommodated, and at a guinea a head, his profit should be even greater than at Mrs. Sartoris'.

If Jenny Lind hadn't already left London on a concert tour Chopin would have had no qualms about asking her assistance now. As an alternative he thought of Pauline Viardot, who was still singing at Covent Garden. However, he feared her close ties with Mme. Sand may have turned her against him.

Once more friends had to intercede for him. One day when he and Broadwood were discussing the concert, Pauline's brother Manuel Garcia, a voice teacher in London, overheard their conversation.[42] Confident that nothing had altered his sister's feelings he spoke to her, and as he expected, she was more than eager to take part on the program.[43] Recently she had converted some of Chopin's mazurkas into songs and performed them at Covent Garden where they were well received. Now, in what she doubtless regarded as a compliment to their composer, she proposed to sing them with her young cousin Antonia de Mendi at his concert. Apparently Chopin didn't object, although it is hard to imagine he was pleased.

On the afternoon of July 7 the summer stillness of St. James's Square was broken by the sharp staccato of horses' hooves and the fitful creaking of carriage wheels as a procession of sleek black broughams and open-roofed landaus approached Lord Falmouth's house. One by one the vehicles stopped to let out their passengers, who walked past the low wrought iron fence and up the short flight of stairs to the entrance. At the door they were greeted by one of the earl's liveried footmen and handed the following program:

Monsieur Chopin's
Second Matinée Musicale
Friday, July 7, 1848
at the residence of
the Earl of Falmouth
No. 2 St. James's Square
To commence at Four o'clock

Programme

Andante Sostenuto et Scherzo (Op. 31) Chopin
Mazourkas de Chopin, arrangées par Madame Viardot Garcia
Mme. Viardot Garcia et Mlle. de Mendi
Etudes (19, 13, and 14) Chopin
Air, "Ich denke dein" Beethoven
Mme. Viardot Garcia
Nocturne et Berceuse Chopin
Rondo, "Non piu mesta" (*Centerentola*) Rossini
Mme. Viardot Garcia
Preludes, Mazourkas, Ballade, Valses Chopin
Airs Espagnoles
Mme. Viardot Garcia et Mlle. de Mendi

To quote the *Daily News,* the "numerous and fashionable assemblage" which graced Lord Falmouth's salon that afternoon was thoroughly "delighted with the entertainment provided for them."[44] The incredible ease with which Chopin glided through the most difficult passages amazed the critic, who gushed over the "liquid mellowness" and "pearly roundness" of his playing.[45] At the same time the *Athenaeum* noted that he exhibited even "more force and *brio*" than at Mrs. Sartoris' two weeks before.[46]

Mme. Viardot Garcia's performance also charmed the reviewer, although he considered her vocal arrangements of Chopin's mazurkas "queerly piquant."[47]

"The *season* is ended at present," Chopin wrote a friend in Paris the day after his concert at Lord Falmouth's. "What are my plans for the future? I wish I knew."[48] He had just cleared another 100 guineas or more from it, but most of that went to pay bills he had already run up. "I have only a little cash on hand," he continued, "and I haven't the least idea what I'm going to do."[49]

Miss Stirling and her sister planned to leave for Scotland later that month, and Chopin considered going along with them even though he wasn't particularly keen on it. As "kind and affectionate" as the two ladies were, they "sometimes bore me to death," he conceded.[50] Besides, he wasn't sure he could stand up to so much traveling. "My health varies from one hour to the next. In the mornings there are times I think I'll absolutely cough myself to death."[51]

His summer in London hadn't been a very restful one. Where he once resented the quiet pace of life at Nohant, he now longed for it. Even more, he longed for George Sand, who understood him so much better than his Scottish ladies. She had recognized the limits of his strength and allowed him the privacy and independence he needed.

For years Miss Stirling had observed her teacher and Mme. Sand together without really comprehending the nature of their relationship. Now that the couple had broken up she saw her opportunity to slip unobtrusively into Mme. Sand's role. Certainly many people expected this to happen, and rumors flew back and forth across the channel that she and Chopin planned to be married. Nothing could have been further from the truth. Jane Stirling, coddled since birth by her older siblings, was an emotionally dependent person who could never offer Chopin the maternal support of a George Sand. What was worse, she didn't know how to be protective without being possessive, and it was her suffocating benevolence that irritated Chopin most.

In spite of all Miss Stirling's well-intentioned kindness it was George who remained uppermost in his thoughts. Whenever possible he asked friends for news of her. She and Solange were still at loggerheads, he heard, while Augustine's father was circulating a malicious pamphlet accusing her of the worst sort of depravity. During the revolution she had been branded a communist because of her sympathy for the working classes, and threats were now being made against her life. Chopin felt sorry for her, but after all, he figured, she had brought it on herself.

By the middle of July Miss Stirling and Mrs. Erskine left for Scotland to visit their brother-in-law, James Sandilands, who had inherited the title of Lord Torphichen shortly after his marriage to their sister Margaret in 1806. Now a widower, he lived alone in Calder House, his country estate a few miles west of Edinburgh. The ladies hadn't been gone long before Chopin decided to join them. Out of concern for his comfort, Henry Broadwood accompanied him to the railroad station in London and paid to keep the seat beside him empty so he wouldn't feel cramped during the long, twelve-hour journey to Edinburgh.

Once in Scotland Chopin found the inhabitants a warmhearted but unattractive lot—if anything, even more philistine than their English cousins. Calder House, though, made a pleasant impression on him, and he liked his host, the amiable old Lord Torphichen. Had the climate been better his stay might have been agreeable enough, but the damp Scottish air stifled him. Some days he could hardly breathe and felt as if he were going to die.

Regardless of this he lingered on until late August, when he had to leave for Manchester where he was to play in a concert on the twenty-eighth. The trip to Manchester involved another tiring train trip of eight hours, but once there, he was able to relax at Crumpsall House, the luxurious home of Mr. and Mrs. Salis Schwabe.[52] Like most wealthy Mancunians, the Schwabes lived several miles outside the smoky, industrial city. A long, shaded drive, bordering a lake, led up to their splendid Georgian mansion and the extensive gardens surrounding it.

The forty-eight-year-old Salis Schwabe was a friend of Chopin's Paris banker, Auguste Léo, and, like Léo, was a German-Jewish convert to Christianity. He first came to Manchester in 1832 after living in Glasgow for fifteen years. By 1848 he owned the Rhodes Print Works, which boasted the biggest chimney in all Manchester. During his spare time this energetic tycoon devoted himself to helping the mentally ill and pursuing the pleasures of music. He was a proficient pianist and organist who enjoyed the company of fine musicians. Neukomm, one of Haydn's pupils and a former court musician to the emperor of Brazil, had been his guest in June, while Jenny Lind was coming to visit him in September on her tour to northern England and Scotland.

Schwabe, along with Auguste Léo's brother Herman, belonged to a wave of German immigrants who settled in Manchester during the early nineteenth century and eventually made the city not only a great industrial metropolis but an outstanding musical center as well.

Just two months before Chopin's arrival Herman Léo had invited Charles Hallé to Manchester. Like Chopin, he too was a victim of the troubled times on the Continent. That fall he played at one of the city's "Gentlemen's Concerts" and stayed on to become their director the next year. The orchestra at that time was a "band made up of the kind of materials brought together at provincial concerts, a mixed company of professors and amateurs, veterans and recruits."[53] Hallé's success in shaping this motley crew into a respectable orchestra was followed by an even greater triumph when he organized his own famous Hallé Concerts in Manchester's Free Trade Hall in 1858.

While Hallé deserves much of the credit for putting Manchester on the musical map, he was building on a tradition that had begun well back in the previous century. As early as 1770 a handful of flutists started congregating on a regular basis at one of the local taverns. Soon singers and other instrumentalists joined them, and by 1771 a hall seating 900 people was built for the group, which now gave a series of twelve so-called Gentlemen's Concerts each year.

In 1831 a new concert hall, accommodating over 1,200, was erected to take the place of the original one. It was there in 1836 that Pauline Viardot's celebrated sister La Malibran sang for the last time. At the end of her performance she collapsed, and nine days later she died in a nearby hotel. She was only twenty-eight.[54]

While the caliber of music at the Gentlemen's Concerts may have varied over the decades, the social prestige of the organization never waned. The subscribers (who included gentlewomen as well as gentlemen) represented the finest of Manchester society. They were limited to 600 individuals who either lived within six miles of the city or maintained a permanent business there. At all performances men were required to wear white tie, while ladies, it was presumed, would dress appropriately without having to be told. Each subscriber was entitled to two tickets for every performance, which cost him (or her) the modest sum of five guineas a year. Out of these 600 subscribers a commmittee of 12 was elected to supervise the management of the hall.[55]

The program planned for August 28 featured three singers along with Chopin. By far the most remarkable of this cast was the contralto Marietta Alboni. A former pupil of Rossini, she made her debut at Milan's La Scala in 1843. Her voice was virtually flawless and her virtuosity incredible. In her youth she was a great beauty but over the years she grew quite obese, causing Rossini to dub her "the elephant who swallowed a nightingale."[56] In 1848 she was at the height of her powers and knew it. That April she pushed up her fees and threatened to cancel all her English contracts if her demands weren't met.

Touring with Mlle. Alboni was another singer, Mlle. Corbari, and their accompanist, the Irish pianist George Alexander Osborne, who had taken part in Chopin's Paris debut. The third singer on the program, Signor Salvi, was another Italian who also enjoyed a considerable following in England. Compared with this popular triumvirate Chopin was a relative unknown, even though news of the "liquid mellowness" and "pearly roundness" of his playing had recently spread from London to Manchester.[57] None of this mattered, however, to the tired and ailing Chopin. The sixty guineas he was about to earn was far more important to him than anything else. "If I were younger," he announced cynically, "I would let myself become a machine and give concerts everywhere, grinding out the most insipid works devoid of any worth as long as it paid off."[58]

The way things were, he knew he could barely expect to get through the few numbers he had agreed to play. Shortly before the concert he begged Osborne not to listen to him. "You . . . who have heard me so often in Paris, remain with those impressions. My playing will be lost in such a large room and my compositions will be ineffective. Your presence at the concert will be painful both to you and me."[59]

At eight o'clock Monday evening, August 28, 1848, Manchester's white-tied gentlemen gathered with their ladies in the neoclassic splendor of the handsome concert hall on Peter Street[60] for the following program:[61]

PART FIRST

Overture, *Ruler of the Spirits* Weber

Terzettino, "Io t'amava" (*Nabuco*) Verdi
Signoras Alboni e Corbari, e Signor Salvi

Recitativo e Cavatina, "Come provar" (*La Cantatrice Villane*) Pacini[62]
Signora Corbari

Romanza, "Ciel Pietoso" (*Oberto*) Verdi
Signor Salvi

Andante e Scherzo, Pianoforte Chopin[63]
M. Chopin

Cavatina e Finale, "Non piu mesta" (*Cenerentola*) Rossini
Signora Alboni

Duetto, "Vieni in Roma" (*Norma*) Bellini
Signora Corbari e Signor Salvi

PART SECOND

Overture, *Prometheus* Beethoven
Duetto, "La Regatta Veneziano" Rossini
Signoras Alboni e Corbari
Romanza, "Una Furtiva Lagrima" (*L'Elisir d'Amore*) Donizetti
Signor Salvi
Nocturne, Etudes, et Berceuse, Pianoforte Chopin[64]
M. Chopin
Duetto, "Un soave non so che" (*Cenerentola*) Rossini
Signora Alboni e Signor Salvi
Aria, "Oh, dischiuso" (*Nino*) Verdi
Signora Corbari
Tyrolienne, "In questo semplice" (*Betly*) Donizetti
Signora Alboni
Trio, "Cruda sorte" (*Ricciardo e Zoraide*) Rossini
Signoras Alboni e Corbara, e Signor Salvi
Overture, *Il Barbiere de Siviglia* Rossini
Leader of the Orchestra, Mr. Seymour[65]

When the critic for the *Manchester Examiner* arrived at the concert he found every seat was taken, "so great was the desire to hear Alboni."[66] Because of this he wasn't able to get inside the hall until the first part of the program was half over. Chopin had just started to play when he entered, and what he heard was a great disappointment to him. Nowhere in Chopin's performance could he detect any "melody or meaning," and he considered it unfortunate that the pianist had insisted on playing his own works. All in all, he concluded, this "*artiste* does not quite come up to our idea of a first-rate pianist."[67]

The *Musical World* was equally unflattering. It too claimed that the large audience at the concert came chiefly to hear Mademoiselle Alboni—"and lastly, M. Chopin, the French-celebrated pianist and composer, who is a novelty in these parts."[68] In line with this order of priorities, the critic (J. W. Davison, a longtime detractor of Chopin) wasn't inclined to waste many words on him. "You must pardon me if I venture to say very little of Mons. Chopin's pianoforte playing. He neither surprised me, nor pleased me entirely. He certainly played with great finish—too much so perhaps . . . but I missed the astonishing power of Leopold de Meyer, the vigour of Thalberg, the dash of Herz, or the grace of Sterndale Bennett."[69]

Only the *Manchester Guardian* suggested hesitantly that Chopin was "perhaps an equal feature of interest with Alboni."[70] Like the other newspapers, it also noted the lack of vigor in his playing, which it attributed to his extreme physical frailty. "He is very spare in frame," the reporter observed, "and there is an almost painful air of feebleness in his appearance and gait."[71]

Osborne, who ignored Chopin's pleas, listened to him from a corner of the hall. There he cheered and applauded even though he realized his friend's premonitions had been right. "His playing was too delicate to create enthusiasm and I felt truly sorry for him."[72]

To friends in Paris Chopin painted a cheerier picture. "I was well received," he claimed, "and called back to the piano three times.[73] The hall was beautiful and 1,200 people showed up."[74]

• CHAPTER FOURTEEN •

Glasgow, Edinburgh, and London 1848

AFTER THE MANCHESTER concert the Schwabes urged Chopin to stay on with them for another week to see Jenny Lind. However, Miss Stirling and Mrs. Erskine had other plans for him. Their oldest sister, Ann, who had married Ludovic Houston, lived at Johnstone Castle, eleven miles southwest of Glasgow, and this was to be the next stop on their itinerary of family calls. Naturally they expected Chopin, as their celebrity-in-tow, to come along.

Mrs. Houston turned out to be a delightful person and Johnstone Castle "an extremely beautiful and opulent" place. "The life led here is most elegant," Chopin observed with his characteristic sensitivity to refinement.[1] However, he soon tired of it. Most of the houseguests ranged from seventy to eighty years of age, while the few young ones present were usually out grouse hunting all day.

Even though Johnstone Castle was run with greater magnificence than Nohant, Chopin was as ill-suited to country life in Scotland as he had been in France. "I'm depressed," he chafed. "The people here wear me out with all their attentions. I can barely breathe or work and feel so alone, alone, alone, despite all the crowd around me."[2]

During his stay at Mrs. Houston's it was suggested that he give a concert in Glasgow. "I don't know if anything will come of it," he remarked as he set out to visit a former pupil, Lady Murray, at Strachur on Loch Fyne.[3] Since he had thought vaguely of playing in Edinburgh later on, he had his mail forwarded to a friend there, Dr. Adam Lyszczyński. While he was still at Strachur word reached him that a concert had definitely been scheduled for him in Glasgow on September 27. This came about through the efforts of some local ladies including two daughters of the Duke and Duchess of Sutherland: the Duchess of Argyll and Lady Blantyre. It was Muir Wood, a Glasgow music dealer, though, who actually took charge of the arrangements.[4]

In his preparations for the concert, Wood reserved the auditorium in the Merchants' Hall on Hutcheson Street and sold tickets for it out of his shop at No. 42 Buchanan Street. The Merchants' Hall in 1848 was a new building only four years old. The organization which it housed, however, went back to the Middle Ages. The original purpose of the Merchants' Hall (or House, as it was often called) was threefold: to elect the local dean of guild, to engage in charitable activities, and to voice opinions on the commercial, political, and civic affairs of Glasgow. Its use as a concert hall was purely incidental.[5]

When it came to fixing the details of his performance Chopin behaved with frustrating indecision. He couldn't make up his mind what to play and made Muir Wood chase back and forth between Glasgow and Strachur trying to put together the program for the printer.

The time set for the performance was 2:30 Wednesday afternoon. This, as it turned out, was a poor choice since few people were free at that hour on a weekday. Furthermore the half-guinea cost of a ticket was considered high outside of London and discouraged all but the most affluent. How many people came isn't certain, but the concert was far from a sellout. The hall, according to widely varying estimates, was from one-fourth to two-thirds empty. Nevertheless, the lineup of carriages caused some afternoon congestion on Hutcheson Street as the aristocracy and gentry from the west of Scotland drove up to hear the famous *artiste* from France.

While he waited for his audience to arrive Chopin milled about the concert hall in a pale gray suit, chatting with friends and looking nervously at his pocket watch. His cadaverous appearance shocked many of those who had never seen him before. As one observer put it, he looked thin, ashen, bent-over, and clearly "marked for doom."[6]

Among those he greeted were Prince and Princess Alexander Czartoryski, who were visiting in Edinburgh only forty-five miles away.[7] For Chopin their presence alone was compensation enough for the poor turnout and made all his effort seem worthwhile. "I felt revived under the influence of these Polish spirits, and that gave me the strength to play," he wrote a friend in Paris.[8]

At 2:30, despite the many vacant seats which still remained, Chopin put away his watch and sat down at the piano. The program, which lasted an hour and a half, included the following:

1. Piano-forte, Andante [Op. 22] et Impromptu [Op. 36] Chopin
   M. Chopin
2. Romanza, "La camelia" Guglielmo
   Mme. Giulietta Adelasio de Marguerittes
3. Piano-forte, Etudes [Op. 25] Chopin
   M. Chopin
4. Melodie et Romance, "Le Lac," Meditation poetique de Lamartine mise en Musique Niedermeyer
   Mme. Adelasio
5. Piano-forte, Nocturnes [Opp. 27 and 55] et Berceuse [Op. 57] Chopin
   M. Chopin
6. Barcaruola, "La notte e bella" Guglielmo
   Mme. Adelasio
7. Piano-forte, Prelude [Op. 28], Ballade [Op. 38], Mazourkas [Op. 7], Valses [Op. 64] Chopin
   M. Chopin[9]

Muir Wood, in addition to everything he had already done for Chopin's concert, also served as accompanist to the sole singer on the program, Mme. Adelasio. She was the daughter of a London physician and had never performed in Glasgow before. Apparently she wasn't very happy to be there and "evinced a certain lack of enthusiasm with which we were not at all charmed," the *Glasgow Herald* observed.[10] The *Glasgow Courier,* on the other hand, was quite pleased with her "beautiful voice" and the "great ease and occasional brilliancy" with which she handled it.[11]

Since the meager audience consisted mostly of Chopin's friends and acquaintances there is little doubt he was warmly applauded. However, he rewarded them with only one encore. This, according to Julius

Seligmann, president of the Glasgow Society of Musicians, was a mazurka he had already played earlier in the program. On repeating it as an encore, though, he gave it an entirely different interpretation than before.

The newspaper reviews were mixed. In the estimation of the *Glasgow Courier,* Chopin showed "the highest musical talent" and played with "grace," "ingenuity," and a "magic touch."[12] The *Glasgow Herald,* however, refrained from commenting on his playing with the tactful explanation that "M. Chopin is evidently a man of weak constitution and seems labouring under physical debility and ill health."[13] This, of course, was noticed by others too. As Seligmann remarked, "His touch was very feeble and while the finish, grace, elegance and delicacy of his performance were greatly admired by the audience, the want of power made his playing somewhat monotonous."[14]

Because of the poor attendance Chopin's income from the concert was somewhere between sixty and ninety pounds—half of what he expected.

Money, however, wasn't on his mind when he returned to Johnstone Castle that evening with Prince and Princess Czartoryski. At the large dinner Mrs. Houston gave in his honor, he relaxed and forgot the strains of the past few weeks. In the company of his Polish guests he came back to life again. But it was a life whose time was now measured in months rather than years.

The exhilaration Chopin felt among his friends at Johnstone Castle didn't last for long. Already it was fall and the days were growing shorter and cooler. Despite the hospitality of the Scots, their country depressed him. He wished he were home in the Square d'Orléans, but with all the bad news coming out of Paris he wondered when he would ever get there. On September 30 the *Glasgow Saturday Post* reported that nearly 100 shops along the rue Royale and the Grands Boulevards were closed and half the houses abandoned. Prices had fallen to rock bottom, and churches everywhere stood empty except for a few women. Why go back to Paris with conditions like that? And yet he was so thoroughly sick of Scotland he knew he couldn't stand it there much longer.

Each morning he stayed alone in his room until he had to dress for lunch. Then, after eating, he sat around gasping and choking during the rest of the afternoon. Worse yet were the evenings when he had to smile silently through an interminable dinner since he didn't know enough English to take part in the conversation. At the end of the meal when the ladies withdrew he was left behind with the men. For the next half hour, as the room filled up with their cigar smoke, he had nothing to do but "watch them talk and listen to them drink."[15] Later, in the drawing room, he was expected to play a bit. By then he would be so worn out his servant had to carry him upstairs to bed.

Oblivious to his suffering, Chopin's zealous hostesses continued to make the rounds of their relatives with him. They were killing him with kindness but he was too polite to object. Toward the end of September they carted him off to Perthshire for a visit to one of their cousins, Sir William Stirling, a well-traveled and knowledgeable young bachelor of thirty.[16] Just the year before, he had inherited Keir, a magnificent country seat belonging to the Stirling family since 1460.[17]

When Chopin arrived he found the large house filled with thirty or so guests. "My! What an assortment of outfits, diamonds, pimply noses, gorgeous hair-dos, and splendid figures," he exclaimed.[18] Life in the "English chateaus" (as he called them) left little to be desired with their fine libraries, art collections, wine cellars, stables, and gardens. Unfortunately, at Keir Chopin wasn't well enough to enjoy any of these luxuries. As a result he didn't mind leaving for Edinburgh a few days later to give the concert he had been planning there.

Naturally Miss Stirling and her sister insisted on coming along. At the railroad station in Edinburgh, however, Chopin managed to escape them when he was met and driven away by Dr. Lyszczyński. For the next several days he remained a guest in the doctor's home, a modest two-story house overlooking a stretch of open fields on the northern edge of the city.

While Chopin welcomed this respite from his "good Scots ladies," he didn't get along very well with his new hostess, Mrs. Lyszczyński. The doctor's wife was clearly disgruntled at having her household upset by her husband's friend, whom she found terribly self-centered and finicky. Even though she moved her children out of their room to accommodate him and ran upstairs with his breakfast every morning, nothing seemed to please him. He complained of everything, including the heat (in Scotland in October!), and spent most of the day fussing over his hair and his clothes.

There can be little doubt Chopin was a very aggravating guest. All his life he had been an extremely meticulous person. Now, constant pain, exhaustion, and shortness of breath made him even more exacting and often petulant. In his weakened state he was forced to rely on others for things he could no longer do on his own, and this only increased his irritability. If, for example, he tried to please Mrs. Lyszczyński by coming downstairs for his meals he knew her husband would have to carry him back to his room later. On the day before his concert he didn't even have the strength to drive over and try out the piano in the hall where he was to play.

The Hopetoun Rooms, which had been selected for the concert, were located at No. 70 Queen Street, just a few blocks north of Edinburgh's famous Princes Street. It was a small auditorium attached to the British Hotel,[19] once described as "by far the most splendid establishment of its kind in Edinburgh."[20] Besides concerts it was used for lectures, religious assemblies, and receptions of various types.

Because there had been little advance publicity for Chopin's concert few tickets were sold ahead of time. This alarmed Miss Stirling so much she bought up 100 of them at half a guinea apiece and distributed them to friends. In this way at least one-third of the hall's 300 seats would be filled. How much she differed from George Sand who, under similar circumstances, would have worried more about Chopin's health than the size of his audience! To Jane Stirling her teacher was a sort of god who somehow transcended the physical limitations of ordinary mortals. She simply couldn't comprehend the gravity of his illness. Where George would have protected him, she pushed him on.

That October Chopin was already so near collapse he hadn't been able to go out and look for other artists to share the program with him. This was to make his Edinburgh concert the only solo recital he ever gave in his life—ironically, at a time when he was least able to meet such a challenge. Surprisingly enough, the result was nothing short of miraculous. The ailing pianist completely captivated his listeners. As the *Scotsman* put it, "Any pianist who undertakes to play alone to an audience for two hours, must, now-a-days, be a very remarkable one to succeed in sustaining attention and satisfying expectation. M. Chopin succeeded perfectly in both."[21]

The works which occupied the two-hour program on October 4 were as follows:

1. Andante et Impromptu
2. Etudes[22]
3. Nocturnes et Berceuse[23]
4. Grande Valse Brillante[24]
5. Andante precédé d'un Largo
6. Preludes, Ballade, Mazurkas et Valses[25]

Among the city's newspapers the *Edinburgh Evening Courant* praised "the sparkling brilliancy" of Chopin's style,[26] and the *Caledonian Mercury* his "simplicity and power."[27] The *Scotsman* carried on grandiloquently about "feelings too deep for tears" that lay hidden in Chopin's music,[28] while the *Edinburgh Advertiser* spoke glowingly of his "refined" performance.[29] Even the *Musical World,* which had so often criticized him in the past, now expressed its appreciation of his "perfectly finished manner."[30]

Thanks in great part to the tickets Miss Stirling had circulated, a "select and highly fashionable audience" filled the Hopetoun Rooms and called Chopin back for five encores.[31] In every respect the concert seems to have been a triumph, but seldom had any performance taken such a toll on Chopin. Fatigue and indifference are apparent in the tone of his letter to Adolf Gutmann on October 16: "I played in Edinburgh," he wrote. "All the aristocracy of the region gathered to hear me. They say it went well—a few compliments and a little cash."[32]

From Edinburgh Miss Stirling hustled her teacher off to Calder House again, but her stifling attentions soon drove him back to the Lyszczyńskis'. After a few days there he felt strong enough to set out for a visit to Lady Belhaven at Wishaw and later the Duke of Hamilton at Hamilton Palace. The duke, who had been ambassador to the Russian court at the time of Catherine the Great, was a very old gentleman by 1848. Still, he liked to think of himself as a young soldier and tramped around his palace grounds in Hessian boots and the faded uniforms of brighter days. His energy amazed Chopin, as did the grandeur of his estate.

By now, though, Chopin had seen enough of Anglo-Saxon country life. As an artist he felt alien in this environment which placed such an emphasis on material comforts. It especially irked him to find that in most homes music wasn't even considered an art. The word "artist," as used by the English, referred only to painters, architects, or sculptors—never to musicians.

Actually he himself had to admit that the musical life of the rural aristocracy didn't really merit being called art. Some of the exhibitions of local talent he was forced to sit through were appalling. Take, for example, the lady who loved to strap on her accordion and squeeze out the most awful tunes from it, or the one who always played the piano standing up. Then there was the *grande dame* who sat hunched over her guitar and whistled as she strummed. "I suppose it's what one has to expect here," he concluded. "It seems to me they're all a bit crazy. Lord help them! What a bunch of crackpots!"[33]

It was a relief to get back to the Lyszczyńskis' at the end of the month, but by then the weather was so chilly Chopin caught cold and spent most of his time in bed. Each day he was there Miss Stirling wrote him. He ignored her letters but still they came. She wouldn't leave him alone. The fact that she kept chasing after him only served to fuel the constant rumors that they were going to be married.

In his polite way Chopin tried to make Miss Stirling understand that there were limits to their friendship. Some things, though, were just too delicate to discuss. For one thing, he felt no physical attraction to the tall, gangly spinster, and even if he had, his pride wouldn't have let him marry her. He had no intention of becoming a parasite on a bride he couldn't support. Besides, in his physical condition he was hardly fit to be a bridegroom. Miss Stirling might as well marry Death, he told a friend. "I'm nearer to a coffin than a wedding bed."[34]

When he left Edinburgh on October 31, Chopin could barely drag himself down to London. The moment he arrived he collapsed in an apartment at No. 4 St. James's Place. For nearly two weeks he secluded himself there, exhausted and miserable. His cough got worse, his head ached, and he could never seem to get enough air to breathe. Every day he flung open the windows of his apartment and then huddled in front of the fireplace to keep warm.

One of the reasons Chopin came back to London when he did was a promise he had made Lord Dudley Stuart to play at a charity ball for the relief of Polish refugees on November 16. This annual event, sponsored by the Literary Association of the Friends of Poland, was to take place in the Guildhall where it had been held for many years. The Literary Association, founded in 1832, was conceived by Prince Adam Czartoryski and Julian Niemcewicz as a means of aiding Polish immigrants who had fled their country during the 1830 uprising. Through public meetings, theatrical performances, private donations, and the annual ball it attempted to raise money for vocational training, medical care, and other forms of assistance needed by the stream of new exiles. When jobs couldn't be found for them, the society provided funds to send them on to New York where they were able to secure "profitable employment . . . the day after their arrival."[35]

In 1834 Lord Dudley Stuart, who was a member of Parliament, succeeded in getting the House of Commons to vote money for the refugees. By 1848, however, the government decided to cut this subsidy in half on the grounds that the Poles had been given time enough to establish themselves and earn their own living.

Parliament's action was the reflection of a wave of anti-Polish sentiment that pervaded the country then. With all the troubles on the Continent that year, the English were thankful for their insular calm and had no desire to get embroiled in the various conflicts across the channel. To many an Englishman it seemed that the Poles were deliberately fomenting strife throughout Europe in the hope that a disruption of the current balance of power might allow Poland to reemerge as an independent nation once more. This sort of attitude soon brought Lord Dudley the derisive title of "King of the Poles" for trying to help the exiles.[36]

In the London papers that fall, the Polish refugees were lambasted as "foreign parasites," "illustrious beggars," and "patriotic batteners on another people's fatness."[37] The forthcoming ball at the Guildhall was singled out for special attack. Why is it, one of the papers argued, that the "lazy Pole, who eschews employment," gets treated to "the substantial crumbs that fall from the well-decked tables of a civic ball," while an

Englishman gets packed off to the workhouse whenever he is down on his luck?[38]

Such outbursts threatened to discourage attendance at the ball. To counteract this, Mr. Carr, the secretary for the association, tried to lure subscribers by advertising the event as one of "unusual splendour," and stressing the fact that "the magnificent decorations and embellishments" from the Lord Mayor's recent inaugural banquet would be held over for the occasion.[39] He also added that "the most eminent vocalists" would perform, knowing that even mediocre singers were far greater attractions than a first-rate pianist like Chopin.

Over the next few days Lord Dudley received warnings that there would be violence at the ball, which prompted him to station "Forrester, the celebrated police officer and his assistants" inside the Guildhall and "a strong body of police" outside on the night of the gala.[40] Fortunately no hecklers showed up, and the evening turned out to be peaceful. However, it lacked the pomp and glitter of earlier years.

"The presence of a few noble lords, of the Lord Mayor and some civic authorities diversified the monotony of the plain misters and mistresses who formed the majority of those present," the *Times* related.[41] All in all the affair was "brilliant and animated without being particularly lively."[42]

The dancing itself took place in the main part of the Guildhall, which was one of the most historic landmarks in the city of London.[43] An "excellent band" directed by a Mr. Adams provided the music.

Chopin's presence at the concert which preceded the dancing didn't seem to lend any particular prestige to it. According to the *Times,* it was "much the same as on former anniversaries."[44] The program, organized by Chopin's former pupil Lindsay Sloper in conjunction with Jules Benedict, was primarily a vocal one. Altogether seventeen singers participated and, like Chopin, all donated their services free.

The concert was relegated, with the refreshments, to a side room (most likely the Common Council Chamber) where Chopin was given a sorry little upright piano on which he probably played several of the shorter compositions from his Glasgow and Edinburgh concerts. For many of the ball's subscribers (who paid a guinea per couple to attend) the concert was the highlight of the evening. "At its conclusion," the *Times* noted, "much of the company departed."[45]

Chopin himself left as soon as he had finished. He "played like an angel," Princess Marcelina Czartoryska claimed.[46] Others must have agreed, since the *Illustrated London News* reported that his "beautiful compositions" were greeted with much applause.[47] The rest of the evening was devoted to dancing, which kept up well into the morning. "At 1:00 o'clock it was at its height," the correspondent for the *Times* wrote.[28]

By then Chopin was back at St. James's Place where he spent a restless night with a bad headache.

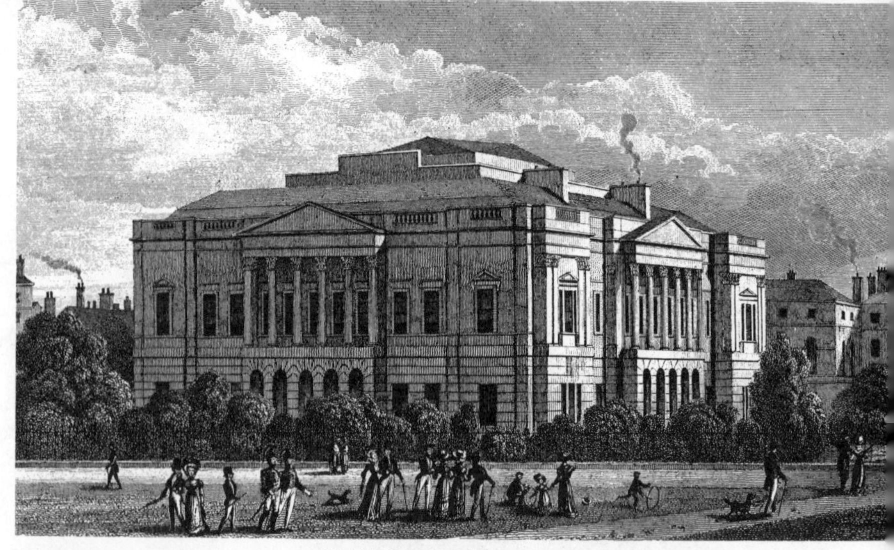

STAFFORD HOUSE, LONDON

ANTONIO TAMBURINI

ADELAIDE KEMBLE SARTORIS (IN THE ROLE OF NORMA)

GIOVANNI-BATISTA RUBINI

THE RESIDENCE OF MRS. ADELAIDE SARTORIS, LONDON

THE RESIDENCE OF LORD FALMOUTH, LONDON

THE GENTLEMEN'S CONCERT HALL,
MANCHESTER

THE COMMON COUNCIL CHAMBER,
GUILDHALL, LONDON

MARIETTA ALBONI

PAULINE
VIARDOT-GARCIA

GEORGE ALEXANDER
OSBORNE

THE GUILDHALL, LONDON

• CHAPTER FIFTEEN •

Paris
1848–1849

"ONE MORE DAY here will drive me mad if it doesn't kill me!" Chopin burst out five days after the Polish ball. "My Scots ladies bore me to tears! God preserve me from them. They've got such a hold on me I'll never get loose."[1] His agony was only compounded by the guilt he felt over his ingratitude toward the two women who sincerely had his best interests at heart.

By the end of the week it was obvious that Dr. Mallan could do nothing more for him. At this point Sir James Clark, Queen Victoria's personal physician, was called in, but there were two things not even the first physician of the realm had the power to change: the English climate and Chopin's state of mind. The best thing Clark could suggest for his patient was to get back to Paris as quickly as possible. Chopin couldn't have agreed more. He was sick to death of England.

During his last few days in London he refused to see anyone but his Polish friends. Princess Czartoryska came to visit him every day, as did Karol Szulczewski and Leonard Niedzwiedzki (two representatives of the so-called Polish government in exile). Together they tended to his various needs. Insofar as he could, Chopin avoided Miss Stirling and Mrs. Erskine. The latter had recently begun reading the Bible to him with the idea of converting him to the Calvinist faith. Paris, though, was far more important to him now than any priggish paradise she could offer him.

On November 23 a puffy-faced Chopin hobbled aboard the channel train for France. His legs were swollen and he had to be helped to his seat. En route he suffered a violent convulsion which frightened his valet and Niedzwiedzki, who were traveling with him. He soon recovered, though, and was able to go on.

Back in the Square d'Orléans his rooms had already been aired and dusted. As he entered he found a warm fire and a vase of fresh violets to welcome him home. For the first time in months he felt cheerful and optimistic. Here at last he would be able to "breathe better, understand what people say, and see some friendly faces."[2]

Unfortunately, the psychological boost of his return to Paris wasn't followed by any physical improvement. Impatiently he switched from doctor to doctor, but the French physicians could do no more for him than the English, and he grew steadily worse.

From his window he watched his neighbors coming and going across the wintry courtyard. George Sand's face, of course, no longer appeared among them. It was nearly a year now since he had last seen her. While the pain of their separation still tortured him, he was too proud to let anyone know. At times he wanted to curse his former mistress, but his anger was never strong enough to destroy the aching need he still felt for her.

Without George his days were lonely even though he had many callers, including Delacroix, the Czartoryskis, Baroness Rothschild, and a host of attentive pupils. Their company meant more to him than ever now that he had little else to occupy his time. Teaching and composing required an effort well beyond his strength. Even playing the piano exhausted him.

As the months passed his income withered away to almost nothing. Friends, like Miss Stirling and her sister, took care of his expenses as inconspicuously as possible. In the spring of 1849 his doctors recommended that he move out to Chaillot, a relatively rural area then with plenty of fresh air. This was accomplished through the charity of another friend, Princess Obreskoff, who paid half the rent without letting him know it. That summer the Czartoryskis sent a servant to look after him while they arranged with the Russian authorities for his sister Ludwika and her family to obtain passports for Paris.

Their arrival on August 9 buoyed Chopin up immensely, but his health continued to decline. By now he was almost completely bedridden. Rarely did he bother to get up and dress anymore.

In September Ludwika's husband returned to Warsaw, irate that his wife refused to leave her dying brother. Around the middle of the month she moved Chopin back to Paris. Again through the generosity of friends, a comfortable apartment was found for him on the east side of the Place Vendôme. There on October 17, 1849, in the dark hours of the early morning, the sylph slipped quietly offstage.

• APPENDIX A •

Chopin's Concerts

WARSAW AND BAD REINERZ 1810–1828

Warsaw, Radziwiłł Palace, February 24, 1818
Warsaw, Charitable Society, February 24, 1823
Warsaw, Protestant Church, mid-May 1825
Warsaw, Conservatory, May 27, 1825
Warsaw, Conservatory, June 10, 1825
Bad Reinerz (Duszniki), Kursaal, August 11, 1826
Bad Reinerz (Duszniki), Kursaal, August 16, 1826

VIENNA 1829

Kärnthnerthor Theater, August 11, 1829
Kärnthnerthor Theater, August 18, 1829

WARSAW 1829–1830

Resursa, December 19, 1829
National Theater, March 17, 1830
National Theater, March 22, 1830
National Theater, July 8, 1830
National Theater, October 11, 1830

BRESLAU, VIENNA, AND MUNICH 1830–1831

Breslau (Wrocław), Resursa, November 8, 1830
Vienna, Redoutensaal, April 4, 1831

APPENDIX A

Vienna, Kärnthnerthor Theater, June 11, 1831
Munich, Philharmonic Society's Hall, August 28, 1831

PARIS 1831–1832

Salle Pleyel (rue Cadet), February 26, 1832
Conservatory, May 20, 1832

PARIS 1833

Salle du Wauxhall, March 23, 1833
Residence of M. Marcelin Lafont, March 30, 1833
Théâtre-Italien (Salle Favart), April 2, 1833
Salle du Wauxhall, April 3, 1833
The Conservatory, December 15, 1833

PARIS 1834–1835

Conservatory, December 7, 1834
M. Franz Stoepel's Music School, December 25, 1834
Salle Érard, February 22, 1835
Salle Pleyel (rue Cadet), March 15, 1835
Salle Favart (Théâtre-Italien), April 4, 1835
The Conservatory, April 26, 1835

PARIS 1836

Residence of Professor D. Levi, February 7, 1836
Salons of the Grand Référendaire of the Court of Peers in the Petit Luxembourg Palace, April 21, 1836

PARIS AND ROUEN 1837–1838

Paris, Salle Érard, April 9, 1837
Paris, Tuileries, February 16, 1838

CHOPIN'S CONCERTS

Paris, Salons de M. Pape, March 3, 1838
Rouen, Hôtel de Ville, March 11, 1838

PARIS 1839–1842

Saint-Cloud, The Royal Palace, October 29, 1839
Salle Pleyel (rue Rochechouart), April 26, 1841
Tuileries, December 1, 1841
Salle Pleyel (rue Rochechouart), February, 21, 1842

PARIS 1843–1848

Residence of Baron James de Rothschild,
January 11, 1843
Salle Pleyel (rue Rochechouart), February 16, 1848

LONDON AND MANCHESTER 1848

London, Stafford House, May 15, 1848
London, The residence of Mrs. Adelaide Sartoris, June 23, 1848
London, The residence of Lord Falmouth, July 7, 1848
Manchester, The Gentlemen's Concert Hall, August 28, 1848

GLASGOW, EDINBURGH AND LONDON 1848

Glasgow, The Merchants' Hall, September 27, 1848
Edinburgh, The Hopetoun Rooms, October 4, 1848
London, The Guildhall, November 16, 1848

• APPENDIX B •

Reviews of Chopin's Concerts

Kuryer dla Płci Pięknej, Warsaw, February 26, 1823[1]

On the 24th of this month the sixth musical evening sponsored by the Administrative Committee of Evening Musicales took place. It is generally conceded that this event was more outstanding than most, not only because the lovely selection of works performed delighted the audience but also because it introduced them to a talent which aroused everyone's admiration, a talent which is especially worthy of our attention because of its perfection, as well as its high degree of development at such an early age. The splendid overture by Paër which opened the evening was followed by Ries' Concerto for pianoforte. In this particular concerto the young performer allowed us to hear the excellence of his talent which we have already mentioned. We can confidently say that we have not heard a virtuoso to date in our capital who could overcome such astonishing difficulties with so much ease and accuracy, who could render the unequaled beauty of the Adagio with such feeling and fine precision, in brief, with such an exquisite talent, brought to an unrivaled perfection at such a tender age. This charming work of Ries was indeed creditably done. The latest issue of the *Leipzig Musical Gazette* called our attention to an article from Vienna which stated that a young artist named List [*sic*] also astonishes everyone there with his excellent, precise, and forceful performance of such works as Hummel's Concerto.—After the sixth evening musicale we will certainly not be envious of Vienna's M. List, for our capital possesses his equal if not his superior in the person of (we see no reason to make a secret of the name of this young man who has attracted such general praise) young M. Chopin.—M. Chopin is not yet 15 [*sic*]. After the concerto an overture by Mozart followed. Next, to everyone's satisfaction, came a septet in which we heard the performer of Cremont's concerto for the second time. The evening closed with an excerpt from the *Four Seasons* by Haydn.

Kurjer Warszawski, Warsaw, May 28, 1825

Yesterday's concert at the Conservatory was interesting from many points of view. In giving well-earned tribute to the esteemed talents of the performers of both sexes, we especially want to mention the following details. The newly composed overture by Józef Nowakowski, a student of composition at the Conservatory, opened the program. His addition to the ranks of composers augurs well for music. The young student who performed Rode's Violin Concerto received copious applause. Another young amateur [Chopin] again attracted the attention of the connoisseurs when he once more performed a Fantasia on the Warsaw-invented instrument called the aeolopantaleon with taste and feeling. The cantata composed by Józef Elsner to the poem "God Save the King, Our Nation's Father" created a most enjoyable impression on the audience. To the voices of the choir and the entire orchestra was added the organ and also the newly acquired majesty of the Warsaw-created instrument the choraleon [probably played by Chopin], which produced an extraordinary effect. The number of amateurs who sang and performed in the orchestra under the direction of M. Jawurek numbered 140 and the audience consisted of 200.

Kurjer Warszawski, Warsaw, June 11, 1825

An audience of 170 spent a delightful evening at yesterday's concert in the Conservatory since all the musical works performed were excellent. Particularly deserving of the applause they received were the Variations for flute performed by the visiting artist M. Kresner, the Adagio for bass viol performed by one of our local artists, the Fantasy performed by the young Chopin on the aeolopantaleon, invented by Długosz, and the second aria sung by Mme. Bianchi, who was heard in Warsaw for the first time.

Allgemeine Musikalische Zeitung, Leipzig, November 16, 1825, no. 46

I will pass over the concerts of the foreign artists heard here some time ago . . . and will mention only one concert which the musical director, Jawurek, organized. The proceeds of this concert, given in the grand salon of the Conservatory of Music, were donated to a charitable cause. At the request of the public, Herr Jawurek scheduled a second concert in which two of the works from the first performance were repeated by popular demand, namely a chorus by Beethoven to which Herr Jawurek added a choraleon accompaniment and a cantata by Professor Elsner based on the song "God Save the King." The first concert began with an overture in the style of Rossini by Nowakowski (a composition student), while the second opened with the overture to *The Magic Flute*. In both concerts Mlle. Sredulanka distinguished herself as an excellent pianist by her execution of the B and A major Rondos of Hummel. Herr Suzurowski and Mlle. Weinnert sang a duet from *Achilles* by Paér and Mme. Wernicke, an aria by Rossini with piano accompaniment. In addition Mme. Bianchi and the flutist Herr Kresner, sojourning in Warsaw, were also heard. The beautiful tonal production and artistry of the latter elicited everyone's applause. Mme. Bianchi proved to be an excellent singer although her voice was somewhat lacking in youthful freshness. Herr von Molsdorf played a Rondo à la Polacca for cello by B. Romberg and Herr Frankowski, the first Allegro of a Violin Concerto by Rode. The student Chopin was heard playing the first Allegro from the F minor Piano Concerto by Moscheles and a free fantasy on the aeolopantaleon. . . . Under the hands of the talented young Chopin, who proved himself a complete master of the instrument, an enormous impression was made through the wealth of musical ideas in his free fantasy. Other gifted amateurs also appeared with the artists. . . .

Kurjer Warszawski, Warsaw, August 22, 1826

A letter recently received from Kudowa Spa in Silesia (about two miles from Reinerz) informs us that the young Polish artist Fryderyk Chopin is spending some time in Reinerz on the orders of his doctors for the benefit of his health. There, when some children became orphaned by the death of their father who had come for the healing waters, M. Chopin, urged by persons acquainted with his talent, gave two fund-raising concerts for which he was highly commended and from which the unfortunate ones received a substantial sum of money. (This young man has been heard at the piano many times in Warsaw and invariably receives the most well-deserved admiration for his magnificent talent.)

Allgemeine Theaterzeitung, Vienna, August 20, 1829

A short while ago a young pianist named Herr Chopin was heard in the Imperial and Royal Court Theater at the Kärnthner gate. Since he has scarcely been mentioned in the musical world until now it is all the more surprising to discover in him not only a fine but truly an outstanding talent. From the style of his playing as well as the characteristics of his compositions one may already detect a spark of genius, at least in regard to his unique forms and striking individuality.

In both his playing and his compositions—of which, to be sure, only the Variations were heard in this performance—the young man displays an extremely modest character. He seems reluctant to show off. Although he could easily execute technical difficulties which, even here in the homeland of piano virtuosity, must command attention, he elected, with almost ironical naïveté, to entertain a large audience with music simply as music. Well, lo and behold, he succeeded! His receptive listeners rewarded him with a deluge of applause.

His touch, though clean and firm, had little of the brilliance which our virtuosos like to exhibit the minute they sit down at the keyboard. Because he lacked that rhetorical *à plomb* which our pianists consider so essential to success, he appeared rather like someone overwhelmed in a crowd of clever people who doesn't get the attention he deserves. He played in the calmest manner without those flourishes which generally distinguish the artist from the dilettante immediately. Nevertheless, our highly refined and sensitive public quickly recognized in the young, unknown foreigner a true musician. He displayed the noblest and most delightful artistic accomplishments without the least trace of pomposity and gave the unbiased observer the pleasure of hearing (as any honest person would have to admit) a genuine connoisseur and a perceptive virtuoso of definite merit.

This young man, however, did exhibit some flaws in his playing—and significant ones at that—among which perhaps the most conspicuous was his failure to place any accent at the beginning of a musical phrase. And yet despite this, we predict that one day, when people have the chance to hear more of him, he will prove to be an artist worthy of the highest praise. He comes from Warsaw and this is his first excursion out of his native city. He did not come here with the intention of giving a concert and is highly surprised and encouraged by the stir his abilities have aroused. In his performance he stood out like a tall, magnificent young tree, full of fragrant blossoms and succulent fruit. His compositions were equally outstanding. Their original phrases, passages, and musical forms were especially evident in the introduction, in the first, second, and fourth variations, and in his treatment of the Mozart theme in the final Polacca. Being somewhat ingenuous, the young virtuoso decided to improvise for our public at the close of his concert even though few outside of Beethoven and Hummel have ever met with a favorable reception in such attempts. However, he demonstrated his excellent grasp of this rare gift and succeeded in thrilling the crowd with his ingenious variations, his fluent development and assured handling of the themes, not to mention his faultless execution throughout.

Herr Chopin brought so much pleasure to his audience today we sincerely hope he will be heard by a larger one the next time. At this performance Mlle. Veltheim, a singer from the royal Saxon court, also proved herself to be a talented artist, singing an aria by Vaccaj and another by Rossini with her charming, supple, and cultivated voice and brilliant style.

Wiener Zeitschrift für Kunst, Literatur, Theater, und Mode, Vienna, August 22, 1829

On the 11th of August Fräulein Veltheim appeared again in an Academy [concert] with an aria by Rossini and a Rondo with variations by Vaccaj for which she was highly applauded, especially in the latter, because of her vocal skill. A Herr Chopin appeared as a pianist and performed first a Rondo and then Variations of his own composition.[2]

He executes the greatest difficulties with accuracy and precision, and all his passages are pervaded by clarity. The audience repaid this adroit artist with loud applause. The concert piece with orchestral accompaniment [the Variations] was especially moving. The second number [Chopin's improvisations or "free fantasy"] was riddled with complexities in which he demonstrated his dexterity to the fullest. He was showered with applause and called back onstage. Beethoven's beautiful overture to *Prometheus* opened the program.

Der Sammler, Vienna, August 29, 1829

In Herr Friedrich Chopin we have a pianist of the highest order. His delicate touch, his effortless execution, his masterly tempi and nuances, exhibit the most profound feeling, while the clarity of his performance and the genius of his compositions are the marks of a naturally endowed virtuoso. He has appeared as one of the brightest meteors on the musical horizon through his genius alone, unaided by any outside influence except for his early lessons with the worthy professor and kapellmeister Würfel, who was living then in Russia [i.e., Russian-controlled Poland]. At the next opportunity we will discuss all this further in greater detail.

Gazeta Warszawska, Warsaw, August 30, 1829[3]

The Warsaw youth M. Chopin displayed his talent in Vienna on the 10th [*sic*] of this month in the theater next to the Kärnthner gate. He performed his own works on the piano, playing a Rondo as well as Variations on a theme by Mozart, and was received with universal acclaim. After each solo he was overwhelmed with applause and acknowledged to be a second Hummel. The following day distinguished personages called at his rooms and insisted that he give another concert.

Allgemeine Musikalische Zeitung, Leipzig, November 18, 1829

. . . Herr Chopin, a pianist from Warsaw who is reputed to be a pupil of Würfel, established himself as a master of the highest order [on

August 11]. The remarkable delicacy of his touch, his indescribable mechanical agility, his consummate tonal shading, so rich in feeling, his seldom-matched clarity, and his highly original compositions—brilliant variations, Rondo, and free fantasy—reveal a most exceptional virtuoso, liberally endowed by nature, who appears unheralded, like one of the brightest meteors on the musical horizon.

Wiener Zeitschrift für Kunst, Literatur, Theater, und Mode, Vienna, August 29, 1829

Tuesday the 18th of August Herr Friedrich Chopin performed again in this theater [Kärnthnerthor] and presented a new Rondo of his own composition for piano with orchestral accompaniment. This work is characterized throughout by a chromatic style and is difficult to appreciate. However, it has moments which are distinguished by depth and skillful development. Its main defect seems to be a lack of variety. The master displayed his ability as a pianist of the highest order and successfully surmounted the most enormous difficulties. A longer stay in Vienna would give him the opportunity to improve his touch as well as his adeptness in playing with an orchestra. He was warmly applauded and brought back for an encore.

After him, the very young and talented violinist Herr Joseph Khayll, a pupil of Herr Jansa, performed a Polonaise for violin by Mayseder which received tremendous applause. At such a tender age he has already acquired a most impressive dexterity and distinguishes himself by the clarity of his double stops and especially his staccato. He deserves to be encouraged and will soon rise to greater heights of virtuosity through his talent. He was likewise heartily applauded and called back onstage.

At the close Herr Chopin today played the Variations on a theme by Mozart which he had already rendered so superbly and successfully in his first concert. The rich and pleasing variety of this piece as well as the splendid performance again earned the artist a loud round of applause. Both the experts and the amateurs enthusiastically expressed their appreciation of his artistic skill. This young man, who is reported to owe his early training to Herr Würfel, displays a serious attempt to weave the orchestra and piano parts of his compositions together in an interesting style.

The orchestra distinguished itself at the outset with its brilliant and vigorous rendition of Lindpaintner's overture to *Der Bergkönig,* for which it was warmly applauded.

Allgemeine Theaterzeitung, Vienna, September 1, 1829

In his second concert the pianist Herr Chopin from Warsaw performed in such a way as to justify this paper's earlier review of his first concert. He is a young man who pursues his own path and does so in a charming manner. His style and method, both in playing and in composing, however, deviate from the usually accepted pattern of other virtuosos. Where he differs is mainly in this: the desire to produce good music is obviously more important to him than the mere urge to please his audience. Despite this Herr Chopin succeeded in pleasing everyone today.

In this second concert by Herr Chopin the young violinist Khayl [*sic*], a pupil of Herr Jansa, also appeared, playing a Polonaise by Mayseder. He gave delightful evidence of his outstanding talent and his progress, which the public acknowledged with a rousing response.

Gazeta Polska, Warsaw, September 16, 1829[4]

M. Chopin, our fellow countryman, gave a second concert in the court theater at Vienna. He was received warmly and the theatrical gazette [*Allgemeine Theaterzeitung*] states that M. Chopin is more concerned with pleasing his audience than in making good music.[5] And he did indeed prove most pleasing.

Kurjer Warszawski, Warsaw, December 21, 1829

The young virtuoso M. Chopin, whose talent was admired more than ever the day before yesterday by a large audience of amateurs and connoisseurs at the old Resursa, improvised on some piano variations on the favorite song "Miotły." [Miotełki] That evening Józef Bielawski, first violinist of the National Theater, played a Beethoven quintet [*sic*], M. Dorwil [*sic*] sang the well-known aria "Santinel," and M. Kopello [*sic*] sang the great aria by Paër from the opera *Achilles*. This musical evening was acknowledged to be a highly enjoyable one.

Kurjer Polski, Warsaw, December 20, 1829

The members of the Merchants' Guild [Resursa], called the Old, held a very pleasant musical evening yesterday in their hall. M. Bielawski began the evening with a concerto to an orchestral accompaniment. Then M. Capello sang with M. Chopin at the piano. M. Soliva served as accompanist to M. Dorville, a French theatrical artist, after which M. Bielawski entertained the audience with a solo. To conclude the evening M. Chopin improvised on various well-known melodies (among them, some from Raimund's *Millionaire Peasant*).

Kurjer Warszawski, Warsaw, December 23, 1829

Last Saturday evening one of the most enjoyable events took place in our capital. This was to a great extent due to the talent of M. Chopin. Our compatriot, who has been praised enthusiastically abroad, has not thus far allowed himself to be heard in *his own native land*. Modesty, although a most beautiful trait in the talented, is not as praiseworthy when it results in this sort of behavior. Isn't M. Chopin's talent the property of his homeland? Isn't Poland capable of appreciating him in a proper manner? The compositions of M. Chopin bear without doubt the imprint of genius. Among his new works is the Concerto in F minor, worthy of being included in the ranks of compositions by Europe's foremost musicians. We hope, therefore, that M. Chopin, as we have so often implored him, will no longer be inclined, to the detriment of his own glory and that of our nation, to deny us the happy conviction that Poland is capable of producing great talent.

Powszechny Dziennik Krajowy, Warsaw, March 4, 1830[6]

One of our musical connoisseurs has drawn my attention to a young talent whose works have been unknown up to now. M. Chopin has so far been recognized only for his excellent piano virtuosity. On Wednesday we had an opportunity to become acquainted with another facet of this man. At his home he had a preview with full orchestra of his excellent compositions, and he himself played his own concerto. Among the listeners of both sexes were connoisseurs, amateurs, and artists including Kurpiński and Elsner. I am not a lover of piano concertos, having always felt that this instrument was introduced into the concert hall by some classicist who liked to exploit its mechanical features to produce the tonal shading and emotional effects that he could not achieve by his own artistry. Then lo and behold! I forgot all my prejudices in discovering the creative genius of this young composer. By stages, he first aroused our curiosity, then he began to astonish us, and finally he ended by moving us profoundly. The originality of his musical ideas is on a par with Beethoven's and he renders them as artfully and pleasingly as Hummel. The Adagio, usually a tiresome part of any piano concerto, delighted everyone, especially in the passage where the whole orchestra played a *tremolando* while the soloist executed a recitative of rich tonal diversity. It reminded me of a similar effect produced by Lipiński although M. Chopin is by no means guilty of having copied him. He also played a fantasia on a theme from Kurpiński's [song] "Laura and Philo." This piece did not pose the technical difficulties of the concerto, but by his unusual development of the accompaniment, he was able to convey the meaning of the entire song without any words. All the audience was highly impressed by these works, and those who knew him most intimately were deeply touched. His old music teacher sat there moved to tears. Elsner radiated joy as he milled about, hearing nothing but praise for the pupil to whom he had taught composition. Even Kurpiński finally let himself be persuaded to direct the orchestra for the young artist. In M. Chopin we have a real talent, a truly outstanding one, and he should allow himself to be heard in public. Of course, in doing so, he must be prepared to cope with the criticism of the envious, an ordeal which mediocre talents never have to face.

Kurjer Warszawski, Warsaw, March 5, 1830

The day before yesterday at the home of M. Szopę [Chopin] there was again a large gathering of artists and music lovers. The young virtuoso played his concerto and a potpourri on various themes, notably that of our Polish song "Już miesiąc zeszedł" [The Moon Has Set] and Kurpiński's *Krakowiak,* etc. We repeat here the opinions expressed by those most qualified to judge: "Young Szopę surpasses all pianists we have heard in this city. He is the Paganini of the piano and his compositions are full of merit and originality."

Pamiętnik dla Płci Pięknej, Warsaw (1830), year 1, 2:46

After prolonged anticipation, M. Chopin was heard in a piano concert in the National Theater. A large audience hailed the young artist with much applause. In the two previous renderings of his concerto [the private rehearsals given at home] he justified the favorable opinions already circulated about him by the foremost musicians and connoisseurs. Both a genius for composition and a truly masterful technique are apparent in his playing. Harmony is the soul of M. Chopin's performances, and it seems that he concentrates on this above all else. To this end he directs all his sensitivity; to this end he forges ahead down his own path, shunning blind imitation; and to this end he even cloaks the tenderness and delicacy of his playing in shades of a plaintive melancholy. His compositions which contain themes from various national songs especially enchanted his listeners, since M. Chopin is able to blend the lovely simplicity of these folk songs with his exquisite playing and ingenious composition so that every note fills the ear with pleasure, stirs the heart, and speaks directly to the soul.

Kurjer Warszawski, Warsaw, March 18, 1830

Yesterday in the National Theater music lovers spent a highly enjoyable evening. There were 880 people present which shows how our public typically turns out to pay its respects to true talent. The young virtuoso delighted all those present and was acknowledged by them to belong in the ranks of the most distinguished maestros. His performance of his concerto and potpourri was showered with well-deserved applause. The Adagio of this concerto drew the attention of the connoisseurs for its excellence not only in the way it was performed but also in the way it was conceived. The Rondo that followed enchanted everyone. The mazurka in this Rondo, with its extremely charming variations, is sure to give pleasure wherever M. Chopin chooses to play it. Also contributing to the enjoyment of this evening were Mme. Meier's vocal variations from *La Bjondyna* as well as the horn playing of M. Gerner and the flawless performance of the overtures from the national operas *Leszek Biały* and *Cecylja Piaseczyńska*. M. Żywny was the piano teacher of this virtuoso who learned the art of musical composition in the local Conservatory from its rector, Elsner. These worthy teachers were delighted with the success of their pupil. Since many people were not able to get boxes or seats for yesterday's concert, a second will be given next Monday.

Gazeta Warszawska, Warsaw, March 18, 1830[7]

M. Chopin was heard three times last night in works of his own composition which are as well conceived as they were executed. All the qualities which characterize a piano virtuoso are combined to the highest degree in M. Chopin: strength, technique, and above all feeling are his principal traits. Each stroke of the keys by him is an expression of the heart. The people of Warsaw know well how to appreciate the rare talent of their compatriot who was recently praised and honored abroad. Showers of applause greeted his arrival and departure. . . . At the end of the performance M. Chopin was called back on stage by universal acclaim. Everyone hopes that before his departure to foreign parts he will be heard once more, and we are confident he will respond to this respectful summons.

Powszechny Dziennik Krajowy, Warsaw, March 19, 1830[8]

The evening before last provided true consolation for lovers of genuine art. Our fellow countryman M. Chopin showed in the composition of his concerto that he has the courage to scorn that weak-willed habit, all too common among us, of blindly imitating certain masters who, for the sake of fashion or through the help of people of so-called good taste and *good style,* have impertinently ascended the throne of European music. On the contrary, M. Chopin owes his brilliance to the sublime Bach, Handel, Gluck, Mozart, Haydn, Cherubini, and Beethoven with whom he is comparable. While he is worthy of these illustrious predecessors, this stalwart youth nevertheless pursues his own path to the temple of Euterpe where the wreath of immortality is bestowed only on those who dare approach the muse by their own route and not in the footsteps of others.

Harmony is at the very heart of M. Chopin's concerto. It permeates each solo from beginning to end. The melodies, already so lovely and pleasing in themselves, become even more beautiful to the listener by being grounded on this well-proportioned harmonic foundation. The typical excesses peculiar to new composers are nowhere to be seen. Each *tutti* is perfectly structured to blend imperceptibly with the solo passages in such a way that the delighted listener can scarcely distinguish the one from the other. . . . The performance was entirely in keeping with the spirit of the composition. Never did the pianist try to exploit the technical difficulties, the bravura passages, or the tender, lyrical melodies in order to shine at the expense of the overall musical effect. Modestly he allowed himself to conform to the greater or lesser glory of the total harmony as one should. His playing seemed to say to the listener: "This is not me; this is music!" . . . M. Chopin's style, both in composition and in execution, is soft and delicate. Even the gayest of his themes assumes an almost melancholy color which he imparts to his listeners through the force of his talent. It would be unnecessary to advise M. Chopin not to deviate from his path. Whoever writes as he does can never find a better guide than his own feelings.

It is also pleasing to the Polish people when reflecting on such a magnificent talent, nay even genius, to remember that in the greater part of his compositions as well as in his performance the spirit of the nation was evident. His playing quite naturally produced great delight, even surprise in certain listeners who discovered that it is possible to derive pleasure from music that is not full of repetitious and monotonous melodies, nerve-shattering orchestral blasts, or shrieking finales which are so prevalent in today's works.

The esteemed Elsner, who has already given so many proofs of his industry, knowledge of art, and skill in training fine composers, was rewarded that evening by being able to say to himself, "*Behold! He too is my pupil.*"

Gazeta Korespondenta Warszawskiego i Zagranicznego, Warsaw, March 19, 1830

On the 17th of this month the young Chopin who had long been heralded by almost all the nation's newspapers appeared in a concert of his own compositions. . . . This young virtuoso who studied music with one of our local professors and composition at our Conservatory certainly justified the renown and praise he received in advance. The large audience showered him with tremendous applause at the end of the first part of the concert. And after the second part, that is, after the Adagio and Rondo, it exhibited unbounded enthusiasm and called him back three times. The prolonged bravos clearly showed how pleased everyone was. Such a brilliant reception not only does honor to those assembled for encouraging national talent, it is at the same time a definite guarantee of the excellence of this young virtuoso since our public is both able and entitled to appreciate and judge the best talents, as proved by its daring opinions of [Maria] Szymanowska, Hummel, and Paganini, opinions which time has substantiated. The talent of young Chopin deserves twofold consideration, for he is both a performer and a composer. As a performer he even surpasses Hummel in both the delicacy of his feeling and the exquisiteness of his taste. If he does not quite equal Hummel in technique and the smoothness of his tempi, he at least is unrivaled by anyone else. As a composer his Adagio and Rondo are worthy of Hummel himself. . . . We deserve to congratulate ourselves that Poland will someday be justly proud of having produced one of the greatest performers and composers in Europe.

Kurjer Polski, Warsaw, March 20, 1830

After a long wait M. Chopin allowed himself to be heard in a public piano concert the day before yesterday. The large audience greeted the young artist with loud applause. Almost since his infancy he has been heralded as a talent that rarely appears on our horizon. Such reports have in no way exaggerated his gifts nor have they disappointed the expectations that many had formed of his playing. Without imitating other youths who have given public concerts, he has managed to overshadow them all through his dedicated pursuit of the secrets of harmony and technique. Prior to appearing in public he waited until he had achieved a maturity of feeling and imagination as well as a full development of his art in order to place himself immediately in the ranks of the foremost virtuosos and composers of his instrument. Vienna, one of the leading capitals of the fine arts and long the abode of famous musical artists, heard Chopin twice and was enthralled. The Viennese papers expressed their appreciation of his laudable talent and rendered numerous compliments to his playing and his compositions. In order not to be suspected of prejudice or chauvinism in placing Chopin among the inner circle of first-rate virtuosos, we will leave it to others who are impartial to suggest anyone more deserving. At his concert the day before yesterday Chopin played works of his own composition. It is difficult to say whether he is better as a composer or a performer. His compositions are particularly characterized by the way he incorporates the lovely originality of his melodies and his bold, brilliant passages (so well suited to the piano with their vibrant coloring and scintillating embellishments) into a unified whole. The listener is struck by the combination of his beautiful gift for composition with his playing, which displays such a depth of feeling and a dexterity that can overcome the greatest difficulties as if they didn't exist at all. Everyone was especially delighted by the performance of the Rondo from the concerto and the Fantasy on national songs. The beautiful themes of the latter brought happy memories of tales from out of the distant past to many. Genuine talent can flourish anywhere. Even though Warsaw is not considered a city where the fine arts attract the greatest attention, Chopin was nevertheless able to receive his musical education from local tutors and masters to whom he owes his early development and progress. Far from those countries famed for their cultivation of the fine arts, Chopin has instinctively understood how to seize upon and utilize that which enriches music and enhances the artist. Because of this he is able to pursue his own path and establish his own style of playing and composition. The land which has given him life by its songs has influenced the character of his music. This is evident in the works of this artist where the sound of many of his melodies seems to be a joyful echo of our native harmony. The simple mazurka becomes transformed at his touch while it still preserves its own peculiar flavor and accent. To capture the charming simplicity of such native refrains as

Chopin does with his exquisite playing and brilliant composition, one has to have a certain sensitivity to the music of our fields and woodlands and the songs of the Polish peasant. Soon he will be leaving his homeland in the prime of his youth. The longing awakened at this moment of separation will greatly influence his musical inspiration and add a new color to his playing and composition. Perhaps, however, before he leaves this place where he has enjoyed his youth he will reveal to us the secret emotions and dreams his heart has experienced here among us. The brilliant reception he received from our public permits us to hope that he will not leave Warsaw without another farewell.

Dekameron Polski, Warsaw, March 31, 1830

On the 17th M. Chopin gave a vocal and instrumental concert attended by a large audience. Mme. Meier delighted those present with her singing as did Gerner with his performance on the French horn. M. Chopin, in our opinion, is truly outstanding. Everyone was full of the highest praise for the extraordinary talent of this young virtuoso. Some even foresaw in him a new Mozart. Indeed, whoever is acquainted with such an inanimate instrument as the piano and then hears M. Chopin can't help but wonder at the intrinsic feeling and originality that inject so much life into his playing. M. Chopin is, in every sense, a product of Poland, having studied music with M. Żywny and composition with our worthy Elsner.

Kurjer Polski, Warsaw, March 24, 1830

M. Chopin's second concert was, in every respect, even more delightful than his first. The compositions which he repeated were better conceived and all the more appreciated than before. The new Rondo, with its melodies reminiscent of the songs of the Carpathian mountaineers, made a very great impression. His formidable talent as a performer was apparent this time since the instrument selected was appropriate to the hall. It was a pity therefore that M. Chopin didn't repeat the Potpourri [Grand Fantasy] with its Polish songs and rhythms which aroused such enthusiasm at the previous concert. . . . The improvisation did not and could not produce the same effect since it was a genuine and not a feigned improvisation. As such, how could it compare with compositions so wonderfully inspired, so skillfully polished and enriched by such captivating harmonies? Let Chopin leave this sort of thing to lesser talents, to those creatures whose blood no longer throbs with life but who function like robots devoid of any feeling. To the listener all his compositions sound like improvisations because he doesn't try to imitate others but always brings forth something new, fresh—in a word, inspired. In the last analysis one can improvise freely only in solitude or in the presence of a single friend or loved one.

MAURYCY MOCHNACKI

Gazeta Warszawska, Warsaw, March 23, 1830[9]

Chopin's second concert was splendid just like the first. . . . In keeping with the wishes of many connoisseurs M. Chopin played this time on a Viennese piano like Hummel ordinarily used in his concerts. It should be noted that the tone of his piano, although less forceful than that of an English instrument, was, however, more expressive. . . . The Adagio and Rondo from the Concerto in F minor composed by Chopin himself, which delighted absolutely everyone at his first concert, including even those who had heard it before, made an incomparably greater impression this time. M. Chopin closed this concert with improvisations which overwhelmingly convinced the audience of his creative and technical skill.

Kurjer Warszawski, Warsaw, March 23, 1830

At M. Chopin's second concert yesterday there was a crowd of nearly 900 people. They greeted the virtuoso with extraordinary applause which was repeated time and again, especially after the Rondo à la Krakowiak. At the end, the artist improvised on those favorite national songs "The Cruel World" and "Strange Customs in the Town," producing the most delightful variations with the touch of a master. Those present unanimously called the virtuoso back, and someone was heard to cry, "Have pity on us and give just one more concert before you leave." Also contributing to the pleasure of last night's concert were

Mme. Meier's excellent performance of one of Soliva's magnificent arias and M. Bielawski's superb rendition of Bériot's Variations. The program opened with the debut of a symphony of M. Józef Nowakowski, who studied musical composition at the local Conservatory. M. Chopin will be leaving shortly to travel abroad. He will go to Berlin first and then on to Paris and London. The sincere wishes of the Polish people on whose soil he was born, raised, and received his musical training will accompany him wherever he goes.

Powszechny Dziennik Krajowy, Warsaw, March 25, 1830[10]

Fate has blessed the Poles with M. Chopin just as she gave the Germans Mozart. M. Chopin is our special property. Therefore it behooves us to be the first to know his works. Whoever has heard M. Chopin's concerto only in the theater has heard but a part of it since our theater, having the worst sort of construction for concerts and operas and especially such types of compositions [as Chopin's], is not at all suited for the presentation of these works. The audience in the orchestra seats heard only the pianist and not the rich lyrical accompaniment of the orchestra (so important in a piano concerto), as it was stifled in the wings. In the boxes, however, the whole of the orchestral part was audible, though not clearly, while the piano could only be heard intermittently.

In order to appreciate Chopin's unique piano style and his composition as a whole it is necessary to hear M. Chopin's concerto several times in the hall to form the best impression of it. We hope therefore that M. Chopin, for the purpose of making his compositions better known to his fellow countrymen, will deign to give several concerts in the Sala Reduta [a smaller auditorium than the National Theater], for why should the Poles be the last to know the superb works of their own compatriot?

Kurjer Polski, Warsaw, March 26, 1830

Allow me to add a few more words about Chopin's second concert. The repeat performance of the first concert by M. Chopin in the National Theater allowed the general public a closer and better appreciation of the full beauty of his compositions. There was not a single person with an ear for music who was not more impressed this time than before because musical works, through the aura of their own beauty, excite us more each time we hear them. Without entering into a detailed analysis I would simply point out that the beauty of each work was related to the orchestral accompaniment, which never distorted or overpowered the principal instrument. On the contrary, the accompaniment served to augment and ennoble its beauty. An Adagio, in order to produce a powerful effect, must be lofty and sublime. It arises only from an energetic burst of feeling which is allowed to develop spontaneously, usually enhanced by an artistic imagination that lends it an exhilarating charm. Such is the Adagio of Chopin's concerto. In order to create and express such a piece one must combine a delicate shading of tones and tempi with a skillful technique that is capable of ranging from the loudest *crescendo* to a hushed *diminuendo*. These special traits are to be found in Chopin's playing, which is a beautiful musical statement that seems to be the natural result of his compositions. Our native songs which appear in his works, far from making them tiresome, serve as an ingenious background of ideas. They offer him a palette of pure but vibrant colors which, in combination with his own ideas and feelings, become transformed into lovely poetic ornaments that are ennobled by art and raised to a new level of existence. They have this common trait, that they all strive to bring forth their own stamp of individuality as well as that of the nation which influenced their character. Is this nothing more than the result of blind chance or the whims of fashion or prejudice? Not at all. It is the path of true talents. They give back to their homeland a part of their inspiration. From what we have heard we can conclude that Chopin's works have a spirit that will not long remain confined to the narrow boundaries of mere concert pieces. He will, in time, move on to the greater tasks of opening new fields for the composer, disseminating new musical ideas, and creating more distinctively Polish songs and harmonies. . . .

Dekameron Polski, Warsaw, April 10, 1830

M. Chopin gave another concert to the great satisfaction of his public. Whoever is familiar with the delightful talent of this young virtuoso likens him to Mozart in regard to the boldness, abundance, and originality of his ideas as well as the diversity of his style and harmonies. Everything about M. Chopin's concert marks him as a talent of the highest order.

Powszechny Dziennik Krajowy, Warsaw, September 24, 1830[11]

We hasten with pleasure to inform the friends of music and our local artists of the following news: Fryderyk Chopin has composed his second magnificent concerto. The day before yesterday, in the intimate surroundings of his own home, he tried it out for the first time with an orchestra before his friends as well as the most exacting masters and connoisseurs of this capital. Rather than carry on at great length in praise of it I can sum it up succinctly in a single sentence: *It is a work of genius.* Its originality and graceful conception, its abundance of imaginative ideas, its perfect orchestration, and last but not least, its masterful execution delighted the audience. . . .

Kurjer Warszawski, Warsaw, October 12, 1830[12]

Yesterday evening was an extremely pleasant experience for music lovers; about 700 of them were present in the audience. The new Concerto in E minor, composed and performed publicly for the first time by M. Szopę [Chopin], was regarded by the connoisseurs as one of the most sublime of all musical works. The Adagio and Rondo were especially received with delight by all. The composer and virtuoso was overwhelmed by a wealth of applause and called back onstage after each solo. The audience also expressed its pleasure at the arias sung by our young artists Mlle. Gładkowska and Mlle. Wołkow. The orchestra gave an excellent rendition of the overture to Rossini's *William Tell.* The concert opened with the symphony composed by M. Görner, a member of this orchestra whose previous compositions have been a source of great enjoyment.

Allgemeine Musikalische Zeitung, Leipzig, September 21, 1831

Herr Chopin, also from the Sarmatian capital [Warsaw], established himself during his visit [to Vienna] last year as a pianist of the first order. The performance of his newest serious effort, the Concerto in E minor [on April 4, 1831], gave us no cause to change our earlier opinion. [Cf. *Allgemeine Musikalische Zeitung,* November 18, 1829.] Anyone who loves true Art so sincerely deserves our highest esteem.

Allgemeine Theaterzeitung, Vienna, June 18, 1831

On June 11, at an Academy [concert] which opened with the overture to Weber's *Euryanthe,* we heard the first movement of a new piano concerto composed and performed by Herr Friedrich Chopin. This young Warsaw musician whose love of music brought him to Vienna some time ago is one of those artists who pursue their own path without trying to win a fleeting notoriety through amusing but trivial musical effects dictated by fashion. . . . His playing is graceful in style and highly polished. His phrases are lucidly developed but he seems to be a little too free with his tempi, and although he has prepared a brilliant and impressive cadenza, some changes in it would seem desirable. All these, however, are matters of secondary importance which should correct themselves in time through practice and experience. The performer was applauded and called back at the end of the first movement of his concerto. He was again greeted with the same response when he subsequently played the Adagio and Rondo, in which melodic passages were combined with dazzling ornamentation in a fascinating manner that gave the artist many opportunities to display his technical skill and expressive style. He used an excellent instrument by Graf, the piano manufacturer to the court. It is our expectation that this young virtuoso will soon take his place among the ranks of the finest pianists. Between the piano portions of the program a very charming vocal quartet was performed with great purity and expressiveness by Messrs. Staudigel, Emminger, Rupprecht, and Richatscheck [*sic*].

F. A. KANNE

Flora: A Journal of Entertainment, Munich, August 30, 1831

On the 28th of this month Herr F. Chopin from Warsaw gave a midday concert in the auditorium of the Philharmonic Society which was attended by a very select audience. Herr Chopin played his Piano Concerto in E minor and showed an outstanding virtuosity in his performance. A lovely delicacy along with a beautiful and individualistic interpretation of the themes was characteristic of his cultivated style. On the whole the work was brilliant and well written but without any particular originality or depth except for the main theme and middle section of the Rondo, which display a unique charm in their peculiar combination of melancholy and light-hearted passages. In closing, the pianist played a Fantasy on Polish national songs. There is something in Slavic folk songs that almost never fails to impress the listener. . . . Herr Chopin's Fantasy . . . aroused applause from all quarters. Herr Bayer sang a cavatina by Schubert with piano and clarinet accompaniment. Herr Bayer performed this tender, deeply moving composition of the immortal Master with an outpouring of fervent feeling. He was more than merely assisted by Herr Bärmann, for it was, in reality, a duo [for clarinet and voice]. That young virtuoso [Bärmann] will certainly reach the highest level of his art, and we cannot give him any greater praise than to say he is already worthy of his famous name. A lovely vocal quartet composed by the conductor, Herr Stunz, was magnificently performed by Mad. Pellegrini and Messrs. Bayer, Lenz, and Harm.

Revue Musicale, Paris, March 3, 1832

To say these days that a pianist has talent or even a *great talent* indicates that he is either the follower or the rival of certain first-rate artists whose names immediately come to mind. . . . Now, though, we have a young man who gives free rein to his natural impressions and makes no effort to copy any of his predecessors with the result that he has achieved, if not a complete rejuvenation of piano music, at least some degree of that for which we have searched in vain for a long time, that is, an abundance of original ideas not to be found anywhere else. This isn't to claim that M. Chopin has the organizational strength or conceptual vigor of a Beethoven. There is a difference between music for the piano, which Beethoven wrote, and music for pianists, a field in which M. Chopin's inspiration has created a revitalization of forms which could carry in their wake a great impact on this type of art.

In a concert which he gave the 26th of this month in the salons of MM. Pleyel et Cie., M. Chopin performed a concerto that aroused as much astonishment as it did pleasure because of the freshness of its melodic ideas as well as its structure, its modulations, and its development in general. Its melodies sang out from the soul, its composition was imaginative, and throughout, its originality was evident. It was not, however, without flaws, i.e., there was an excessive richness in its modulations, a certain lack of order in its development which sometimes gave one the impression of listening to an improvisation rather than a finished work of music. Faults like these, though, can be blamed on the age of the artist. With the acquisition of experience they should disappear. If M. Chopin's subsequent works fulfill the promise of his debut, there can be no doubt that he will achieve a brilliant and well-deserved reputation.

As a performer the young artist also deserves praise. His playing is elegant, effortless, graceful, and possesses brilliance as well as clarity. He doesn't draw a lot of volume from the piano. In this regard he is similar to most German pianists. But his studies with M. Kalkbrenner cannot fail to endow him with those qualities which will strengthen his performance and allow him to derive greater expressiveness from the piano.

Besides the concerto which I have just mentioned, two other outstanding works were also heard. One is the Quintet for violin performed with that feeling and inspiration which are characteristic of M. Baillot's talent. The other, a piece for six pianos composed by M. Kalkbrenner and performed by the composer and MM. Chopin, Stammati [*sic*], Hiller, Osborne, and Sowinski. This piece, in which the instruments are utilized with great finesse and the style of which is full of grace and elegance, had already been heard and well received in Pleyel's rooms several years ago. It was no less a pleasure to hear it again this time.

An oboe solo by M. Brod, whose talent is already well recognized, and several pieces sung by M. Boulanger and Mlles. Isambert and Toméoni completed this musical evening, one of the most enjoyable of the year.

Revue Musicale, Paris, May 26, 1832

One sometimes finds worthy noblemen who perform good deeds. But there aren't many who can perform good music as well—at least we know only a few of this sort. M. le prince de la Moscowa [*sic*] does both at the same time by paying the expenses for charity concerts at which his compositions are given. Moreover these works of his are not mere romances, fantasies, or those trifles that fall under the heading of "amateur music," but a complete mass: Kyrie, Gloria, Credo, Sanctus, and Agnus. Written for four voices with chorus and a full orchestra, it lacks nothing! Honorable indeed is this distinguished gentleman who makes noble use of his fortune, his abilities, and his time! . . .

The performance of the mass, directed by M. Girard, with great control and intelligence, produced a most satisfying effect, and there was more coordination than one ordinarily expects from students in the orchestra and chorus, who were limited to only one rehearsal.

During the concert the first portion of a piano concerto, composed and performed by M. Chopin of Warsaw, was heard. This concerto had already been given in Pleyel's rooms where it was a brilliant success. It was less well received on this occasion, which must be attributed, no doubt, to the somewhat heavy orchestration combined with the rather weak tone Chopin elicits from the piano. It seems to me, nevertheless, that the music of this young musician will rise to great heights in the public's opinion when it is better known.

An oboe solo performed by M. Brod enchanted the audience with the charm which is typical of his playing.

It is appropriate here to indicate Dabadie's progress in softening the quality of his voice, especially in the high registers. During the concert he sang an aria from *Tamerlan* by Winter with great purity. Mlle. Michel was also heard in an aria by Rossini. She left something to be desired in the accuracy of her pitch, but she nevertheless demonstrated skill in the art of singing.

L'Europe Littéraire, Paris, April 12, 1833, 1:79

M. Henri Herz, our brilliant and scintillating pianist, made all the fashionable carriages headed for Longchamps turn around and go in the opposite direction. So many stunning coaches with their gleaming lanterns brightened up the somber rue des Marais and the often-deserted surroundings of the Wauxhall. The beautiful room was well lighted and the ladies were conspicuous for their charm and elegant dress (something most essential to the success of such occasions, which perceptive virtuosos would do well to recognize). M. Herz was heard three times; at first in one of his own concertos. . . . He then played a fantasy on the march from *Otello* most admirably . . . and finally appeared at the head of a quartet of pianists playing an eight-hand work for two pianos. The chorus of the conspirators from *Crociato* served as the theme for their prodigious exercise in agility. It was marvelous to hear the rapid passages burst forth under the fingers of Herz and Liszt. MM. Jacques Herz and Chopin played the second piano and provided a worthy counterpart to the first-rate performance of their formidable partners. Within the first eight measures they established a complete rapport and then continued to perform together with a unity difficult to achieve on keyboard instruments. This unique combination was received enthusiastically. By thus augmenting the sounds of the piano an impressive effect was obtained, and M. Herz was able to keep the accompaniment appropriately subordinated to the melodic line. . . . Mmes. Tadolini, Vigano, and Boucaulx and MM. Bordogni and Géraldi performed the vocal portions of the program. The trio from *L'Inganno Fortunato,* beautifully sung by Mme. Tadolini and MM. Bordogni and Géraldi, was highly applauded. The other pieces added little to the concert, and their performance wasn't good enough to excuse this defect. M. Gambati rendered a trumpet solo on Bellini's cavatina in which he would have done better to leave out the Andante. This number, granting the performer's undeniable talent, would have sounded much better with an orchestral accompaniment. The piano simply wasn't up to the job in this case. M. Human [*sic*], one of our most distinguished virtuosos, played a violin fantasy on a beautiful romance by M. Lambert and an aria by M. Auber. This young violinist executes the most difficult passages with absolute perfection fit for the ears of Paganini himself.[13]

CASTIL-BLAZE

Revue Musicale, Paris, December 21, 1833

. . . M. Hiller deserves credit . . . for his devoted and untiring efforts to rehabilitate the old but admirable music of Bach, the taste for which has become *passé* although it has lost nothing of its freshness and beauty for those musicians and music lovers endowed with a certain delicacy of feeling. . . . Bach is less than 300 [*sic*] years old. Why don't we appreciate him? One concerto of Bach is worth far more than an air and variations by Herz! The fragment for three pianos played by MM. Hiller, Liszt, and Chopin afforded us a rare pleasure. These three artists performed this piece, we can assure you, with an understanding of its character and a perfect delicacy. . . .

EDOUARD FÉTIS

Gazette Musicale, Paris, December 28, 1834

. . . [Berlioz] is above all a poet. . . . Out of the richest treasures of the musical language, his artistic genius creates an expression of overwhelming sincerity which moves us as it originally moved him and fills us with the same inspiration that he himself experienced. . . . So much for our opinion of Berlioz's music in general. As to its performance, we will confine ourselves to saying that it was most satisfying although certain details were not always rendered with the utmost precision. We would like to mention that M. Urhan played his solo much better this time than at the last concert. . . . We owe special praise to Mlle. Heinefetter, who sang a most difficult aria with the greatest artistry and beauty of expression. The public displayed its appreciation of her performance in a highly flattering manner. We would also like to mention M. Boulanger, who, in performing one of M. Berlioz's compositions, showed that besides his expressive voice and exquisite style, he understood the spirit of the work entrusted to his talent.

To conclude, M. Chopin, that sublime composer and inimitable pianist, played an adagio [*sic*] of his own composition. It is a work that created a beautiful effect which compared favorably with the compositions performed before and after it. It is very well constructed and extremely rich in delicate nuances, which contrast sharply with the colossal weight of M. Berlioz's orchestral productions.

P. R.

Gazette Musicale, Paris, December 28, 1834

Although the system of afternoon musicales hardly fits into our idea of art or the way it should be cultivated and although we attach little importance to reviewing such occasions, we must, however, make an exception in the case of those mentioned above [i.e., the "matinée" musicales of M. Ernst on December 23 and M. Stoepel on December 25]. Both were outstanding not only because of the perfect performances rendered but also because they provided an opportunity to gather together the most distinguished artists in the capital. . . . [A review of M. Ernst's concert follows with the conclusion that, from an artistic point of view, M. Stoepel's was the more interesting event.]

. . . Messieurs Liszt and Chopin opened it [M. Stoepel's concert] in a brilliant manner with the Grand Piano Duo for four hands by Moscheles. We feel it is superfluous to say that this work, one of the composer's masterpieces, was performed with a rare degree of perfection by the two greatest piano virtuosos of our era. The brilliancy of the performance combined a refined delicacy with a consistently high level of quality, a rapturous vivacity with a calm serenity, and a playful grace with a sombre gravity. It would be impossible to hope for anything more than this collaboration of two artists equally sublime and equally endowed with such a profound sensitivity of their art.

The most enthusiastic applause testified better than our own words could how much MM. Liszt and Chopin charmed their audience, whom they electrified a second time with their performance of the Duo for two pianos composed by M. Liszt. This composition is a work of great stature which we don't feel competent to review in detail after only one hearing. On the whole, though, we admired its beautiful and extraordinary melodies and its rich and original harmonies as well as other features which do the greatest honor to M. Liszt's talent as a composer. Only an imagination as fertile and vibrant as his could create such a work. One can easily understand why the charming value of such a piece can be appreciated at this stage by only a select few. In spite of this everyone in the audience applauded the performance of the two artists. M. Ernst provided new proofs of his talent in a violin solo accompanied by M. Liszt with his usual skill. In concluding our observations on the instrumental portion of the program we must mention Mme. de La Hye, who improvised on the harmonium. She brought out all the resources of the instrument with great taste, demonstrating a well-grounded knowledge of music with the imagination of an improviser. As for the vocal portion, it was happily distinguished by M. Richelmi, Mlle. Heinefetter, and Mme. Degli-Antoni. The well-liked talent of M. Richelmi has been recognized for a long time and earned him new acclaim from the public. Mlle. Heinefetter, who for four years has delighted the habitués of the Théâtre-Italien as much by her beautiful voice as the expressiveness of her singing, seemed worthy in our opinion of taking her place today among the foremost prima donnas of our era. . . . Mme. Degli-Antoni sang two arias with all the charm of her gorgeous voice and style. The wild applause of the audience should indicate to the singer how much they appreciated her worth.

Revue Musicale, Paris, March 8, 1835

On Sunday the 22nd of February the beautiful rooms of M. Érard contained within its walls—covered by mirrors and magnificent works of ancient masters garnered from one of the finest galleries of Europe—all the leading artists and music lovers whom M. Hiller had invited to hear his latest compositions. First on the list were musicians, those older ones who have achieved glory and the young ones who yet await it. Then there were painters, since painters love and understand music; next, writers and poets, who are less appreciative in general of the beauties of this art but like to appear familiar with it; elegant and fresh-faced ladies; grave and serious-mannered men, diverted for a day from the bustle of public affairs; and finally journalists, who are, after all, the most important guests at these functions.

All the pieces performed on this interesting program were by M. Hiller, who has shown a great breadth of talent. They included an instrumental trio and quartet, some études and a piano duo, two vocal pieces sung by Mme. Dorus-Gras, and several choruses performed by the Germans who are now playing at the Opéra-Comique in *Robin des Bois* [Weber, *Der Freishütz*].

The trio with MM. Baillot, Franchomme, and Hiller produced an excellent impression owing to the clarity and elegance with which it is written and the intricate details with which it abounds. It came off admirably.

The quartet performed by MM. Baillot, Vidal, Franchomme, and Sauzay is also remarkable in many of its passages, particularly in the second movement where much originality of form is evident. . . . There were some charming études among those he played which are not only useful to study but delightful to hear. In general, they exhibit a great deal of diversity. The Duo for two pianos is a most brilliant composition, too brilliant perhaps. MM. Hiller and Chopin [*sic*] played it in a sparkling manner.

"Le Songe," a vague, melancholy, and yet charming piece, was sung by Mme. Dorus-Gras with an abundance of feeling, understanding, and accuracy. The extremely difficult passages with which this poorly defined piece abounds (it is neither a romance, an aria, or a rondo) did not present any obstacles to Mme. Dorus-Gras, who, on the contrary, managed it magnificently and displayed an equal talent in "La Fiancée du Pêcheur," a beautifully melodic creation.

"Vanitas, Vanitatum, Vanitas!" "La Chanson Suisse," and "La Chanson à Boire," with words by Goethe, were listened to and applauded politely. But the German choir sang them in a style that must have absolutely devastated M. Hiller as they were more off-key than at the Opéra-Comique and even worse than the choruses at the Théâtre des Variétés and the Théâtre-Italien. . . .

Le Ménestrel, Paris, March 22, 1835

The last concert given in the salons of M. Pleyel was very brilliant. Outstanding figures from the social, literary, and artistic worlds came to hear our musical celebrities, MM. Herz, Chopin, Osborne, Hiller, and Reicha, Mmes. Camille [*sic*] Lambert, and Leroy, and M. Hamati [Stamaty], a young pianist who has never before appeared in our salons. This pianist played various pieces which won the approval of all. The Variations by Kalkbrenner on the cavatina "Di Tanti Palpiti" were especially well received.

Gazette Musicale, Paris, April 12, 1835

M. Chopin, we assume, was not a stranger to the planning of the evening's program which was devoted to the relief of his unfortunate fellow countrymen. As a result, the affair was brilliant. Nourrit and Mlle. Falcon carried the vocal part of the program alone. In an aria from the *Siege of Corinth* and a duet from *William Tell* they were both vigorously applauded. The pieces by Schubert which Nourrit sang, at first with the orchestra and later with Liszt at the piano (as a substitute for the orchestra), did not produce as much effect as hoped for. In a vast theater the delicate nuances are lost, and what affects one deeply in a small salon or concert hall passes unnoticed. On the contrary, Chopin's piano concerto, so full of originality and ingenious details, written in such a colorful style with a wealth of refreshing new themes, was an enormous success. It is indeed difficult to keep a piano concerto from seeming monotonous, and music lovers should thank M. Chopin for the pleasure that he rendered them, while musicians must admire the talent that enabled him to succeed in rejuvenating such a worn-out form. The Duo for two pianos by Hiller was equally remarkable for its firmness of style and its beautiful melodic organization. Liszt and the composer performed it magnificently. M. Ernst, in a violin solo of his own composition, gave new evidence of the steady progress of his talent. He seemed to us to have acquired more skill in his rapid trills and greater assurance in his upper tones since the last time he appeared in public. M. Dorus played his flute solo in a manner worthy of a pupil of Tulou; it was scintillating and well executed, with the tone as pure as the pitch was accurate, although it sometimes lacked a little in smoothness and fullness. The two overtures from *Oberon* and *William Tell*, performed by the orchestra under Habeneck's direction, did not live up to expectations. This may have been due to the size of the theater, which was too large for the small orchestra.

Revue et Gazette Musicale, Paris, February 14, 1836

M. Schunke, one of the great pianists of our epoque, whose overwhelming performances arouse the most incredible enthusiasm, astonishment, and admiration, remains the same as ever. And yet if you could see inside his soul for several hours or days before one of his public performances you would be amazed at the frightful torments and unheard-of terrors which hardly seem possible when you merely glance at his powerful physique, so similar to that of [the pianist]

Dussek. Such, however, is the artist with all his inner mysteries, known only to his intimate friends, while the public remains unaware—indeed without even the least suspicion—of their existence.

M. Schunke's fingers race with incomparable strength and fluidity over the keyboard. In the endless flow of joyful notes, however, the meaning of a piece is never lost nor its nuances obliterated. Everything is clearly defined and delicately expressed, all with an irrepressible verve that is truly magical. Each of the pieces performed by him last Sunday (especially the Variations on the galop from *La Tentation*) merely served to increase our wonder and amazement at his talents.

M. Ernst, the young violinist of such capable and powerful abilities, also garnered his share of the honors in a Duo on a theme from *Oberon* composed and performed by him [with M. Schunke at the piano] as well as in his Variations for violin alone. M. Chopin joined forces with M. Schunke in a four-hand Sonata by Moscheles, and you can doubtless imagine the effect of this superb piece when played by two such magnificent artists. M. Batta and his cello, M. Lewi and his horn, which he used to create previously unheard-of effects, MM. Boulanger, Lanza, and their voices, together and separately, completed the brilliant soirée given in the superb salons at No. 17 rue de Lille to which one was admitted only by invitation.

S. G.

Revue et Gazette Musicale, Paris, May 1, 1836

On the 21st of April M. le duc Decazes gave a most brilliant concert in the salons of the *grand-référendaire* in which the choice of works competed with their execution to give satisfaction to all. Outstanding was the vigorous and sonorous voice of M. Géraldy [*sic*] in the part of Marcel from the trio of *Les Huguenots*. A Nocturne by Clapisson was sung by MM. Boulanger and Baron Christophe in a most delightful manner. We must also mention a Waltz by M. Chopin, which was performed by the composer with a delicacy for which he is famous.

But the honors of the evening went to a Venetian lady, Mme. Crescini, an amateur singer, whose contralto voice recalls the energetic precision of Mme. Pisarroni and who excels above all in her declamatory ability. She was heard in a cantata written specially for her by one of our most promising composers, M. Alary, an Italian who has studied for some time at the Conservatory in Milan. This cantata, entitled *Eloisa nel Chiostro,* is an extremely melodious and sensitive work. Several striking and original passages aroused the approval of all, and the singer shared the applause and praise of the aristocratic audience with the composer. . . .

Journal des Débats, Paris, February 19, 1838

M. Schopin [*sic*], the celebrated pianist, had the honor of playing several of his compositions before Their Majesties last Friday [the sixteenth]. His remarkable talent was evident throughout the performance. The Variations which he improvised on a theme suggested by Her Royal Highness the Princess Adélaïde created an overwhelming effect on his audience, and the gifted artist was repeatedly congratulated by the Queen and the princesses. The same day Mlle. Bazin, a young singer endowed with a most beautiful voice, sang several French romances for the royal family with a skill that elicited all the charm of that genre.

Revue et Gazette Musicale, Paris, February 25, 1838

M. Chopin, that pianist who is as extraordinary as he is modest, was recently summoned to the court to be heard in an intimate circle. There the young composer's outstanding merit was as fully appreciated as it is among his fellow musicians. He was particularly admired for his inexhaustible improvisations, which were virtually enough in themselves to make the evening worthwhile and earned him the enthusiastic applause of everyone present.

Revue et Gazette Musicale, Paris, March 11, 1838

. . . It cannot be denied that the piano plays a very important role in our social order. Everyone spends a part of his income on one. You will find them in the back room of a small business shop as well as in the drawing rooms of the aristocracy. The piano has become the symbol of civilization and equality. It assists us in the pursuit of social and musical refinement. But it is frightening to find it becoming a substitute for all other instrumental art. We mention this only to draw attention to the absolute deluge of [piano] fantasies and variations which has inundated us during this Lenten season. However, this is not intended to apply in any way to the concert given by M. Alkan in M. Pape's rooms on Saturday, March 3, which delighted a most distinguished audience.

A Trio for violin, piano, and cello by Mayseder opened the concert in an admirable fashion. It was performed with verve and excellent coordination by M. Ernst, the beneficiary [Alkan], and M. Batta. Mlle. d'Hennin, Mme. Maria [Marix], and M. Alizard distinguished themselves in the vocal portions of the program. We would advise the latter in the interest of his career as well as that of our lyric theaters not to follow the school of French bass singers but to practice in order to give his voice greater flexibility, purity, and sonority. Levassor, the leading tenor of M. Dormeuil's theater [the Palais Royal], sang several short songs in a most humorous fashion. . . . All this he does in a manner which—if not terribly musical—is at least highly amusing.

M. Alkan then performed two of his own études. . . . The concert ended with the Andante and Finale of the Symphony in A arranged for two pianos and eight hands. In spite of the skill of the arrangement and the importance of the piano which we have just commented on (illustrated so well by the able performance of MM. Chopin, Zimmerman, Alkan, and Gutmann), we don't think it's a good idea to tamper in such a way with the monumental works of Beethoven. The melody which is so flowing and full of melancholy when played on the cello in the Andante of the symphony can't help but lose its angelic nature when transposed to the piano. . . . Those who profess a genuine respect for the creation of a great man would call this a sacrilege.

All things considered, though, this brilliant evening retained for M. Alkan that double reputation he has already acquired of being a capable pianist and excellent composer. The large crowd which came at his invitation gave frequent and unequivocal indications of its pleasure at hearing the young artist and the gifted musicians who assisted him.

HENRI BLANCHARD

Revue et Gazette Musicale, Paris, March 25, 1838

The following is an event which is not without importance for the musical world. Chopin, who hasn't allowed himself to be heard in public for several years [*sic*], Chopin, who confines his charming genius to an audience of five or six persons, Chopin, who resembles those enchanted isles rarely visited by outsiders and of whom so many marvelous things are told that it is difficult to believe they can be true, Chopin, who can never be forgotten once he has been heard, the same Chopin just gave a magnificent concert in Rouen before 500 people for the benefit of a Polish professor. Nothing more than the opportunity to do a good deed along with the memory of his homeland was required for him to overcome his aversion to playing in public. And, indeed, his success was enormous! All those ravishing melodies, those indescribable delicacies of execution, those inspired passages full of melancholy and passion, all that poetry which overwhelms the imagination as well as the heart, all these stunned, moved, and intoxicated the 500 listeners in the same way they have affected the 8 or 10 chosen few who have listened to him religiously for hours at a time. Throughout the entire performance the hall quivered with electricity and rippled with murmurs of ecstasy and astonishment which are the "bravos" of the soul. On, Chopin! On! May this triumph convince you not to be selfish any longer. Spread your wonderful talent on the winds. Admit that you are who you are. Stop this great debate which is dividing the artistic world. Henceforth when the question is asked, "Who is the foremost pianist in Europe, Liszt or Thalberg?" let all the world be able to reply, like those who have heard you, "It is Chopin!"

Revue et Gazette Musicale, Paris, October 31, 1839

The King invited MM. Moscheles and Chopin last Tuesday to come to Saint-Cloud, and these two great artists played before the assembled court. In the presence of this small royal gathering they played the delightful études recently composed by them. Moscheles' Grande Sonata for four hands produced such an effect that the queen asked to hear the Andante a second time. Chopin then improvised on *La Folle* by Grisar, and Moscheles on various Mozart themes, notably the overture from *The Magic Flute* in which he displayed his double talent as a pianist and composer. These two great artists held the attention and shared the enthusiasm of the court for the whole evening.

Revue et Gazette Musicale, Paris, May 2, 1841

Last Monday at eight o'clock in the evening the salons of M. Pleyel were magnificently lit up. To the foot of the stairway covered with carpets and perfumed with flowers numerous carriages brought the most elegant ladies, the most fashionable young men, the most celebrated artists, the richest financiers, the most illustrious peers, indeed all the elite of society, all the aristocracy of birth, fortune, talent, and beauty.

A grand piano stood open on a stage with a crowd pressing around it trying to get the nearest seats. Even before the concert began people were settled and ready to listen, telling themselves they could not afford to miss one chord, one note, one nuance or thought, by the person who would soon seat himself there. And they were right to be so avid, so attentive, so devoutly moved, for he whom they awaited, whom they longed to see and hear, to admire and applaud, was not only an able virtuoso, a pianist expert in the technique of his art, a musician of great renown, he was all that and more; he was Chopin.

Having arrived in France around ten years ago, Chopin never competed in any way for first or second place among the hordes of pianists who surge all around us today. He has seldom allowed himself to be heard in public; the eminently poetic nature of his talent is not suited to that. Similar to those flowers which open their fragrant calyces only in the evening, he requires an atmosphere of tranquillity and composure in order to yield up the melodic treasures which repose within him. Music was his language, the divine tongue through which he expressed a whole realm of sentiments that only the select few can appreciate. As with that other great poet Mickiewicz, his compatriot and friend, the muse of his homeland dictates his songs, and the anguished cries of Poland lend to his art a mysterious, indefinable poetry which, for all those who have truly experienced it, cannot be compared to anything else. If his name is surrounded by less fame, if his brow is illuminated by a less brilliant aureole, it is not because he lacked the same energy of thought, the same depth of sentiment, as the illustrious author of *Konrad Wollenrod* and the *Pilgrims* but rather because his means of expression were too limited, his instrument too imperfect. The piano alone was not sufficient to reveal all that lies within him. This, if we do not deceive ourselves, is the origin of his secret but constant sorrow, his reluctance to express himself in public, his melancholy which hides behind a mask of gaiety. In short, he is a most remarkable individual who commands our highest degree of devotion.

Thus, as we have said, it has been but rarely and then only at widely separated intervals that Chopin has played in public. But this, which would have resulted in almost certain neglect and obscurity for anyone else, has, on the contrary, assured Chopin a reputation far above the caprices of fashion and shields him from rivalries, jealousies, and injustices. He resides outside the maelstrom which, for several years, has tossed performing artists everywhere into a chaotic and competitive battle for survival. He has always remained surrounded by his faithful followers, enthusiastic pupils, and warmhearted friends, who, while guarding him from bitter struggles and painful rebuffs, have not ceased circulating his works coupled with an admiration for his genius and respect for his name. Thus this exquisite celebrity, highly placed and supremely aristocratic, remains free from all attack. All criticism has been silenced in regard to him as if posterity had already made its pronouncement. And as for the brilliant audience which flocked around the poet, who for too long has remained silent, there was no reticence, no reserve, only praise on every tongue.

We won't attempt a detailed analysis of Chopin's compositions here. Without any specious striving for originality the composer has remained himself both in the style and conception of his works. To new ideas he has given new forms. A certain wild and rugged flavor of his native land can be detected in his bold dissonances and strange harmonies, while the delicacy and grace which characterize his personality are apparent in the endless shadings and ornamentation of his inimitable imagination.

In Monday's concert Chopin performed for a select few those of his works which are most removed from the classical forms. He did not play any concerto, sonata, fantasy, or variations but rather preludes, études, nocturnes, and mazurkas. Addressing himself to society rather than the public, he could, with impunity, reveal his true nature, that of an elegiac poet, profound, pure, and pensive. He had no need to shock or to show off. He sought to elicit delicate sentiments rather than thunderous emotions. Let us hasten to add, however, that it was not because he lacks those emotions. From the first note, he established a close communication between himself and his listeners. Two études and a ballade were given encores, and had it not been for the fear of adding to the exhaustion already evident in his pallid face, the audience would have requested an encore to every piece on the program.

Chopin's preludes are unique compositions. They are not simply, as their title would suggest, pieces intended as an introduction to something further; they are poetic preludes similar to those of a great contemporary poet [Lamartine] which gently ease the soul into a golden dream world and then whisk it away to the highest realms of the ideal. Admirable in their diversity, they require scrupulous examination of the workmanship and thought which have gone into them before they can be properly appreciated. Even then they still retain the appearance of spontaneous improvisations produced without the slightest effort. They possess that freedom and charm which characterize works of genius.

What can one say about the mazurkas, those little masterpieces so capricious and yet so polished? "A perfect sonnet is worth more than a long poem," said an authority on the finest century of French literature. We are indeed tempted to say the same of these muzurkas if not more. For us some of them are worth more than certain *very long* operas.

After all the bravos cast at the feet of the king of the evening's entertainment, M. Ernst proved expert in obtaining some well-merited ones for himself also. He played an elegy in an expansive and grandiose style with intense feeling and a purity worthy of the masters, which made a vivid impression on the audience.

Mme. Damoreau, who lent her charming assistance to this *fashionable* concert, was, as always, ravishing in her perfection.

Before concluding these few lines we must add something which lack of time forces us to say briefly. The fame and success which crown talent and genius are, in part, the product of fortuitous circumstances. But sustained success is seldom an accident. Nevertheless, since justice is perhaps the rarest quality of the human spirit, the result is that success comes easily for certain artists, while for others it remains beyond their grasp. It has been said that every tenth wave of the sea's tide beats more violently against the shore than the others. So it is in the ways of the world; only those individuals who ride the tenth wave of fortune are carried higher and farther than others who may be their equals or, indeed, their superiors. Chopin's genius, however, is not at all due to any such special circumstances. His success, great as it is, nevertheless remains inadequate to what he truly deserves. Still, we insist with the utmost conviction that he need envy no one. Is not the noblest and most justifiable satisfaction an artist can experience that sense of being above and beyond his fame, superior even to his success, greater still than his glory?

F. LISZT

La France Musicale, Paris, May 2, 1841

There are those individuals whose heart is uneasy in the midst of the world's clamor. They are born for solitude and contemplation just as glistening pools of dew are meant for cool shadows and the song of the warbler.

Look at Schubert, whose all-too-brief life was passed in tears far from the world of love songs and dirges. The glare of lights burned his eyes; the bustle of the crowd stifled his heart and suffocated him. Accolades and applause dizzied him and dried up the flow of soft, tender melodies in his soul. And yet didn't Schubert go right on expressing those passions which stir the whole world? . . . We have spoken of Schubert because there is no one else so similar to Chopin. The one has done for the piano what the other has done for the voice. Both have drawn their many-splendored, tender, sad, and passionate inspirations from the same well. Their characters even resemble each other. Listen to Chopin and you will quickly see that he does not bow to fashion or vulgarity to achieve fame and fortune. This artist, this poet, has not, like so many others over the past fifteen to twenty years, striven by every means imaginable to please the public. On the contrary, he has avoided pretensions, preferring the quiet life devoid of ostentation, competitiveness, or emotional displays. While so many artists strive for notoriety he dreams away in silence, turning inward to his soul for thoughts of youth and love, for objects of beauty and endearment. Poetry is such a noble companion in solitude!

Any sort of commotion horrifies Chopin. He doesn't dare play before a large crowd if he isn't sure of being understood because he fears the hubbub that might result. What pains, what struggles, he goes through in his mind and heart before resolving to face the gaze of his judges—or rather, one should say his admirers. The artist—or to be more exact—the poet has given in at last. He appeared, was heard and applauded, so much so that now, after nearly a week, it is hard to realize that it actually took place before our very eyes and ears.

Chopin is a pianist of conviction. He composes for himself and performs for himself. What he writes and plays the world listens to with interest, fascination, and infinite pleasure. Don't expect his hands to produce any loud or startling effects of those *tours de force* that make your head rattle. Chopin doesn't care for that blustery kind of music which accomplishes nothing but to drown out the orchestra. On the contrary, pay attention to how he dreams, how he weeps, how he sings so sweetly, tenderly, and with such sorrow, how he expresses to perfection everything that is heartfelt and noble. Chopin is the pianist of feeling par excellence.

One can say that Chopin has created his own school of piano technique and composition. From the first moment that he runs his fingers over the keyboard nothing can rival the lightness and delicacy of his touch, nor can anything match his compositions, so full of originality, distinction, and grace. Chopin is indeed a unique pianist who cannot be compared with anyone. The Andante and Scherzo which he played on his program are two examples of his exquisite style. The melodies are original and distinctive. The Scherzo, above all, is full of elegant simplicity and warmth. His études are not any the less remarkable. The audience made him repeat three of them and with good reason. But the pieces which aroused the most enthusiasm were the Ballade, a Mazurka, and the Polonaise which climaxed the evening. These three delightful compositions, the latest which Chopin has published, are all masterpieces, destined to become as popular as the most beautiful of Schubert's melodies.

It would be unfair not to mention the four preludes which were also highly appreciated.

The concert was a festive occasion attended by an aristocracy of talent and wealth. Two artists whose names alone would have been sufficient to attract a brilliant crowd in the spectacular salons of M. Pleyel joined M. Chopin. Mme. Damoreau and M. Ernst took part on the program. Mme. D. sang in a ravishing manner (as only she can do) two arias from M. Ad. Adam's last opera, *Rosa de Pérrone.* Both the music and the singer were showered with applause. These arias are much in vogue around town today. With Mme. D.'s endorsement their popularity can only increase.

M. Ernst played his *Élégie.* He too is an artist and poet who can move and charm you without twisting his face into horrible contortions. Melody pours out of him effortlessly. Perhaps he allowed himself to be a little too overcome with melancholy on this occasion, but at least he has an original and clear-cut style. If you want to hear a violin weep, listen to M. Ernst. He wrings such heartrending, passionate sounds from his instrument that you fear any minute the violin will literally shatter in his hands. It would be difficult to achieve any greater expression of sorrow, suffering, or despair.

ESCUDIER

Le Ménestrel, Paris, May 2, 1841

It is nigh on to several years since we have had the opportunity to hear this sensitive pianist. Has he changed? Not at all, for Chopin is not concerned with mechanical tricks. There isn't the least bit of charlatanism in him. Such a gifted nature would gain nothing from it. It is his heart and genius alone which speak to us. To appreciate Chopin fully one must have a feeling for beautiful imagery and the poetry of love. To understand Chopin one must read a strophe by Lamartine.

Chopin's compositions are even more impressive than the delicate nuances of his playing. Schubert was never more inspired. And we can assure you that in Chopin's works one finds the same delightful perfection of harmony and melody. This is what makes us prefer him to Listz [*sic*], although the latter, now that he has put aside his original compositions, is beginning to give us some idea of what his talent can do in arranging the works of our celebrated composers. . . . Chopin, on the contrary, is pure imagination and creativity. We are not trying to claim that Chopin is the greatest pianist in the world. Not at all. Nevertheless, he has his own unique style as does Listz, whose fiery nature and astounding technique are certainly beyond all rivalry.

The études and mazurkas stand out among Chopin's compositions. The inspiration in each is developed just enough to captivate the public without boring it for a single moment. This is what makes Chopin so immensely successful! We must add that Pleyel's pianos suit this pianist well, although they wouldn't be able to stand up under the onslaught of Listz's fingers or even those of less violent pianists. . . . Mme. Damoreau and Ernst rival each other in talent and charm. In short, we didn't leave this evening with the feeling of having been overpowered by a display of high drama which is all the rage today. On the contrary, each listener returned home filled with delight and a profound sense of satisfaction.

Revue et Gazette Musicale, Paris, December 5, 1841

The second concert given by HRH the Duke of Orléans was the most brilliant imaginable. The vocal part consisted of a selection of Italian operatic works by Mozart, Rossini, Donizetti, Carafa, and Païsiello, performed by Lablache, Mario, and Mesdames Grisi and Persiani. There was only one instrumental soloist but that artist was Chopin, who began with a delightful Ballade of his own composition (the third) played with that marvelous talent so characteristic of him. Next he improvised as only he can do. It is scarcely necessary to add that his success equaled his talent and the extraordinary charm of his performance. The excellent Pleyel piano on which he played contributed to the successful effect which he produced.

La France Musicale, Paris, December 5, 1841

The concert which took place at Mgr. the Duke of Orléans the first of December was magnificent. The artists from the Théâtre-Italien, Mmes. Grisi and Persiani, MM. Lablache and Mario, were heard there.

Only Tamburini was missing. We note this absence with regret. The instrumental part was represented by Chopin, the pianist-poet whose absolutely extraordinary genius has remained so far without rival or imitator. He played one of his ballades and then improvised with a grace, elegance, and ease which his royal audience marveled at. After the second piece the Queen approached M. Chopin and paid him the most flattering compliments. Pianists in general, when they are heard in public, have the habit of playing on new pianos. Chopin didn't hesitate to play on the Pleyel grand piano, sold to the court five or six years before, and he drew from it sounds of admirable purity which testify to the durability of M. Pleyel's pianos. This is an observation which has already been made and which we are pleased to confirm.

La France Musicale, Paris, February 27, 1842

[After a lengthy preamble in which the critic discusses some behind-the-scene aspects of a Paris musical season, he finally acknowledges that "our main purpose is to discuss M. Chopin's concert with the reader."]

Those who don't know the Polish pianist couldn't form any idea of his exceptional talent from a simple review. Those who have heard him and are acquainted with him have no need of our praise in order to appreciate his worth and character. Therefore we could do our job quickly by merely saying that Chopin is a pianist out of the ordinary, a pianist that few if any can equal. However, we have an obligation to express our thoughts in detail, and we would like to discuss M. Chopin's concert at length if space, time, and our readers will allow.

Chopin provided a most enchanting evening in the salon of M. Pleyel, an event filled with adoring smiles, tender, rosy-cheeked faces, and delicate, shapely white hands; a magnificent affair where simplicity was combined with grace and elegance; where good taste served as a pedestal for riches. Those awful black ["stovepipe"] hats which make men look as disgusting as possible were fortunately scarce. Golden ribbons, delicate blue veils, strands of shimmering pearls, the freshest roses and tiny carnations, in short a collection of the gayest and loveliest adornments were assembled and arranged in every conceivable fashion over the perfumed coiffures and bare shoulders of the most charming ladies for whose favor the salons of the aristocracy vie with one another. The first accolades of the evening went to Madame Georges [*sic*] Sand. From the moment she appeared with her two charming daughters she was the center of attention.[14] Other people would have been flustered under the gaze of so many eyes beaming down at them like stars. But Georges Sand simply lowered her head and smiled. What must it feel like to be such a literary celebrity?

Chopin played eight pieces in all.[15] Each resembled the other in form; only the thought expressed by them varied, which is what makes them so stunning. Chopin is a poet, and above all a tender one, a true master of the art. He accomplishes the most prodigious feats of technique but never to the detriment of his melody which is always simple and original. If you follow the pianist's hands you will see with what marvelous facility he executes the most graceful passages, bridges the distances of the keyboard, and achieves a shading from *piano* to *forte* and back again! The magnificent instruments of M. Pleyel lend themselves admirably to these diverse functions. In listening to all those sounds and nuances which pour forth one after the other, weaving about each other only to disengage and then reunite once more as they give shape to the melody, one cannot help but think he is hearing the faint voices of fairies sighing under silver bells or showers of pearls falling on crystal tables. The pianist appears to have an infinite number of fingers; it doesn't seem possible that two hands alone could produce such feats of velocity in so accurate and natural a manner. Don't expect Chopin to imitate the massive sounds of the orchestra on a piano. That type of performance isn't in keeping with his musical concepts. He has no desire to dazzle you with tricks of speed or the startling originality of his mazurkas, nor does he try to generate hysteria or make you faint on the spot. His style is pure poetry, tender and simple. Don't expect of him those great thunderous chords or diabolical variations; his aim is to speak to the heart and not to the eyes; he wants to caress his audience and not devour it. As a result the public grows ecstatic, their enthusiasm reaches its peak, and Chopin has achieved his goal.

At this delightfully planned evening, Mme. Pauline Garcia-Viardot and M. Franchomme also took part. Mme. Viardot sang several of Handel's works with admirable expression, one especially which included the loveliest passages ever created for the voice. Her choice of an aria by M. Dessauer was unfortunate. This is a good example of why one should never try to perform trivial music. . . . M. Franchomme is a supremely excellent artist, as everyone knows; one might even consider him the foremost cellist in Paris. He doesn't resort to affected gestures, elaborate embellishments, or sentimental, dreamy posturing to impress or win over his audience. He remains almost invisible when he plays as if he were part of his instrument. He is repeatedly applauded because he understands his feelings and how to communicate them. He performs in a pure and noble style which cannot but satisfy the most stringent demands of people with good taste and intelligence.

ESCUDIER

Revue et Gazette Musicale, Paris, February 27, 1842

If music is really an architecture of sounds as a famous lady has ingeniously said, then one must acknowledge that M. Chopin, the pianist-composer, is indeed an elegant architect. The originality of forms dreamed up by his delightful imagination is well known. His unusual, delicately wrought little masterpieces stimulate our interest more and more each time we hear them. Despite ourselves they conjure up fantasies of the Alhambra, the Generalife, and all those superb caprices which the Arab genius has incorporated into the marvelous monuments of Grenada. The mind is thrilled by the spectacle of this tasteful opulence, which never fails to exhibit order in its richness! This is above all the distinctive characteristic of M. Chopin's creations. His fertile imagination weaves a certain connecting thread through the most brilliant digressions so that the diverse portions of his work remain skillfully bound together in a unified whole.

M. Chopin's style is, moreover, eminently aristocratic. He exhales it like a perfume of the finest quality; it is, if you will pardon the well-worn phrase, something exquisite and fashionable. There is nothing banal in its character as a whole or vulgar in its detail. If anything, a picayune critic could perhaps complain that he has gone too far in the opposite extreme. Striving for too much refinement and delicacy can sometimes lead to pretentiousness and lack of feeling. Music is like a beautiful lady that one adores to see in a divinely elegant *ensemble* at the same time it is also pleasant to surprise her occasionally *en négligé*.

However, far be it from us to start a quarrel with M. Chopin. He is highly charming when he wants to be, that is to say, when he doesn't abuse his astonishing ability in an effort to discover new types of ornamentation which sometimes become a little mannered. And aren't we all aware that it is simply the exaggeration of certain features which results in imperfections? But when all is said and done, those little defects disappear into the shadows if we view a talent from its bright side. With M. Chopin, his melodic genius has such an expressive, tender, and distinguished character and his harmonic style is so richly endowed that the first impression—invariably irresistible—disarms the critic who, waiting like a knight in armor, is prepared to rush into the field, his visor pulled over his face and his pen ready to do battle.

You see, therefore, what success M. Chopin encounters on those rare occasions when he appears in public. You can imagine how people press to find ways of hearing him; artists and music lovers alike throng around him. Ah! he is more to them than merely an object of adulation. It is not only the composer that they come to applaud but also the virtuoso, the beguiling pianist who speaks an enchanting language through his fingers and unburdens his soul in a performance, which truly leaves nothing to be desired. His exceptional playing reveals a personality to which no other can claim the secret. It is as if the piano is transformed in some manner and actually becomes a different instrument, in response to the searing touch of a tender and passionate genius. Liszt and Thalberg, as we know, can transport us by the thundering violence of their styles. Chopin can also do the same but in a more subdued, less fiery manner, precisely because he is able to strike the most intimate strings of the heart and arouse its deepest emotions. The former pianists create a euphoria which whips up their audiences into loud bursts of bravos and applause. But the latter produces a more profound effect. The sentiments which Chopin excites are less obvious and less overwhelming but just as delightful and much more substantial. All you need to do is ask anyone who attended last Monday's concert at the Salle Pleyel.

As a virtuoso M. Chopin hardly needs any comment. Indeed,

words, as always, would be inadequate. He completely won over the vast crowd of distinguished listeners who came to hear him. We will not attempt to add anything to the admiration and praise that were heaped upon him by everyone there—to which we happily contributed our part. . . . We shall therefore finish with M. Chopin, whose reputation is great enough at this time to gain little from our praise. Moreover we still have other compliments to distribute to M. Franchomme's extremely pure and polished talent, as well as to the thrilling voice of Mme. Viardot-Garcia. Like Piccini's *Dido* this young singer can justly say, "Ah! how I was inspired!" And we can hardly deny it, as she sang with feeling, beauty, and an extraordinary facility. Her first number was a composition as well known as it is lovely, "La Felice Donzella" by Dessauer; next she offered two pieces by the long-departed but still sublime Haëndel [*sic*], and finally "Le Chêne et le Roseau," which had to be encored. There is no doubt that Mme. Viardot aspires to equal the singing of her wonderful sister. While she has also composed several charming things we hope that Mme. Viardot will continue down the road of success upon which she is already launched without becoming sidetracked as a composer, for her true vocation is to be a singer.

MAURICE BOURGES

Journal des Débats, Paris, April 13, 1842

Chopin always keeps himself aloof. You will never see him in the theaters or at a concert. It has been said that he is afraid of music and musicians. Once a year, though, he comes down off his cloud and can be heard briefly in the salon of M. Pleyel. Only then does he permit the public and other artists to admire his magnificent talent. For the rest of the year—unless you are a prince, minister, or ambassador—you might as well give up all hope of hearing him. So many others jump at the chance to play in public whenever they can. In Chopin's case, is it shyness or is it the desire to remind his admirers of Florian's fable *The Nightingle and the Sparrows*? The success of his last concert was such that only a philosopher could resist the temptation to keep repeating it as often as he could. Chopin's playing is invariably full of mercurial grace, refinement, and originality, while his compositions are second to none in their harmonic richness and melodic sweetness.

HECTOR BERLIOZ

La France Musicale, Paris, January 15, 1843

The salons have opened early this year and judging by the brilliant soirées given in the past week, the winter season promises to be full of delightful events. The first of the mansions to be lit up was that of M. de Rostchild [*sic*], the illustrious banking tycoon. Just look! Look at those glass portals, those regal tapestries, those magnificent paintings, those furnishings swathed in gold! On all sides there's a magical brilliance that overpowers you. It's like an incredible dream. Such fairy-tale luxury is within the realm of kings and princes alone. All of those women, glittering with beauty and wealth, just look at them, smiling blissfully. M. de Rostchild has brought the greatest artists of the world to play for them. Listen! There's Lablache. Do you hear him? And there's Mme. Grisi, the queen of songstresses. They're singing the duet from *Don Pasquale.* Then there's Mme. Pauline Viardot-Garcia, that superb young artist, offering you an aria by Balfe with such admirable expression followed by the duet from *Semiramide* with Mme. Grisi. Next we have Mario, that singer with such a seductive voice, who sighs like a poet as he renders the serenade from *Don Pasquale,* "Com'e gentil la notte a mezz' April." After that comes Chopin, the poetical pianist who, with M. Filtsch, performs a ravishing concerto of his own composition. Then we have Mme. Grisi once more, singing the delightful cavatina from *Don Pasquale*. Then . . . next . . . Ah! *Mon Dieu*! Here, let me give you the whole program of the evening so you can judge for yourself how satisfying it was and how worthy of applause: cavatina from *Don Pasquale* sung by Mme. Grisi; duet from *Semiramide* sung by Mesdames Grisi and Viardot; serenade from *Don Pasquale* sung by Mario; piano concerto performed by MM. Chopin and Filtsch; aria sung by Mme. Viardot; Romance by Schubert sung by Mario; duet from *Don Pasquale* sung by Mme. Grisi and M. Lablache; romances sung by Mme. Viardot; quartet from *Bianca e Faliero* sung by Mesdames Grisi and Viardot and MM. Mario and Lablache. The piano, a beautiful instrument by Pleyel, was played by Tadolini [to accompany the singers].

ESCUDIER

Revue et Gazette Musicale, Paris, February 20, 1848

A concert by the *Ariel* of pianists is something much too rare to be treated like any other concert where the doors are open to anyone who wants in. In this case a special list was drawn up. But even those on the list were not certain of getting one of the precious tickets. Only the favored few were admitted into the holy of holies to deposit their offering, which consisted of a mere louis. Surely there is no one who would not be able to find a louis somewhere in his purse when it is a matter of being able to listen to Chopin.

That being the case, it was only natural that Pleyel's rooms should have been filled on Wednesday with a select flowering of the most distinguished aristocratic ladies in the most elegant finery. In addition there was also present another aristocracy, that of artists and music lovers, all overjoyed to catch the flight of this musical sylph who had promised to let himself be seen and heard once more if only for a few hours.

The sylph has kept his promise and with what success, what enthusiasm! It is easier to recount the reception he received and the delirium he aroused than to describe, analyze, and reveal the mysteries of a performance that has no equal in our earthly realm. Even if we possessed that pen which traced the delightful marvels of Queen Mab (hardly bigger than the agate which gleams on the finger of an alderman) and her chariot drawn by her diaphanous steeds, it would still be impossible to give an accurate impression of such a talent—one so ideal it hardly seems to belong to the crass world of material things. To know Chopin is to understand him. Everyone who attended Wednesday's performance will attest to that.

The program began with a Trio by Mozart which Chopin, Alard, and Franchomme rendered in such a manner that one despairs of ever hearing it as well done again. Then Chopin played some études, preludes, mazurkas, and waltzes. Next he did his gorgeous Sonata with

Franchomme. Don't ask how all these varied masterpieces were presented. As we said at the beginning we won't attempt to describe the infinite nuances of an extraordinary genius who has such powers at his command. We will state only that his charm never ceased for an instant to hold his audience completely entranced and that its spell lingered after the concert itself was over.

Let us add that Roger, our brilliant tenor, sang with his most expressive voice the beautiful prayer inserted into *Robert le Diable* by the composer himself at the time of Mario's debut at the Opéra. In addition Mademoiselle Antonia de Mendi, the young and beautiful singer, aroused her share of bravos by a talent which has much promise for the future. . . .

Illustrated London News, London, May 20, 1848

Chopin's pianoforte playing before Her Majesty at Stafford House on Monday created a great sensation: Lablache, Mario and Tamburini sang the trio from Rossini's "Guillaume Tell" admirably: M. Benedict was the accompanist at this concert given by the Duke and Duchess of Sutherland to celebrate the christening of their infant daughter.

Illustrated London News, London, July 1, 1848

M. Chopin

This famous pianist, a Pole by birth, gave a matinée at the house of Mrs. Sartoris in Eaton Place on the 23rd ult. He had been a resident in Paris and has composed many charming pieces for the pianoforte. His school, both in composition and playing is perfectly original. There is a charm in his touch which is indescribable and has not been rivalled by any other executant of the present day. Although labouring for years under ill health, when he is at his instrument his poetic fancy is awakened and he plays with the greatest energy.

Athenaeum, London, July 1, 1848

It is not too much to say that, at a period when so many sources of pleasure appear to be exhausted,—when mechanical skill, too, has been carried to a point precluding the hope of much further discovery—M. Chopin gave his audience yesterday week an hour and a half of such musical enjoyment as only great beauty combined with great novelty can command. We have had by turns this great player and the other great composer,—we have been treated to the smooth, the splendid, the sentimental, the severe in style, upon the pianoforte, one after the other. M. Chopin has proved to us that the instrument is capable of yet another "mode"—one in which delicacy, picturesqueness, elegance and humour may be blended so as to produce that rare thing, a new delight. His treatment of the pianoforte is peculiar; and though we know that a system is not to be "explained in one word" we will mention a point or two so entirely novel that even the distant amateur may in part conceive how from such motions an original style of performance, and thence of composition must inevitably result. Whereas other pianists have proceeded on the intention of equalizing the power of the fingers, M. Chopin's plans are arranged so as to utilize their natural inequality of power,—and if carried out, provide varieties of expression not to be attained by those with whom evenness is the first excellence. Allied with this fancy are M. Chopin's peculiar mode of treating the scale and the shake, and his manner of sliding with one and the same finger from note to note, by way of producing a peculiar *legato,* and of passing the third finger over the fourth finger. All of these innovations are "art and part" of his music as properly rendered; and as enacted by himself, they charm by an ease and grace which, though superfine, are totally different from affectation. After the "hammer and tongs" work on the pianoforte to which we have of late years been accustomed, the delicacy of M. Chopin's tone and the elasticity of his passages are delicious to the ear. He makes a free use of *tempo rubato*; leaning about within his bars more than any player we recollect, but still subject to a presiding sentiment of measure such as presently habituates the ear to the liberties taken. In music not his own we happen to know that he can be as staid as a metronome; while his Mazurkas etc. lose half their characteristic wildness if played without a certain break and license,—impossible to imitate, but irresistible if the player at all feels the music. This we have always fancied while reading M. Chopin's works:—we are now sure of it after *hearing* him perform them himself.

The pieces which M. Chopin gave at his *Matinée* were *Notturni*—Studies—"La Berceuse" (a delicate and lulling dream with that most matter-of-fact substratum, a ground bass)—two *Mazurkas* and the two new Waltzes. Most of these might be called "gems" without misuse of the well-worn symbol. Yet if fantasy be allowed to characterize what is essentially fantastic, they are not so much gems as pearls—pearls in the changeful delicacy of their colour,—in the occasional irregularities of form, not destructive, however, of symmetry—pearls in their *not* being the products of health and strength. They will not displace and supersede other of our musical treasures, being different in tone and quality to any possessions we already enjoy; but inasmuch as Art is not final, nor Invention to be narrowed within the limits of experience, no musician, be he ever so straight-laced or severe—or vowed to his own school—can be indifferent to their exquisite and peculiar charm. It is to be hoped that M. Chopin will play again; and the next time some of his more developed compositions—such as Ballads, *Scherzi* etc. if not his *Sonatas* and *Concerti*. Few of his audience will be at all content by a single hearing.

Examiner, London, July 8, 1848

The sole performers, on the occasion of M. Chopin's first matinée were Chopin himself, with Mario, accompanied by that consummate musician, Signor Alary. The repose which arises from the certainty of hearing nothing disturbing or incongruous, or rather nothing but what is exquisite in its kind, was therefore complete. And what could at once contrast and assimilate more finely with Chopin's complicated and delicate harmonies, than Mario's purity and melodiousness of song? Of him it is unnecessary to say anything in London; but there is still need to call the attention of the public to the finished instrumentalist, in a capital where we cannot but hope that there is a greater number of hearers capable of sympathising with him than in any other city of Europe. . . .

M. Chopin played none but his own works. It is yet too soon to express our estimate of him as a composer. One thing we will say, which implies a good deal: he *is* a composer. His works are not mere exercises. . . . On the present occasion, the attention and deep interest of the audience were secured by the first piece, a Largo in G-Minor, introducing the Andante, Op. 22. . . . In the Berceuse there was a mysterious soothing, like moonlight, which prepared the way admirably for the coruscations of the Impromptu that followed. Perhaps there is no one who at all knows the works of Chopin, but knows and loves the Ballade in F Major, Op. 38. It opens with a tone repeated and swelled like a sound of nature—a breeze or a stream—out of which a song develops itself, as the witch of the Alps is shaped from the rainbow of the waterfall; but it still retains the character of a thing that grows up and is not made. It is short, simple, single; always fresh. In the last piece, this was set between the graceful whim of the Mazurka, first of Op. 5th, and the marvellous intertexture of an undulating Valse. At the close, the general feeling was of pure gratification for the audience, and of a complete success for the performer.

Chopin's style of execution is the result of the most steadfast following out of principle. As he does not seek to make the pianoforte do the work of a violin or of a drum, but of a piano; so he does not use the arm like a couple of levers connected by a ball joint, but like a human arm; nor the fingers like five little hammers of equal length and power, but like the unequal mutually-adjusted members of a human hand. "Continue the living organism into the dead machine; do not let the machine stiffen the live limb into a part of itself." Hence an entire system; of which possibly Monsieur Chopin may give us some future occasion to speak.

John Bull, London, July 8, 1848

M. Chopin, the celebrated pianist, gave a *Matinée Musicale* yesterday at the residence of the Earl of Falmouth in St. James's Square. He played a variety of his own compositions in which he displayed not only wonderful powers of execution, but that exquisite finish and refinement of style which distinguishes him from all other performers on his instrument. Madame Viardot Garcia and Mdlle. de Mendi increased the attraction of the entertainment by singing some charming pieces of Spanish national music. The room was filled by a most fashionable audience.

London Daily News, London, July 10, 1848

M. Chopin's Matinée Musical: This celebrated pianist and composer gave a performance on Friday at the residence of the Earl of Falmouth in St. James's Square, which, *more anglice,* was called a *matinée* though it began at four in the afternoon. There was a numerous and fashionable assemblage, who were delighted with the entertainment provided for them. M. Chopin performed an "Andante Sostenuto e Scherzo" from his opera 31, a selection from his celebrated studies, a "Nocturne et Berceuse" and several of his own preludes, mazurkas and waltzes. In these various pieces he showed very strikingly his original genius as a composer, and his transcendental powers as a performer. His music is as strongly marked with individual character as that of any master who has ever lived. It is highly finished, new in its harmonies, full of contrapuntal skill and ingenious contrivance; and yet we have never heard music which has so much the air of unpremeditated effusion. The performer seems to abandon himself to the impulses of his fancy and his feelings—to indulge in a reverie, and to pour out unconsciously, as it were, the thoughts and emotions which pass through his mind. We have never heard any public performance so remote from anything like exhibition or display. M. Chopin does not seek to astonish by loudness of sound or mechanical dexterity. He accomplishes enormous difficulties, but so quietly, so smoothly, and with such constant delicacy and refinement, that the listener is not sensible of their real magnitude. It is this exquisite delicacy, with the liquid mellowness of his tone and the pearly roundness of his passages of rapid articulation, which are the peculiar features of his execution, while his music is characterized by freedom of thought, varied expression, and a kind of romantic melancholy which seems the natural mood of the artist's mind. Mme. Viardot Garcia and her young relative Mdlle. de Mendi, sang several quaint and beautiful Spanish duets, to the great delight of the audience.

Athenaeum, London, July 15, 1848

M. Chopin's Second Matinée—Little is to be added to the general character of this charming and individual artist which we gave on a former occasion. But M. Chopin played better at his second than at his first *Matinée*—not with more delicacy (that could hardly be) but with more force and *brio*. Two among what may be called M. Chopin's more serious compositions were especially welcome to us—his *Scherzo* in B-flat minor and his Study in C-sharp minor. The former we have long admired for its quaintness, grace and remarkable variety,—though it is not guiltless of a needlessly crude and hazardous modulation or two;—the latter again is a masterpiece—original, expressive and grand. No individual genius, we are inclined to theorize, is one-sided—however fondly the public is apt to fasten upon one characteristic and disproportionately to foster its development; and if this crotchet be based on a sound harmony, M. Chopin could hardly be so intimately and exquisitely graceful as he is if he could not on occasion be also grandiose. At all events the remark is eminently illustrated by certain among his *Polonaises* (let us instance those in A and A-flat major), and by several of his Studies—that in C minor not forgotten, as well as the one which has here tempted us to generalize. The other attraction of M. Chopin's *Matinée* was the singing of Madame Viardot-Garcia; who besides her inimitable Spanish airs with Mdlle. de Mendi and her queerly piquant Mazurkas, gave the "Cenerentola" *rondo,* graced with great brilliancy,—and a song by Beethoven, "Ich denke dein". . . . No singer of our acquaintance could have given this fine composition so much vocal charm as Madame Viardot, whom increasing experience disposes us more and more to consider as the greatest artist of her time. . . .

Illustrated London News, London, July 15, 1848

M. Chopin—This celebrated pianist's *matinée musicale,* given at the residence of the Earl of Falmouth, St. James's Square, was fashionably attended. M. Chopin played andantes, scherzos, preludes, mazurkas and waltzes of his own composition, developing not only his original genius as a composer, but his novel and striking style as an executant. Ingenious contrivance and contrapuntal skill, richness of harmony, spontaneity of melody are exhibited in his inspirations whilst the charm of his touch and the fluency of his executive powers are indescribably attractive. The delight of the auditory was unbounded. Mme. Viardot and her cousin, Mdlle. de Mendi, sang their Spanish airs between the instrumental pieces with marvellous effect.

Manchester Courier, Manchester, August 30, 1848

. . . Mons. Chopin played in the first part, an andante and scherzo of his own composition. He has been known in this country for many years as a composer of refined taste and original genius of the French school, though deeply imbued with the German, but his music cannot be strictly traced to any particular school, as he is perfectly original, and not a copyist of any one. We can, with great sincerity, say that he delighted us. Though we did not discover in him the vigour of Thalberg, yet there was a chasteness and purity of style, a correctness of manipulation combined with a brilliancy of touch, and a delicate sensibility of expression which we never heard excelled. He played, in the second act, Nocturne, études et Bergeuse [*sic*], and elicited a rapturous encore. He did not however repeat any part, but treated the audience with what appeared to be a fragment of great beauty. . . . The concert, in consequence of the engagements announced, created much sensation, and the room was filled to overflowing by a most brilliant audience.

Manchester Examiner, Manchester, September 5, 1848

It was with the greatest difficulty that we could get a ticket for the concert, yesterday week, so great was the desire to hear Alboni. Indeed, we did not succeed till more than half the first part was over, and, consequently, cannot speak as to the merits previous to the performance of M. Chopin who had just commenced playing when we entered the room. This *artiste* does not quite come up to our idea of a first-rate pianist; it is true he plays very difficult music (provoking one almost to say with Dr. Johnson, "would that it were impossible!") with beautiful delicacy and precision of finger but there is no melody or meaning in it; you are continually wondering when he will begin something, and before you can resolve the question he comes to an end, leaving your ideas in a complete state of confusion as to the intention of the composer. We should like to have heard him play some classical *sonata* of Beethoven's, which we have no doubt he would, from his great delicacy of touch, be able to render admirably. It is a pity that performers of his ability think it incumbent on them to astonish rather than please their audiences with *concertos* written by themselves, apparently for the express purpose of cramming into them elaborate passages, chromatiques and next-to-impossible cadenzas, all of which have no beauty in themselves, but should only be sparingly used to relieve what would be otherwise, perhaps, too monotonous a concord of sweet sounds. He pleased us better in the second part. . . . The concert concluded shortly after ten.

Musical World, London, September 9, 1848

Music in Manchester: The concert given on Monday evening (August 28) by the directors attracted a very elegant and numerous assemblage of visitors. The causes of attraction were many. First there were the vocalists, of whom the chiefest was Mademoiselle Alboni, decidedly the greatest contralto that ever appeared in this country, and one of the greatest artists of the day; Signor Salvi, the celebrated tenor, who yields to none but Mario in celebrity; the Signora Corbari, an engaging and delightful singer, who has won no small degree of repute by her performances at the Royal Italian Opera in two seasons; and lastly, M. Chopin, the French-celebrated pianist and composer, who is a novelty in these parts.

The programme was brilliant if not unexceptional. Not to be hypercritical, it was a capital concert programme—and so the audience appeared to fancy, as the majority of the pieces were encored. . . .

. . . You must pardon me if I venture to say very little of Mons. Chopin's pianoforte playing. He neither surprised me, nor pleased me entirely. He certainly played with great finish—too much so, perhaps, and might have deserved the name of *finesse* rather—and his delicacy and expression are unmistakeable; but I missed the astonishing power of Leopold de Meyer, the vigour of Thalberg, the dash of Herz, or the grace of Sterndale Bennett. Notwithstanding, Mons. Chopin is assuredly a great pianist, and no one can hear him without receiving some amount of delectation. . . .

Manchester Guardian, Manchester, August 30, 1848

The concert of Monday evening was the most brilliant and interesting which the directors have given during the season; and there was a larger audience than we remember to have seen here since the celebrated Grisi and Alboni concert in September last.

Of course, the lustrous-eyed and liquid-voiced Alboni was the chief attraction of the concert. . . . With the more instrumental portion of the audience, Mons. Chopin was perhaps an equal feature of interest with Alboni, as he was preceded by a high musical reputation. Chopin appears to be about thirty years of age. He is very spare in frame, and there is an almost painful air of feebleness in his appearance and gait. This vanishes when he seats himself at the instrument, in which he seems for the time perfectly absorbed. Chopin's music and his style of performance partake of the same leading characteristics—refinement rather than vigour—subtle elaboration rather than simple comprehensiveness in composition—an elegant, rapid touch, rather than a firm nervous grasp of the instrument. Both his compositions and his playing appear to be the perfection of chamber music—fit to be associated with the most refined instrumental quartets and quartet-playing—but wanting breadth and obviousness of design and executive power to be effective in a large concert hall. These are our impressions from hearing Mons. Chopin for the first time on Monday evening. He was warmly applauded by many of the most accomplished amateurs in the town, and he received an encore in his last piece, a compliment thus accorded to each of the four London artistes who appeared at this concert. Several of the vocal pieces were accompanied by Mr. Osborne, an able composer and pianist.

Glasgow Herald, Glasgow, September 29, 1848

M. Chopin's Concert—On Wednesday, M. Chopin the great French pianist gave a *matinée musicale* in the Merchants' Hall under the patronage of the most distinguished ladies of the nobility and gentry of the West of Scotland. At half-past two P.M. when the concert was to commence a large concourse of carriages began to draw up in Hutcheson Street and the streets adjoining. The audience which was not large, was exceedingly distinguished. Of M. Chopin's performance and of the style of his compositions it is not easy to speak so as to be intelligible to unscientific musicians. His style is unique and his compositions are very frequently unintelligible from the strange and novel harmonies he introduces. In the pieces he gave on Wednesday, we were particularly struck with the eccentric and original manner in which he chose to adorn the subject. He frequently took for a theme a few notes which were little else than the common notes of the scale. Those who were present for the entertainment would observe this in the Nocturnes et Berceuse. This simple theme ran through the whole piece and he heaped on it the strangest series of harmonies, discords and modulations that can well be imagined. Again in another subject, one single note of the key was heard with its monotonous pulsations moving through just as peculiar a series of musical embellishments. One thing must have been apparent to every one of the audience, namely the melancholy and plaintive sentiment which pervaded his music. Indeed if we would choose to characterize his pieces in three words we would call them novel, pathetic and difficult to be understood. M. Chopin is evidently a man of weak constitution and seems labouring under physical debility and ill health. Perhaps his constitutional delicacy may account for the fact that his musical compositions have all that melancholy sentiment which we have spoken of. We incline to the belief that this master's compositions will always have a far greater charm when heard *en famille* than in the concert-room; at the same time we know that they possess certain technical peculiarities which must render them sealed treasures to by far the greatest number of amateur pianoforte performers. Madame Adelasio who sang three pleasing little vocal compositions—one by Niedermeyer and two by Guglielmo—showed much vocal ability. But she evinced a certain lack of enthusiasm with which we were not at all charmed. This was her first public appearance in Glasgow, probably, and we believe, she will gain in public estimation the oftener she is heard.

Glasgow Courier, Glasgow, September 28, 1848

M. Chopin's Concert—Yesterday, the distinguished pianist, assisted by Madame Giulietta Adelasio de Marguerittes, gave a matinée musicale, at half-past two o'clock, which was numerously attended by the beauty and fashion, indeed the very elite of our west end. The performance was certainly of the highest order in point of musical attainment and artistic skill and was completely successful in interesting and delighting everyone present for an hour and a half. Visited as we are now by the highest musical talent, by this great player and the other eminent composer, it must be difficult for each successive candidate for our patronage and applause, to produce in sufficient quantity that essential element to success—novelty; but M. Chopin has proved satisfactorily that it is not easy to estimate the capabilities of the instrument he handles, with so much grace and ingenuity, or limit the skill and power whose magic touch makes it pour forth its sublime strains to electrify and delight anew the astonished listener. M. Chopin's treatment of the piano-forte is peculiar to himself, and his style blends in beautiful harmony and perfection the elegant, the picturesque and the humorous. We cannot at present descend to particular illustrations in proof of these observations, but feel persuaded we only express the feelings of all who attended yesterday when we say that the pianist produces without extraordinary effort, not only pleasing but new musical delights. Madame Adelasio has a beautiful voice which she manages with great ease and occasional brilliancy. She sang several airs with much taste and great acceptance. We may mention that the pieces were all rapturously applauded, and the audience separated with expressions of the highest gratification.

Scotsman, Edinburgh, October 10, 1848

M. CHOPIN'S SOIREE MUSICALE—On Wednesday evening the Hopetoun Rooms were filled with company to hear this celebrated performer. Any pianist who undertakes to play alone to an audience for two hours, must, now-a-days, be a very remarkable one to succeed in sustaining attention and satisfying expectation. M. Chopin succeeded perfectly in both. He played his own music, which is that of a musician of genius. His manner of playing it was quite masterly in every respect. In his peculiar touch and manner of expression, he reminds us more of John B. Cramer than of any other pianist we have heard. . . . M.

Chopin's compositions have a peculiar charm, which, however, is only brought out by his own exquisite manner of playing them. We suspect that many of the salient points of melody in his compositions are reminiscences of the popular airs of Poland—of his own ill-fated land, and that the touching expression he gives to these arises from "feelings too deep for tears." The infinite delicacy and finish of his playing, combined with great occasional energy *never overdone,* is very striking when we contemplate the man—a slender and delicate-looking person, with a marked profile, indicating much intellectual energy.

Edinburgh Evening Courant, Edinburgh, October 7, 1848

Chopin's Soirée Musicale—This talented pianist gratified his admirers by a performance on Wednesday evening in the Hopetoun Rooms when a select and highly fashionable audience assembled to welcome him to this, his first appearance in Edinburgh. The first piece was an "Andante et Impromptu"; the opening movement being in three parts, with the theme standing out in alto relievo, as it were, from the maze of harmony with which it was surrounded. This was followed by his "Etudes" which had more the character of ideas flitting across the mind than of studies, and were strung together in the most airy and graceful manner imaginable being executed with that equality of touch and smoothness of style so peculiar to the performer. Among so much musical excellence, it would be difficult to judge, but to our taste, the most delightful performance of the whole was the "Nocturnes et Berceuse". The recurrent air in the minor key conveyed to the mind the idea of night with its silence and repose, while the introduced *motif* fell on the ear as a lullaby, the beautiful simplicity of the melody, with all its sleepy softness, prompting the idea of a cradle song. It was, indeed, a charming morceau, exquisite alike in its composition and its performance. The "Andante et Largo" were also very beautiful, introducing two Polish melodies, somewhat peculiar in style, yet very pleasing. That they went home to the hearts of such of the performer's compatriots as were present was evident from the delight with which they hailed each forgotten melody with all its early associations, as it rang in their ears. The concluding piece was also national, the ballad, reminding us somewhat of one of the choruses in Mendelssohn's "St. Paul", ("How lovely are the Messengers", we think) and consequently having less originality than the other; however the mazourkas which followed had that quality to a degree. There was a quaintness about them quite peculiar. . . . The waltz which followed came from the fingers of the performer with a crispness and sparkling brilliancy of style peculiar to himself. . . . Of his executions we need say nothing further than that it is the most finished we have ever heard. He has neither the ponderosity nor the digital power of a Mendelssohn, a Thalberg or a Liszt; consequently his execution would appear less effective in a large room; but as a chamber pianist he stands unrivalled. Notwithstanding the amount of musical entertainment already afforded the Edinburgh public this season, the rooms were filled with an audience who, by their judicious and well-timed applause, testified their appreciation of the high talent of Monsieur Chopin.

Caledonian Mercury, Edinburgh, October 12, 1848

Soirée Musicale—(from a correspondent)—In addition to the numerous matters of interest of which Edinburgh has been the scene during the past week [this review of Chopin's concert was wedged between accounts of the annual meeting of the London Missionary Society and an accident on the North British Railway], the fashionable world have [*sic*] been gratified by the performance of M. Chopin, the celebrated composer. This distinguished individual has for some weeks been resident in Scotland, and we trust that he has found amidst the magnificent scenery of the north, and the hospitality of the nobility and gentry, that repose for the exercise of his genius which the disturbed state of the Continent denies to men of the most peaceful habits and pursuits. We believe that his public appearances in Britain have been limited in number, we may therefore take it as a high compliment to the taste of the inhabitants of the Scottish metropolis, that he was induced to give a "Soirée Musicale" at the Hopetoun Rooms, on the evening of Wednesday last. It is by no means our intention to write an elaborate "critique" on the compositions of M. Chopin, or on his style of playing them. His name affords a sufficient guarantee for their interest and originality. Were we, however, asked to point out the distinguishing features of both, we should say that their great charm consisted in their reality, their utter want of all charlatanism and false pretention. His music is always the result of principle, his performances therefore are certain to be the development of the living genius within. He never attempts to make the piano do that for which it was not intended, but arrests the attention and interests the sympathy of his audience by the purity of his music, and the simplicity and power of his execution. To any person of common discernment it is evident that M. Chopin's talent cannot be confined to any one accomplishment, and of him it may be fairly said that the mind from which such music proceeds is more interesting than even the music itself. We most heartily congratulate the admirers of music in general on the opportunity which has been afforded them of rendering homage to one so distinguished by his amiable deportment and high genius. The piano M. Chopin played on was one of Broadwood's finest toned instruments.

Edinburgh Advertiser, Edinburgh, October 6, 1848

M. Chopin's Soirée Musicale—This eminent Pianiste gave a "Soirée Musicale" on Wednesday evening in the Hopetoun Rooms and we have rarely seen such a display of rank and beauty congregated at a similar entertainment. Most of the *elite* of our Edinburgh society were present as well as a considerable sprinkling of strangers. This speaks volumes for the increase of musical taste amongst us. The performances of M. Chopin are of the most refined description; nothing can equal the delicacy of his tone, or rival the lightness of his passages. They fall most deliciously on the ear accustomed to the "hammer and tongs" work of the modern school. Our limits will not admit of our entering into any lengthened description of his system, but we may mention that, while all other pianistes strive to equalize the power of the fingers, M. Chopin aims to utilize them; and, in accordance with this idea are his treatment of the scale and the shake, as well as his mode of sliding with one and the same finger, from note to note, and of passing the third over the fourth finger. The gem of the performance, in our opinion, was the Berceuse, although the most popular were the Mazourkas and Valses, with which M. Chopin concluded one of the most delightful musical evenings we have ever spent.

Musical World, London, October 14, 1848

Chopin at Edinburgh—FREDERICK CHOPIN, the eminent pianist and composer, who has been staying for a short time in Scotland, gave the musical public in Edinburgh an opportunity of hearing him play a selection of his own compositions at the Hopetoun Rooms on Wednesday evening. The attention and delight with which M. Chopin's performance was listened to by a brilliant and judicious audience may be taken as proof that his talent is properly appreciated here. The selection included an *Etude* in F minor, Mazurkas, a Ballad, Berceuse, Grand Valse and other *morceaux*. These named were encored. So much has been written about the peculiar beauty of Chopin's playing, that any additional praise from this part of the world can hardly be necessary. It may be sufficient to say, that the exquisite delicacy of his touch and the consequent beauty of tone, and the perfectly finished manner in which every passage is played can scarcely be surpassed. . . .

M.

Illustrated London News, London, November 18, 1848

The Annual Grand Dress and Fancy Ball and Concert in aid of the funds of the Literary Association of the Friends of Poland was held at Guildhall on Thursday: and in spite of the strong, and we might say uncharitable remarks of our contemporaries upon the subject, we were pleased to observe that the attendance on Thursday was not inferior to the average of that on former occasions.[16] Amongst those who were early in the Hall were observed the Lord and Lady Mayoress.

The elegant decorations with which the hall was fitted up for Lord Mayor's Day were retained for the present occasion: and the vast apartment when brilliantly lighted, presented a "coup d'oeil" of singular beauty.

The concert was conducted by Mr. Benedict and Mr. Lindsay Sloper, who, as well as all the other performers, generously volunteered their gratuitous services. Among the vocalists who came forward on this occasion to offer their aid were Miss Poole, Mrs. Weiss, Miss Bassaro, Miss Ramsford, Miss Messent, Misses A. and M. Williams,

Miss Dolby, and Miss Miron; Mr. Sim Reeves, Mr. W. H. Harrison and Mr. Charles Braham, Mr. Whitworth, Mr. Weiss, Signor Burdini, Mr. Williams and Mr. Frank Bodda.

Mr. Chopin, the celebrated pianiste, was also present, and performed some of his beautiful compositions with much applause.

The dancing commenced soon after 9 o'clock, and was continued with unabated vigour till an advanced hour in the morning. The refreshments were furnished on a very elegant scale by Messers. Younghusband and Son of Basing Lane.

NOTES

Preface

1. Chopin may have had some aristocratic blood from his mother, who is said to have been a distant cousin of the Skarbek family, Polish counts from the district of Mazovia.

2. Franz Liszt, *Frédéric Chopin,* p. 84.

3. *Ibid.*, p. 84.

1. Żelazowa Wola and Warsaw, 1810–1818

1. Nicholas Chopin was born in the French province of Lorraine and came to Poland at the end of the eighteenth century. In deference to his adopted country he often spelled his family name according to Polish phonetics, i.e., "Szopę."

2. Żywny, although a Czech, grew up in the Austrian Empire, hence his "Teutonic tastes."

3. Krystyna Kobylańska, *Chopin in His Own Land,* p. 41.

4. The so-called Kingdom of Poland was actually nothing but a puppet state assigned to Czar Alexander I by the Congress of Vienna in 1815.

5. Despite his antipathy toward the Poles, Constantine fell in love with a Polish commoner and married her. Because of this he forfeited his right to the Russian throne.

6. Henri Troyat, *Alexander of Russia: Napoleon's Conqueror,* p. 283.

7. The Belvedere Palace once belonged to a former king of Poland, Augustus II, who happened to be an ancestor of Chopin's subsequent mistress, George Sand.

2. Warsaw and Bad Reinerz, 1818–1828

1. Krystyna Kobylańska, *Chopin in His Own Land,* p. 46.

2. *Allgemeine Musikalische Zeitung,* June 15, 1825.

3. When Chopin published this work in 1831, he dedicated it to the German cellist Josef Merk rather than Kaczyński.

4. The new school, officially known as the Institute of Music and Declamation, eventually became a part of the Royal University of Warsaw.

2. WARSAW AND BAD REINERZ, 1818–1828

5. Kobylańska, *Chopin in His Own Land,* p. 61.

6. Ibid.

7. Kobylańska thinks that Chopin may have also played again at a Charitable Society concert on March 17, 1823. *Ibid.*

8. The Kazimierzowski Palace in which the Lyceum was located consisted of a central building with two detached wings. The Chopins' apartment was in the south wing.

9. The tiny Kingdom of Poland which emerged from the Congress of Vienna was a constitutional government in name only.

10. Kobylańska, *Chopin in His Own Land,* p. 105.

11. *Ibid.*

12. The life of the Conservatory was brief. It survived only nine years before being shut down during the uprising of 1830. For a while the buildings served as barracks and later as a theater. In their last days they housed a small zoo before being torn down in 1843 to make way for a viaduct on the new east-west throughway.

13. Kobylańska, *Chopin in His Own Land,* p. 102.

14. *Ibid.*

15. The first musical score ever based on Goethe's *Faust* was written by Prince Radzwiłł.

16. *Allgemeine Musikalische Zeitung,* November 16, 1825, no. 46.

17. *Kurjer Warszawski,* May 28, 1825.

18. F. J. Fétis, *Biographie universelle des musiciens,* p. 406 (under "Bianchi, Eliodoro").

19. *Allgemeine Musikalische Zeitung,* November 16, 1825, no. 46.

20. *Ibid.*, March 1, 1826, no. 9.

21. *Ibid.*, November 16, 1825, no. 46.

22. The concert of June 10 opened with Mozart's overture to *The Magic Flute* rather than Nowakowski's "Rossini-styled" one and included the following works not on the previous program: a Rondo à la Polacca by Bernard Romberg, performed by the cellist von Molsdorf, a Rossini aria sung by Mme. Wernicke, and a bass viol solo executed by an unnamed amateur.

23. With the change of political boundaries the spa now lies in southwestern Poland and is called Duszniki Zdrój.

24. The warm spring today bears Chopin's name.

25. Wanda Tomaszewska, "Chopin w Dusznikach," p. 93.

26. The Chopins actually spent their first six days in a hotel and didn't move into Bürgel's house until August 9.

27. Today Duszniki's main promenade between the spa and the town is called Avenue Fryderyk Chopin.

28. Frédéric Chopin, *Correspondance de Frédéric Chopin,* 1:65.

29. The spa's little theater, with a seating capacity of around 270, is today the site of an annual Chopin Festival held every August in Duszniki Zdrój.

30. The accuracy of these dates is open to some question.

31. Wiktor Zielony, *Polanica Zdrój,* p. 22. While Chopin had finished a funeral march (in C minor) by 1827, there is no record that he composed any études at that time.

32. Julius Bloschke, "Chopin in Bad Reinerz," p. 211.

33. *Kurjer Warszawski,* August 22, 1826.

34. Chopin, *Correspondance,* 1:65.

3. Vienna, 1829

1. Because of a feud between Elsner and Carlo Soliva, head of the vocal department, the Conservatory had been split into two administrative departments.

2. Würfel probably gave Chopin some piano lessons also, since Elsner was weak in keyboard technique.

3. Robert Schumann, *On Music and Musicians,* p. 126.

4. Frédéric Chopin, *Correspondance de Frédéric Chopin,* 1:100.

5. *Ibid.*, 1:102.

6. Earlier Haslinger had also exploited Schubert by paying him only a pittance (one florin apiece) for many of his songs.

7. The other "imperial and royal" theater was the Burg Theater in Michaelerplatz at the entrance to the Hapsburgs' Vienna residence, the Hofburg.

8. Today the Hotel Sacher occupies the site of the old Kärnthnerthor Theater, while the Vienna Opera stands on the ground where the bridge from the Kärnthner gate once spanned the former moat.

9. *Allgemeine Theaterzeitung,* August 20, 1829.

10. Therese, who was "indisposed" on the night of Chopin's concert, gave birth the next month to a child, presumably by Gallenberg.

11. Fanny's real name was Franziska. Both her father and her grandfather had been employed by the composer Josef Haydn as house steward and valet respectively.

12. The Duke of Reichstadt or the king of Rome (also known as L'Aiglon) was the son of Napoleon by his second wife, Marie Louise. His maternal grandfather, the Austrian Emperor Franz, was still reigning in 1829.

13. This is a corrected program and not the one printed up for the audience that night. The latter showed Chopin's Rondo following the Beethoven overture and his Mozart Variations coming after the Rossini aria by Fräulein Veltheim.

14. More people probably came later just to see the ballet.

15. One of Chopin's schoolmates who accompanied him to Vienna.

16. The lawyer who chaperoned Chopin and his friends to Vienna.

17. Chopin, *Correspondance,* 1:107.

18. *Allgemeine Theaterzeitung,* August 20, 1829.

19. *Der Sammler,* August 29, 1829.

20. *Wiener Zeitschrift für Kunst, Literatur, Theater, und Mode,* August 22, 1829.

21. *Der Sammler,* August 29, 1829.

22. Chopin, *Correspondance,* 1:107.

23. *Allgemeine Theaterzeitung,* August 20, 1829.

24. *Gazeta Warszawska,* August 30, 1829.

25. Thalberg claimed to be the illegitimate son of Dietrichstein and the Baroness von Wetzler. Whether he was or wasn't is still a moot question.

26. Chopin didn't take Count Lichnowsky's offer. Instead he used another Graf piano for his second concert.

27. Chopin, *Correspondance,* 1:110.

28. The conductor was Franz Lachner (1803–1890), a close friend of Franz Schubert.

29. Chopin, *Correspondance,* 1:111.

30. *Wiener Zeitschrift für Kunst, Literatur, Theater, und Mode,* August 29, 1829.

31. *Allgemeine Musikalische Zeitung,* November 18, 1829.

32. *Allgemeine Theaterzeitung,* September 1, 1829.

33. *Wiener Zeitschrift für Kunst, Literatur, Theater, und Mode,* August 29, 1829.

4. Warsaw, 1829–1830

1. Prince Clary's mother was related to the Potockis in Warsaw, which is how Chopin gained an introduction to the family.

2. Frédéric Chopin, *Correspondance de Frédéric Chopin,* 1:131.

3. This was the Piano Concerto in F minor, which has come to be known as Chopin's "second" concerto since it was not published until after its successor, the so-called Concerto No. 1 in E minor.

4. Alexander Kraushar, *Resursa Kupiecka w Warszawie,* p. 7.

5. Today the Zajdler (Sedler or Seidler) Palace, also known as the Młodziejowski, Morsztyn, or Igelström Palace, houses the Polish Scientific Publishing firm.

6. In a letter to Tytus Woyciechowski on November 14, 1829, Chopin mentions the possibility of playing the Variations (which, incidentally, were dedicated to Tytus) in the Resursa on November 21.

7. *Kurjer Polski,* December 20, 1829.

8. *Kurjer Warszawski,* December 23, 1829.

9. The middle section of Chopin's first Scherzo is an adaptation of the Polish Christmas carol "Lulajże, Jezuniu."

10. *Gazeta Polska,* February 12, 1830, quoted in Krystyna Kobylańska, *Chopin in His Own Land,* p. 240.

11. Besides his concerto Chopin also played one of his earlier compositions, the Grand Fantasy on Polish Airs for piano and orchestra, while Kurpiński conducted several of his own works.

12. *Kurjer Warszawski,* March 5, 1830.

13. *Powszechny Dziennik Krajowy,* March 4, 1830, quoted in Kobylańska, *Chopin in His Own Land,* p. 240.

14. In November of 1830 the theater was closed down as a result of the uprising that took place in Warsaw then. In 1833 it moved into a wing of the newly built Grand Theater on Senatorska Street.

15. The marking "Adagio" was subsequently changed to "Larghetto" when the concerto was published in 1836.

16. Chopin brought his own piano from home for the concert.

17. *Pamiętnik dla Płci Pięknej* (1830), year 1, 2:46.

18. *Gazeta Warszawska,* March 18, 1830.

19. *Dekameron Polski,* March 31, 1830.

20. *Powszechny Dziennik Krajowy,* March 19, 1830, quoted in Kobylańska, *Chopin in His Own Land,* p. 243.

21. Chopin, *Correspondance,* 1:146.

22. *Powszechny Dziennik Krajowy,* March 19, 1830, quoted in Kobylańska, *Chopin in His Own Land,* p. 243.

23. This *Air Varié,* the only non-Polish work on the program, was written by Charles Auguste de Bériot (1802–1870), the Belgian violinist and composer who married the famous singer La Malibran in 1836.

24. Chopin, *Correspondance,* 1:147.

25. *Kurjer Polski,* March 24, 1830.

26. *Kurjer Warszawski,* March 23, 1830.

27. *Powszechny Dziennik Krajowy,* March 25, 1830, quoted in Kobylańska, *Chopin in His Own Land,* p. 245.

28. Chopin, *Correspondance,* 1:152.

29. *Pamiętnik dla Płci Pięknej* (1830), year 1, 2:59, and *Kurjer Warszawski,* April 17, 1830.

30. Chopin, *Correspondance,* 1:158.

31. *Ibid.*

32. *Ibid.*, 1:148.

33. *Ibid.*, 1:172.

34. *Ibid.*, 1:185.

35. *Ibid.*, 1:198.

36. *Kurjer Warszawski,* September 23, 1830.

37. *Powszechny Dziennik Krajowy,* September 24, 1830, quoted in Kobylańska, *Chopin in His Own Land,* p. 249.

38. While Chopin thought the theater looked full, the critic for the *Kurjer Warszawski* estimated the crowd at 700, i.e., about 200 less than at his March 22 concert.

39. Chopin, *Correspondance,* 1:207.

40. *Ibid.*

41. *Ibid.*, 1:208.

42. "O, quante lagrime per te versai."

43. Chopin, *Correspondance,* 1:208.

44. *Kurjer Warszawski,* October 12, 1830.

5. Breslau, Vienna, and Munich, 1830–1831

1. Frédéric Chopin, *Correspondance de Frédéric Chopin,* 1:204.

2. *Ibid.*, 1:210.

3. It came as a great surprise to Konstancja many years later to learn how much Chopin had adored her. By then she had given up her singing career and was happily married. Unfortunately she went blind at an early age.

4. Today the city is again Polish and called Wrocław.

5. Another of Raimund's works had been the basis of *The Millionaire Peasant,* the musical comedy on which Chopin improvised eleven months earlier at the Warsaw Resursa.

6. Chopin, *Correspondance,* 1:211.

7. *Ibid.*, 1:213.

8. *Ibid.*, 1:212.

9. *Ibid.*, 1:214.

10. The six requiems included ones by Mozart, Cherubini, Winter, Jomelli, Lauchery, and Schnabel himself. H. Feicht, "Chopin we Wrocławiu," p. 13.

11. Chopin, *Correspondance,* 1:217.

12. Later, after Tytus returned to Poland, Chopin moved up to the floor above in order to economize still further. Today a plaque marks the site of this building at No. 9 Kohlmarkt, just across from the popular Demel's Café.

13. Chopin, *Correspondance,* 1:224.

14. *Ibid.*, 1:229.

15. The Redoutensaal was divided into a large and a small auditorium. Which one Mme. Garcia-Vestris used is uncertain.

16. Franz Wild (1792–1860) had just come back to Vienna in 1829 after studying opera with Rossini in Paris.

17. Sabine Heinefetter (1809–1872) and her two sisters, Klara (1816–1857) and Kathinka (1820–1858), were an outstanding trio of singers in the early nineteenth century. Sabine, who was the most gifted of the three, studied under Tadolini and was a protegée of Spohr.

18. Chopin, *Correspondance,* 1:250.

19. *Ibid.*, 1:263.

20. Wagner wasn't particularly pleased with Tichatschek's performances and didn't use him in his later operas.

21. Ivor Guest, *Fanny Elssler,* p. 40.

22. *Allgemeine Theaterzeitung,* June 18, 1831.

23. Chopin, *Correspondance,* 1:258.

24. Chopin had a letter of introduction to Salomon Rothschild in Vienna but doesn't seem to have taken advantage of it.

25. Felix Schiller, *Munich: Its Treasures of Art and Science, Manners and Customs,* p. 175.

26. *Ibid.*

27. This handsome building was destroyed by the RAF on the night of April 25, 1944. However, it was restored after the war and now houses the Ministry of the Interior.

28. *Flora: A Journal of Entertainment,* August 25, 1831.

29. *Ibid.*, August 30, 1831.

6. Paris, 1831–1832

1. The possibility of offering the crown of Poland to a Hapsburg archduke was considered briefly to gain Austrian support.

2. In his despair Chopin is also reputed to have written his "Revolutionary" Étude (op. 10, no. 12, in C minor) at this time.

3. Chopin's anger at the French failed to alter his determination to continue on to Paris.

4. Frédéric Chopin, *Correspondance de Frédéric Chopin,* 2:40.

5. *Ibid.*, 2:17.

6. In 1833, when Chopin published his E minor concerto, he dedicated it to Kalkbrenner in gratitude for the kindness he had shown him during those first difficult months in a strange city.

7. Chopin, *Correspondance,* 2:43.

8. *Ibid.*, 2:61.

9. *Ibid.*, 2:44.

10. *Ibid.*, 2:61. Sowiński, who once studied with Czerny, was probably a much better pianist than portrayed by these harsh words. He sincerely admired Chopin and dedicated his Duo for piano and violin to him.

11. The Quintet in C major, op. 29, for two violins, two violas, and cello.

12. The Tilmant quartet finally broke up during the revolution of 1848.

13. Brod's name was often spelled Brodt.

14. Dr. Véron was a physician of sorts and a capitalist par excellence who made a fortune manufacturing patent medicines before he entered the musical world.

15. *Revue et Gazette Musicale,* February 17, 1836.

16. The reason why Mendelssohn didn't appear on the program is unknown, but it may have had to do with the death of his close friend the violinist Edouard Rietz, on January 23, 1832.

17. Mendelssohn's presence would indicate that it wasn't illness, travel, or prior commitments that prevented him from being on the program.

18. Kalkbrenner probably played the orchestral part for both the concerto and the Mozart Variations on a second piano.

19. Ernest Boulanger also sang but was not listed on the program.

20. Arthur Hedley, *Chopin,* p. 48.

21. Franz Liszt, *Frédéric Chopin,* p. 147.

22. *Revue Musicale,* March 3, 1832.

23. *Ibid.*

24. *Ibid.*

25. Chopin, *Correspondance,* 2:68. One of the orchestra's assistant conductors was Chopin's new friend the violinist Théophile Tilmant.

26. *Ibid.*, 2:66.

27. *Ibid.*, 2:64.

28. *Ibid.*, 2:67.

29. *Ibid.*, 2:70.

30. George Sand, *Correspondance,* 2:73n., quoted from *Histoire de ma vie.*

31. *Ibid.*

32. Paganini earned nearly 10,000 francs from this concert, all of which he turned over to victims of the cholera.

33. Besides the salons of the wealthy Polish émigrés, Chopin also frequented the British embassy where he acquired several pupils from the English colony in Paris.

34. *Revue Musicale,* May 26, 1832.

35. *Ibid.*

7. Paris, 1833

1. *Journal des Débats,* May 23, 1832.

2. Robert Schumann, *On Music and Musicians,* p. 81.

3. Prince Walenty was the younger brother of Prince Antoni Radziwiłł.

4. Frédéric Chopin, *Correspondance de Frédéric Chopin,* 2:83.

5. *Ibid.*, 2:85.

6. *Ibid.*, 2:43.

7. Today the "poetry, fire, and spirit" seem to have gone out of Hiller's works, which are seldom performed anymore.

8. This duo was based on themes from Meyerbeer's *Robert le Diable.*

9. Galignani, *Picture of Paris,* p. 280. London also had a Vauxhall Gardens, while Paris, for a time, had a second pleasure park located in the Bois de Boulogne, called the "Ranelagh."

10. *Revue Musicale,* June 30, 1832.

11. The Concerto No. 5, op. 73 (*Emperor*).

12. *Revue Musicale,* March 16, 1833.

13. Amédée Méreaux, *Variétés littéraires et musicales* (quoted in the introduction by Antoine François Marmontel), p. 3.

14. According to Marmontel, Méreaux and Chopin played the duo in public "several times" (Méreaux, *Variétés,* p. 3), but I can find no documentation of this other than the present concert.

15. In 1820 Mme. Catalani gave the ten-year-old Chopin a gold watch on one of her concert tours in Warsaw.

16. Chopin, *Correspondance,* 2:46.

17. Charles Hervey, *The Theatres of Paris,* p. 18.

18. *Le Charivari,* June 6, 1838.

19. Under Louis-Napoléon the rue de Rivoli was extended further east, past the Hôtel de Ville to the rue de Sevigne. At that time the house numbers on the street were changed so that today's No. 18 rue de Rivoli lies far east of the building where Méreaux's concert was given.

7. PARIS, 1833

20. In Paris at this time there were two horn players named Mengal: Martin-Joseph and his younger brother Jean. The latter was first horn soloist at the Paris Opéra and a member of the orchestra of the Société des Concerts.

21. For the next two years Fétis' son Edouard took over the management of the *Revue Musicale* until it merged with Maurice Schlesinger's *Gazette Musicale* in 1835.

22. Hector Berlioz, *The Memoirs of Hector Berlioz,* p. 95.

23. *Ibid.*, p. 98.

24. Berlioz later took evening courses in English and became reasonably fluent in the language.

25. Berlioz, *Memoirs,* p. 220.

26. Mlle. Duchenois' real name was Catherine Rafuin.

27. Léon Guichard, *La musique et les lettres au temps du romantisme,* p. 69.

28. *Revue et Gazette Musicale,* June 1, 1845.

29. *Ibid.*, April 20, 1845.

30. Chopin, who could never be considered rich at any time in his life, eventually earned up to 100 francs a day for his teaching; 300 francs, therefore, was a rather paltry nest egg.

31. Berlioz, *Memoirs,* p. 222.

32. Adolphe Boschot, *Un romantique sous Louis-Philippe: Hector Berlioz, 1831–1842,* 2:208. "Trilby" here does not refer to Du Maurier's famous heroine (his novel wasn't published until 1894) but to the hero of Charles Nodier's 1822 novelette, also entitled *Trilby.* This Trilby was a male spirit who befriended a fisherman and performed all sorts of tasks for his lovely wife.

33. Herz's sentimental salon pieces were such a sensation in their time that he was able to demand—and get—four times the price per page asked by other composers.

34. The actual directors of *La France Musicale* were the Escudier brothers, Léon and Marie.

35. On one of his programs Herz considered having forty pianos perform simultaneously, but this idea collapsed under its own weight.

36. The review in *L'Europe Littéraire* (April 12, 1833) indicates that Herz's concert took place on April 10. However, *Le Charivari* states, on April 6, that it had already occurred "avant-hier" which would put it on April 4. If we take the liberty of assuming the critic was writing the day before the journal went to press we come up with the date of April 3, which coincides with the dates mentioned in *L'Europe Littéraire* (April 3, 1833), the *Revue de Paris* (March 1833, 48:351), and *Le Charivari* (March 30, 1833).

37. Charming, well-dressed ladies, the reviewer went on to point out, were a "most essential element to the success of such occasions, which perceptive virtuosos would do well to recognize." *L'Europe Littéraire,* April 12, 1833.

38. Giulio Marco Bordogni, 1788–1856, a tenor at the Théâtre-Italien from 1819 to 1833 and later a professor at the Conservatory.

39. A pupil of the renowned Manuel Garcia.

40. A pupil of Tamburini.

41. *Illustrated London News,* May 13, 1848.

42. The following is an incomplete list of the works performed without regard to their order:

Fantasy on the march from *Otello* by Rossini, performed by Henri Herz

Duo for 8 hands based on the chorus of conspirators from *Il Crociato in Egitto* by Meyerbeer, performed by Henri and Jacques Herz, Liszt, and Chopin

A Concerto by Henri Herz, performed by the composer

Trio from *L'Inganno Fortunato* by Donizetti, performed by Mme. Tadolini and MM. Bordogni and Géraldi

Trumpet solo based on a cavatina by Bellini, performed by M. Gambati

Violin Fantasy based on an aria by Auber, performed by M. Hauman

Violin solo: Romance by M. Lambert, performed by M. Hauman

Aria from *Chiara di Rosemberg* by Luigi Ricci, performed by Mme. Boucaulx

The *Journal des Débats* (April 1, 1833) states that the oboist Henri Brod and the baritone Francesco Graziani were also on the program, but their performances as well as a solo by Mme. Vigano were dismissed by *L'Europe Littéraire* as adding little to the occasion.

43. *L'Europe Littéraire,* April 12, 1833, 1:79.

44. George Sand, Chopin's later mistress, first met her husband, the Baron Casimir Dudevant, at the Café Tortoni.

45. *Revue de Paris* (1835), 15:115.

46. The banker Laffitte (father-in-law of the prince de la Moskowa) began his career at Perregaux's bank on the corner next to Chopin's apartment.

47. Hoffmann eventually married one of Chopin's pupils, Emilia Borzęcka.

48. Pixis' hopes of marrying his charge never materialized.

49. As evidence of their friendship Pixis dedicated his Variations for a Military Band to Chopin in 1833, while the latter reciprocated by dedicating his Grand Fantasy on Polish Airs to Pixis in 1834.

50. "Si m'abandoni."

51. An Air and Variations of his own composition.

52. The orchestral portion was conducted by François-Antoine Habeneck.

53. *Revue Musicale,* December 21, 1833.

8. Paris, 1834–1835

1. Frédéric Chopin, *Correspondance de Frédéric Chopin,* 2:127.

2. In 1842 Chopin dedicated his Polonaise in A-flat, op. 53, to Auguste Léo and his Ballade in F minor, op. 52, and his Waltz in C-sharp minor, op. 64, to Baroness Nathaniel Rothschild (James' daughter Charlotte). In 1838 he honored Mlle. A. d'Eichthal with the dedication of his Waltz in F major, op. 34, no. 3.

3. This waltz was actually written three years earlier, in 1831.

8. PARIS, 1834–1835

4. Schlesinger was so furious at Chopin for dealing with Pleyel he bought the waltz back from his competitor and published it himself.

5. Berlioz himself was an editor on the *Gazette Musicale* at that time.

6. *Gazette Musicale,* December 7, 1834.

7. The advance programs published in the *Gazette Musicale* and *Le Ménestrel* state that Mlle. Boucaulx and Mme. Gay-Saintville sang arias, but the singers mentioned in the *Gazette Musicale*'s review are M. Boulanger and Mlle. Heinefetter. According to *Le National* (December 5, 1834), "un grand air" from Berlioz's *Sardanapale* was to be performed. This may have been the aria sung by Mlle. Heinefetter.

8. *Gazette Musicale,* December 28, 1834.

9. *Ibid.*

10. Hector Berlioz, *The Memoirs of Hector Berlioz,* p. 436.

11. Eugène Delacroix, *The Journal of Eugène Delacroix,* p. 96.

12. The Hôtel de Gèvres, a veritable cultural emporium, also housed the Athenée des Familles, which gave courses in literature, languages, science, commerce, and the fine arts.

13. *Revue et Gazette Musicale,* January 15, 1837.

14. François-Joseph Fétis, *Biographie universelle des musiciens.*

15. *Revue et Gazette Musicale,* January 15, 1837.

16. *Revue de Paris* (1835), 15:216.

17. *Gazette Musicale,* December 28, 1834.

18. This duo was based on a theme by Mendelssohn. Liszt's arrangement of it was never published and has since disappeared. At Stoepel's concert the Liszt Duo and the Moscheles Duet (No. 7 on the program) were actually reversed.

19. Liszt provided the piano accompaniment for Ernst's solo.

20. *Gazette Musicale,* December 28, 1834.

21. *Ibid.*

22. Liszt and Franchomme also resigned from the Chantereine Society at the same time. Their joint action may well have been a late repercussion of the Herz-Schlesinger lawsuit. Henri Herz was an active member of the society, while Chopin and Liszt had served as witnesses against him in the trial.

23. Over the years Chopin gradually lost his squeamishness in money matters and became a tough, hard-boiled businessman when it came to dealing with his publishers.

24. Herz's repetition mechanism (mentioned earlier in this book) was a further development of Érard's device.

25. *Revue de Paris* (1835), 15:346.

26. Mme. Dorus-Gras (née Julie-Aimée-Josephe Van Steenkiste) sang for years under her mother's maiden name of Dorus until her marriage to M. Gras, a violinist in the Opéra orchestra.

27. *Revue Musicale,* March 8, 1835.

28. At his Edinburgh concert in 1848 Chopin was not only the sole composer but the sole performer on the program.

29. Chopin, *Correspondance,* 2:48.

8. PARIS, 1834–1835

30. Berlioz had been engaged to Mlle. Moke prior to marrying Harriet Smithson.

31. *Revue de Paris* (1840), 14:147.

32. *Le Ménestrel* of March 22, 1835, states that Reicha took part in the program, although it doesn't say specifically in what capacity.

33. Chopin, *Correspondance,* 2:53.

34. *Gazette Musicale,* March 29, 1835.

35. Mme. Émile de Girardin, née Delphine Gay (1804–1855), was the daughter of Sophie Gay (1776–1852). Both women were writers of fiction and contributors to the Paris journal *La Presse,* which had been founded by Mme. de Girardin's husband.

36. *Gazette Musicale,* March 29, 1835.

37. *Le National,* March 28, 1835.

38. *Journal des Débats,* April 6, 1835.

39. Mlle. Falcon's debut was in 1832. She was therefore not part of the opera's original 1831 cast, which so impressed Chopin on his arrival in Paris.

40. Charles Hervey, *The Theatres of Paris,* p. 19.

41. Other composers like Halévy, Auber, and Rossini also wrote operas for Nourrit. Among those by Rossini were *The Siege of Corinth, Count Ory, Moses,* and the classic favorite, *William Tell.*

42. Garcia's daughters Maria (La Malibran) and Pauline Viardot-Garcia became two of the most celebrated singers of Europe.

43. The Théâtre-Italien was located on the site of today's Opéra-Comique.

44. Favart and his wife, Mlle. Chantilly, were once part of a theatrical company maintained by the maréchal de Saxe, an ancestor of Chopin's later mistress, George Sand.

45. The order of the program is not exact. In all probability one of the overtures opened the concert and the other closed it.

46. *Gazette Musicale,* April 12, 1835.

47. Berlioz, *Memoirs,* p. 106.

48. The *Gazette Musicale* of April 26, 1835, stated that Nourrit was to sing an aria from *La Juive.*

49. *Gazette Musicale,* April 26, 1835.

9. Paris, 1836

1. Karlsbad in 1835 was part of the Austrian Empire. Today it belongs to Czechoslovakia and is called Karlovy Vary.

2. M. Meurice was probably the owner of the famous Hôtel Meurice on the rue de Rivoli.

3. Late in 1835 Fétis' *Revue Musicale* merged with Schlesinger's *Gazette Musicale* to form the *Revue et Gazette Musicale.*

4. *Revue et Gazette Musicale,* February 14, 1836.

5. Besides being a journalist and writer of fiction, Mme. Gay was also a musician and composer who wrote words and music for a number of songs.

6. *Revue et Gazette Musicale,* February 14, 1836.

7. When performing four-hand music Chopin almost always insisted on taking the bass part.

8. *Revue et Gazette Musicale,* February 14, 1836.

9. *Ibid.*

10. It is also quite likely that M. Lewy was a cousin of Professor Levi.

11. The "Monster Trial" derived its name from the "monstrous" number (3,000) of insurrectionists who were arrested. Only 100 or so of these actually came to trial.

12. *Revue de Paris* (October 1837), 46:122.

13. *Ibid.*

14. *Ibid.*

15. Crescini's libretto for *I Briganti* was based on Schiller's *Die Räuber* and, according to the *Journal des Débats* of March 24, 1836, was "not good at all." Mercadante had wanted Romani to write the libretto and employed Crescini only as his second choice.

16. Lady Catherine Charlotte Jackson, *The Court of the Tuileries from the Restoration to the Flight of Louis-Philippe,* 2:332. Countess Merlin was the wife of Count Philippe-Antoine Merlin, a prominent jurist in the French revolutionary and Napoleonic periods. He was banished during the Restoration but returned to France with Louis-Philippe in 1830.

17. *Revue de Paris* (June 1836), 30:63.

18. *Revue et Gazette Musicale,* May 1, 1836.

19. *Ibid.*

20. *Ibid.*

10. Paris and Rouen, 1837–1838

1. *Revue et Gazette Musicale,* April 9, 1837.

2. Adam Zamoyski claims that Chopin never played in this concert, having reneged on his promise to Liszt (*Chopin,* p. 152), but in the Franz Liszt Museum at Weimar there is a program from the concert which indicates that Chopin did take part in it.

3. Sebastian Lee (1805–1887) was a German cellist who arrived in Paris in 1832 and became solo cellist at the Opéra in 1837.

4. *Journal des Débats,* April 8, 1837.

5. Frédéric Chopin, *Correspondance de Frédéric Chopin,* 2:93.

6. While Sydow et al. date this letter "the beginning of July, 1836" in their French edition (Chopin, *Correspondance,* 2:194), Sydow's later Polish edition places it "the 2nd or 9th of July, 1837." Bronisław Sydow, *Korespondencja Fryderyka Chopina* (Warsaw: 1955), p. 426.

7. "Le Journal de Chopin," p. 552.

8. *Revue et Gazette Musicale,* February 4, 1838.

9. *Les Guêpes* (February 1847), 4:325.

10. *Ibid.*

11. *Le National,* February 24, 1838.

12. *Ibid.*

13. Louis-Philippe-Joseph Girod de Vienney, Baron de Trémont (1799–1852), was an amateur violinist who often gave concerts at his home in the rue Saint-Augustin.

14. *Journal des Débats,* February 19, 1838.

15. *Ibid.*

16. There was another entrance at No. 10 rue de Valois.

17. *Le Ménestrel,* April 1, 1838.

18. In 1936 the building which housed the Salle de Pape from 1824 to 1853 was destroyed to make way for an extension of the Banque de France.

19. No one actually witnessed Alkan's death, and the two people most apt to know the facts gave conflicting stories. The other version is that he was found dead in front of his kitchen stove, apparently in the process of cooking a meal.

20. *Le Ménestrel,* April 1, 1888.

21. In the Square d'Orléans where Chopin moved in 1842.

22. Chopin's *Piano Method* was, in fact, barely begun and Alkan never developed it.

23. Wilhelm von Lenz, *The Great Piano Virtuosos of Our Time from Personal Acquaintance,* p. 70.

24. *Revue et Gazette Musicale,* February 25, 1838.

25. Alizard substituted for Dérivis in the actual performance and probably sang other numbers than the ones listed on the program.

26. *Revue et Gazette Musicale,* March 11, 1838.

27. *Le National,* March 20, 1841.

28. *Revue et Gazette Musicale,* March 11, 1838.

29. Chopin, *Correspondance,* 2:129.

30. *Revue et Gazette Musicale,* March 24, 1838.

31. *Ibid.*

11. Paris, 1839–1842

1. The Palace of Saint-Cloud was left in ruins after the Franco-Prussian War of 1870–71 and finally razed in 1891.

2. Charlotte Moscheles, *Life of Moscheles,* 2:59.

3. The *Revue et Gazette Musicale* of October 31, 1839, claimed that Moscheles' variations were based on the overture to *The Magic Flute,* while the *Journal des Débats* of November 2 and 3, 1839, stated that he played variations on themes from *Don Giovanni.*

4. Moscheles, *Life of Moscheles,* 2:29.

5. *La France Musicale,* November 10, 1839.

6 Prior to the trip to Majorca Pleyel had given Chopin a 500-franc advance on the Preludes. This was the second time Chopin sold his compositions to Pleyel rather than Schlesinger.

7. Moscheles had the same idea in 1838, but at the last minute he got cold feet and brought in some singers to keep his audience from getting bored.

II. PARIS, 1839–1842

8. Liszt himself was an editor of the *Revue et Gazette Musicale,* as were George Sand and a young German composer named Richard Wagner who had just arrived in Paris in the fall of 1839.

9. *Revue et Gazette Musicale,* March 21, 1841.

10. *Ibid.,* April 1, 1841.

11. *La France Musicale,* April 4, 1841.

12. *Les Guêpes* (May 1841), 2:97.

13. In later life Marie d'Agoult achieved a modest literary fame. Like George Sand, she also chose a masculine *nom de plume,* publishing her works under the pseudonym of Daniel Stern.

14. Frédéric Chopin, *Correspondance de Frédéric Chopin,* 3:41.

15. Marie d'Agoult spent a great deal of her life in a state of suppressed anger. Sainte-Beuve once described her as "six feet of lava hidden under six inches of snow." Dominique Desanti, *Daniel, ou Le visage secret d'une comtesse romantique, Marie d'Agoult,* p. 20.

16. In March of 1841 Chopin attended Rubinstein's Paris concert.

17. George Sand, *Correspondance,* 5:282.

18. *Ibid.,* 5:283.

19. *Revue et Gazette Musicale,* May 2, 1841.

20. *La France Musicale,* April 25, 1841.

21. Some of the works performed by Chopin that night were the Mazurkas of op. 41, the Ballade in F major, op. 38, the Scherzo in C-sharp minor, op. 39, and the Polonaise in A major, op. 40, no. 1.

22. Adolphe-Charles Adam is better known today for his music to the ballet *Giselle,* written in 1841.

23. *La France Musicale,* May 2, 1841.

24. *Ibid.*

25. *Les Guêpes* (May 1841), 2:97.

26. *La France Musicale,* May 2, 1841.

27. *Le Ménestrel,* May 2, 1841.

28. *Revue et Gazette Musicale,* May 2, 1841.

29. Chopin, *Correspondance,* 3:73.

30. Hippolyte Chatiron was the illegitimate son of Mme. Sand's father and a local servant girl. He and George were childhood playmates and she remained fond of him all her life. He died of alcoholism on Christmas Day, 1848.

31. Mme. Sand's great-great-grandfather had been Friedrich-August II, elector of Saxony and King of Poland. Through this family line she was distantly related to the last three Bourbon kings, Louis XVI, Louis XVIII, and Charles X.

32. *Galignani's New Paris Guide,* p. 163.

33. *Revue et Gazette Musicale,* January 30, 1840.

34. Thiers was later president of France's Third Republic.

35. De Musset had been a lover of George Sand before Chopin.

36. Both Delacroix and Scheffer did well-known portraits of Chopin.

37. *Journal des Débats,* December 3, 1841.

38. Tadolini also composed and was said to have written parts of Rossini's *Stabat Mater.*

39. In 1840 Giuditta Grisi died at the age of thirty-five.

40. Charles Hervey, *The Theatres of Paris,* p. 158.

41. Giulia Grisi was unable to marry Mario because she had been previously married and couldn't get a divorce.

42. Chopin, *Correspondance,* 2:44.

43. *Revue et Gazette Musicale,* December 5, 1841.

44. *La France Musicale,* December 5, 1841.

45. Sand, *Correspondance,* 5:522.

46. Chopin, *Correspondance,* 3:96.

47. *Ibid.,* 3:95.

48. *Ibid.*

49. *Journal des Débats,* April 13, 1842.

50. *La France Musicale,* May 9, 1841.

51. The operas composed for Pauline Viardot included Meyerbeer's *Le Prophète,* Gounod's *Sapho,* and Saint-Saëns' *Samson et Dalila.*

52. *Revue et Gazette Musicale,* February 13, 1842.

53. There were four nocturnes altogether, including those in F-sharp minor, op. 48, no. 2, D-flat major, op. 27, no. 2, F major, op. 15, no. 1, and a fourth unidentified one.

54. One of the preludes was the D-flat major, op. 28, no. 15.

55. There were three études from op. 25 (A-flat major, F minor, and C minor).

56. The mazurkas were in A-flat major, B major, and A minor (opus numbers not given).

57. The Impromptu in G-flat major, op. 51.

58. *Journal des Débats,* February 14, 1842.

59. *La France Musicale,* February 27, 1842.

60. *Ibid.*

61. *Ibid.*

62. *Revue des Deux Mondes* (April 1, 1842), 4th series, 30:159.

63. *Revue et Gazette Musicale,* February 27, 1842.

64. *Ibid.*

65. *La France Musicale,* February 27, 1842.

66. *Revue et Gazette Musicale,* February 27, 1842.

67. *La France Musicale,* February 27, 1842.

68. *Revue et Gazette Musicale,* February 27, 1842.

69. Cherubini was born in 1760, only four years after Mozart.

12. Paris, 1843–1848

1. Frédéric Chopin, *Correspondance de Frédéric Chopin,* 2:53.
2. The rue Faubourg du Roule is today's rue Faubourg Saint-Honoré.

12. PARIS, 1843–1848

3. *Journal des Débats,* March 23, 1842.

4. Chopin's affection for Delacroix didn't extend to his paintings, which were too romantic for his taste.

5. This was Liszt's first visit to Weimar where he would later settle for many years.

6. Chopin charged Filtsch twenty francs a lesson as he did all his pupils. He knew that this put no burden on the boy's family since the money came from Karl's rich patroness, the countess Bánffy.

7. Fryderyk Chopin, *Selected Correspondance of Fryderyk Chopin,* p. 226.

8. *Ibid.*

9. By coincidence the Rothschild house happened to be in the same block as the Hôtel de France where Chopin and George Sand first met six years earlier.

10. Anka Muhlstein, *Baron James: The Rise of the French Rothschilds,* p. 73.

11. The premiere of Donizetti's *Don Pasquale* had just taken place in Paris on January 4, 1843, at the Théâtre-Italien. The opera quickly became the rage of the musical season.

12. *La France Musicale,* January 15, 1843.

13. *Ibid.*

14. *Ibid.*

15. Filtsch's concert took place on April 24, 1843. In it he performed the Chopin concerto again, this time with an orchestra. Later in the season he played the concerto again in London where he copied out all the orchestral parts from memory.

16. The Nocturnes of op. 55 in F minor and E-flat major.

17. *La France Musicale,* March 3, 1844.

18. Not until 1848 did Chopin indicate that he was aware of what George had tried to tell him in her novel.

19. *La France Musicale,* December 6, 1846.

20. *Revue et Gazette Musicale,* March 21, 1847.

21. Chopin, *Correspondance,* 3:308.

22. The most expensive tickets at the Opéra by then still cost only twelve francs.

23. Since the king's sister, Mme. Adélaïde, had just died the royal family was in mourning and didn't attend the concert. Their tickets, though, were undoubtedly distributed to friends in high places.

24. Chopin, *Correspondance,* 3:319–320.

25. *Ibid.,* 3:318.

26. Chopin's Sonata for piano and cello, op. 65, was written for and dedicated to Franchomme.

27. *La France Musicale,* February 21, 1847.

28. The Waltz in D-flat, op. 64, no. 1.

29. *Revue et Gazette Musicale,* February 20, 1848.

13. London and Manchester, 1848

1. The child, a girl, died when she was only a few days old.

2. George Sand, who was related to both French and Polish royalty, also had a distinguished lineage, but one which the bourgeois society of nineteenth-century Europe considered blemished by the stigma of illegitimacy.

3. Although Chopin spoke French from childhood on, it was always with an accent. He never achieved complete mastery of the language and especially disliked having to write in French.

4. Frédéric Chopin, *Correspondance de Frédéric Chopin,* 3:341.

5. *Ibid.,* 3:345.

6. *Ibid.,* 3:347.

7. *Ibid.,* 3:349.

8. Jane Stirling was a great friend of Samuel Hahnemann, the founder of homeopathy. Through her influence Chopin began consulting many homeopaths in his last years.

9. The Marquis of Douglas' mother was the Duchess of Hamilton, whom Chopin had met in Paris.

10. The house today is known as Lancaster House. The English prime minister Disraeli described it in one of his novels, *Lothair,* where he called it Creçy House.

11. The Duke of Sutherland, *The Story of Stafford House,* p. 4.

12. Queen Victoria's own daughter Princess Louise had been christened just two days earlier in the same chapel.

13. *Record,* May 17, 1848.

14. The Prince of Prussia later became King Wilhelm I of Prussia and father-in-law of Queen Victoria's oldest daughter.

15. Chopin, *Correspondance,* 3:367.

16. *Record,* May 17, 1848.

17. According to the *Illustrated London News* of May 20, 1848, Mario, Lablache, and Tamburini sang the trio from Rossini's *William Tell.*

18. Jules Benedict also accompanied the singers that evening.

19. Chopin, *Correspondance,* 3:347.

20. *Record,* May 17, 1848.

21. *Illustrated London News,* May 20, 1848.

22. Chopin, *Correspondance,* 3:343.

23. Hugo Cole, "Proud Look Back: The RPS and Its Orchestras."

24. Chopin, *Correspondance,* 3:356.

25. Henry Fowler Broadwood was the son of James Shudi Broadwood, whom Chopin visited in 1837. At that time Henry was already head of the firm, having taken over its management in 1834.

26. Chopin, *Correspondance,* 3:370.

27. *Ibid.,* 3:378.

28. In addition to his paid performances at Stafford House, Lady Gainsborough's, and the Marquis of Douglas', Chopin also played in the drawing

rooms of Lady Blessington, the Duchess of Somerset, the Duchess of Cambridge, and the Thomas Carlyles. However, these performances appear to have been informal affairs for which he received no money.

29. Her father, Charles Kemble, took over the management of Covent Garden the next year, 1842.

30. H. F. Chorley, *Thirty Years of Musical Recollections,* p. 137.

31. During the summer of 1848 Mrs. Sartoris' sister, the actress Fanny Kemble, was living in Lenox, Massachusetts, where she wandered around the countryside in men's clothes. Her behavior was considered of a "low moral order."

32. Chopin, *Correspondance,* 3:352.

33. *Ibid.*

34. Fryderyk Chopin, *Selected Correspondance of Fryderyk Chopin,* p. 322.

35. Mario was not accompanied by Chopin, but rather by a Signor Alary, whom the London *Examiner* of July 8, 1848, called "a consummate musician."

36. *Examiner,* July 8, 1848.

37. *Athenaeum,* July 1, 1848.

38. *Ibid.,* June 24, 1848.

39. In a letter to his family, mailed August 19, 1848, Chopin complains that all the papers gave his London matinees (i.e., at Mrs. Sartoris' and later at the Earl of Falmouth's) good notices except Davison at the *Times.* Most biographers have interpreted this to mean that Davison wrote bad reviews on these occasions. However, in the *Musical World* Davison specifically states he didn't attend the concert in Eaton Place, and I can find no review in either the *Musical World* or the *Times* concerning the concert at Lord Falmouth's. Therefore what Chopin apparently meant was that Davison had simply ignored his performances altogether. Oddly enough, this virulent critic who shunned Chopin's concerts in London turned up at his funeral in Paris the following year.

40. Chopin, *Selected Correspondance,* p. 322.

41. Lord Falmouth lived at No. 2 St. James's Square until his death in 1852. During the Second World War the house was destroyed by bombs.

42. In medical circles Manuel Garcia is remembered for having invented the laryngoscope, an instrument used to examine the vocal cords.

43. The extent of Pauline Viardot's devotion to Chopin is indicated by the fact that she already had a commitment to sing at Covent Garden on the same morning as his concert at Lord Falmouth's.

44. *Daily News,* July 10, 1848.

45. *Ibid.*

46. *Athenaeum,* July 14, 1848.

47. *Ibid.*

48. Chopin, *Correspondance,* 3:354.

49. *Ibid.*

50. *Ibid.*

51. *Ibid.*

52. Crumpsall House was demolished in 1934.

53. *Manchester Courier,* August 30, 1848.

54. La Malibran's death was related to injuries sustained earlier in a fall from her horse.

55. Chopin's host, Salis Schwabe, was a subscriber but not a member of the musical committee.

56. Henry Pleasants, *The Great Singers from the Dawn of Opera to Our Own Time,* p. 219.

57. *Manchester Courier and Lancashire General Advertiser,* August 23, 1848.

58. Chopin, *Correspondance,* 3:379.

59. George A. Osborne, "Reminiscences of Frederick Chopin," p. 101.

60. Today the Midland Hotel stands on the site of the former Gentlemen's Concert Hall.

61. *Manchester Guardian,* August 30, 1848.

62. Susanna Brookshaw (*Concerning Chopin in Manchester*) claims that Corbari substituted a "simple Swiss-like air."

63. The original program read "Nocturne et Berceuse" with a correction on the back stating that Chopin had decided to substitute an "Andante e Scherzo" instead.

64. The original program read "Mazourka, Ballade et Valse," again with Chopin's last-minute substitutions written on the back.

65. The specific compositions Chopin played, according to Brookshaw, were probably: the Andante Spianato (opus 22), the Scherzo in B-flat minor (opus 31), the Nocturne in E-flat major (op. 9, no. 2—known in England as "Murmurs of the Seine"), the Études in C-sharp minor (op. 25, no. 7) and F minor (op. 25, no. 2) or the one in A-flat major (op. 25, no. 1), and the Berceuse. *Concerning Chopin in Manchester,* p. 25.

66. *Manchester Examiner,* September 5, 1848.

67. *Ibid.* These harsh comments distressed the editors of the *Examiner* so much they called in a second critic, Carl Engel, who wrote a highly complimentary account of Chopin's "musical genius and executive powers" in the same issue. Since Engel's article was a general critique of Chopin's playing and not a specific review of the concert, it is not included in the Appendix of this book.

68. *Musical World,* September 9, 1848.

69. *Ibid.* This last comparison was particularly cutting since Bennett was originally a violinist who later took up the piano as a second instrument.

70. *Manchester Guardian,* August 30, 1848.

71. *Ibid.*

72. Osborne, "Reminiscences," p. 101.

73. The newspapers mentioned only one encore, which was identified merely as a "fragment of great beauty" by the *Manchester Courier* of August 30, 1848.

74. Chopin, *Correspondance,* 3:382.

14. Glasgow, Edinburgh, and London, 1848

1. Frédéric Chopin, *Correspondance de Frédéric Chopin,* 3:383.

14. GLASGOW, EDINBURGH, AND LONDON, 1848

2. *Ibid.*, 3:384.

3. *Ibid.*

4. John Muir Wood (1805–1892) was not only a music dealer but an accomplished pianist who had studied with Kalkbrenner, J. P. Pixis, and Czerny.

5. In 1870 the Merchants' Hall was incorporated into the Sheriff Court House for Lanarkshire and extensively remodeled. Most of the original interior was destroyed at the time, including the hall where Chopin played.

6. Audrey Bone, *Jane Wilhelmina Stirling*, p. 74.

7. Prince Alexander was the nephew of Prince Adam Czartoryski. His wife, Marcelina, was formerly a Radziwiłł and one of Chopin's most talented pupils.

8. Chopin, *Correspondance*, 3:387.

9. The opus numbers were not printed on the original program. They were added in ink later, probably by Muir Wood since this program, published by Bone (Bone, *Jane Wilhelmina Stirling*, p. 79), had once been in the possession of Wood's son Herbert.

10. *Glasgow Herald*, September 29, 1848.

11. *Glasgow Courier*, September 28, 1848.

12. *Ibid.*

13. *Glasgow Herald*, September 29, 1848.

14. J. C. Hadden, *Chopin*, p. 146.

15. Chopin, *Correspondance*, 3:389.

16. Sir William (whom Chopin incorrectly called an uncle rather than a cousin of Miss Stirling) later changed his name to Stirling-Maxwell, which is how he is remembered by historians for his scholarly studies on painters of the Spanish school.

17. The house Chopin stayed in wasn't the original one but a later Georgian mansion erected in the first half of the eighteenth century.

18. Chopin, *Correspondance*, 3:391.

19. The establishment was also known as Cockburn's Hotel.

20. Robert Chambers, *Walks in Edinburgh*, p. 199.

21. *Scotsman*, October 7, 1848.

22. Études nos. 1, 2, and possibly 7 of op. 25.

23. The Nocturnes op. 9, no. 2, and op. 55, no. 1.

24. Op. 18 in E-flat major.

25. The second Ballade, in F major, op. 38. Among the mazurkas was op. 7, no. 5, and among the waltzes, probably op. 64, no. 1.

26. *Edinburgh Evening Courant*, October 12, 1848.

27. *Caledonian Mercury*, October 12, 1848.

28. *Scotsman*, October 7, 1848.

29. *Edinburgh Advertiser*, October 6, 1848.

30. *Musical World*, October 14, 1848.

31. *Edinburgh Evening Courant*, October 7, 1848.

32. Chopin, *Correspondance*, 3:394.

33. *Ibid.*, 3:395.

34. *Ibid.*, 3:398.

35. *Address of the Literary Association of the Friends of Poland to the Poles*, p. 39.

36. *John Bull*, November 18, 1848.

37. *Ibid.*

38. *Ibid.*

39. *London Times*, November 13, 1848.

40. *Ibid.*, November 17, 1848.

41. *Ibid.*

42. *Ibid.*

43. The Guildhall was originally built in 1411, although much of it was damaged by the Great Fire and subsequently reconstructed in the seventeenth century. The Common Council Chamber where Chopin is thought to have played was demolished in 1908.

44. *London Times*, November 17, 1848.

45. *Ibid.*

46. Adam Zamoyski, *Chopin*, p. 307.

47. *Illustrated London News*, November 18, 1848.

48. *London Times*, November 17, 1848.

15. Paris, 1848–1849

1. Frédéric Chopin, *Correspondance de Frédéric Chopin*, 3:403.

2. *Ibid.*, 3:402.

Appendix B. Reviews of Chopin's Concerts

1. Krystyna Kobylańska, *Chopin in His Own Land*, p. 61.

2. This statement by the critic was obviously based on the original program and not the actual performance.

3. An essentially identical review appeared in the *Kurjer Warszawski* on August 29, 1829.

4. Kobylańska, *Chopin in His Own Land*, p. 174.

5. The *Allgemeine Theaterzeitung* had actually said just the opposite, i.e., that "the desire to produce good music is obviously more important to him [Chopin] than the mere urge to please his audience." Wierzyński suggests that this was an intentional mistranslation by the Warsaw journalist to put Chopin in a bad light (*The Life and Death of Chopin*).

6. Kobylańska, *Chopin in His Own Land*, p. 240.

7. A Czartkowski and Z. Jeżewska, *Chopin Żywy*, p. 138.

8. Kobylańska, *Chopin in His Own Land*, p. 243.

9. Czartkowski and Jeżewska, *Chopin Żywy*, p. 148.

10. Kobylańska, *Chopin in His Own Land*, p. 245.

11. *Ibid.*, p. 249.

12. *Ibid.*, p. 263.

13. Paganini was, in fact, present at the concert Castil-Blaze was reviewing.

14. The second "daughter" must have been George Sand's cousin Augustine Brault, who later became her adopted daughter.

15. According to the *Revue et Gazette Musicale,* Chopin played at least fifteen pieces at this concert.

16. The day before, the *London Times* commented twice on the poor attendance at the ball compared with previous years.

BIBLIOGRAPHY

NEWSPAPERS AND PERIODICALS

Allgemeine Musikalische Zeitung, Leipzig, 1825, 1826, 1829, 1831
Allgemeine Theaterzeitung, Vienna, 1829, 1831
Athenaeum, London, 1848
Caledonian Mercury, Edinburgh, 1848
Charivari, Le, Paris, 1833, 1838
Courrier de l'Europe, Echo du Continent, London, 1841
Dekameron Polski, Warsaw, 1830
Edinburgh Advertiser, Edinburgh, 1848
Edinburgh Evening Courant, Edinburgh, 1848
L'Europe Littéraire, Paris, 1833
Flora: A Journal of Entertainment, Munich, 1831
France Musicale, La, Paris, 1839, 1841, 1842, 1843
Gazeta Korespondenta Warszawskiego i Zagranicznego, Warsaw, 1830
Gazeta Warszawska, Warsaw, 1829, 1830
Gazette Musicale, Paris, 1834, 1835
Glasgow Courier, Glasgow, 1848
Glasgow Herald, Glasgow, 1848
Glasgow Saturday Post, Glasgow, 1848
Guêpes, Les, Paris, 1841, 1847
Illustrated London News, London, 1848
John Bull, London, 1848
Journal des Débats, Paris, 1835, 1836, 1837, 1838, 1839, 1840, 1842
Kurjer Polski, Warsaw, 1829, 1830
Kurjer Warszawski, Warsaw, 1825, 1826, 1829, 1830
London Daily News, London, 1848
London Examiner, London, 1848
London Record, London, 1848
London Times, London, 1848
Manchester Courier, Manchester, 1848
Manchester Examiner, Manchester, 1848

Manchester Guardian, Manchester, 1848
Ménestrel, Le, Paris, 1834, 1835, 1838, 1841, 1848, 1888
Moniteur Universel, Paris, 1833
Musical World, London, 1848
National, Le, Paris, 1834, 1835, 1838, 1841
Pamiętnik dla Płci Pięknej, Warsaw, 1830
Presse, La, Paris, 1842
Revue des Deux Mondes, Paris, 1839
Revue et Gazette Musicale, Paris, 1836, 1837, 1838, 1839, 1841, 1842, 1845, 1848
Revue Musicale, Paris, 1832, 1833, 1834, 1835
Revue de Paris, Paris, 1835, 1837, 1840
Sammler, Der, Vienna, 1829
Scotsman, Edinburgh, 1848
Wiener Zeitschrift für Kunst, Literatur, Theater, und Mode, Vienna, 1829

OTHER SOURCES

Address of the Literary Association of the Friends of Poland to the Poles (*Odezwa do Polaków*). Drawn up by Lord Dudley Coutts Stuart, M.P. London: E. Detkens, 1850.

d'Agoult, Marie. *Mémoires (1833–1854).* Paris: 1927.

Almanach des 25,000 addresses des principaux habitans de Paris, année 1840.

Appleton, William. *Madame Vestris and the London Stage.* New York: Columbia University Press, 1974.

Atwood, William G. *The Lioness and the Little One: The Liaison of George Sand and Frédéric Chopin.* New York: Columbia University Press, 1980.

Barry, Joseph. *Infamous Woman: The Life of George Sand.* Garden City, N.Y.: Doubleday, 1977.

Barzun, Jacques. *Berlioz and His Century.* New York: Meridian Books, 1956.

Beaumont, Cyril W. *Fanny Elssler (1810–1884).* London: Beaumont, 1931.

Berlioz, Hector. *Les années romantiques: 1819–1842.* Paris: Calmann-Levy, 1904.

Berlioz, Hector. *The Memoirs of Hector Berlioz.* David Cairns, ed. and tr. New York: Norton, 1969.

Bihrle, H. *Die Musikalische Akademie.* Munich: 1911.

Bloschke, Julius. "Chopin in Bad Reinerz." *Neue Musik-Zeitung* (1910), no. 10.

Bone, Audrey E. *Jane Wilhelmina Stirling, 1804–1859*. Chipstead, Eng.: Sharrock Services, 1960.

Bonnet-Roy, F. *La vie musicale au temps romantique*. Paris: 1929.

Bory, Victor. *La vie de Frédéric Chopin par l'image*. Paris: Horizons de France, 1951.

Boschot, Adolphe. *Un romantique sous Louis-Philippe: Hector Berlioz, 1831–1842*. Paris: 1908.

Boschot, Adolphe. *Une vie romantique: Hector Berlioz*. Paris: Plon, 1920.

Bourniquel, Camille. *Chopin*. New York and London: Grove Press, Evergreen Books, 1960.

Brion, Marcelle. *Daily Life in Vienna of Mozart and Schubert*. Jean Stewart, tr. New York: Macmillan, 1962.

Brockett, O. G. *History of the Theatre*. Boston: Allyn and Bacon, 1968.

Brockway, Wallace and Herbert Weinstock. *Men of Music*. New York: Simon and Schuster, 1950.

Brombert, Beth Archer. *Christina: Portrait of a Princess*. New York: Knopf, 1977.

Brookshaw, Susanna. *Concerning Chopin in Manchester*. Privately published, 1951.

Castelot, André. *The Turbulent City: Paris, 1783 to 1871*. Denise Folliot, tr. New York: Harper and Row, 1962.

Cate, Curtis. *George Sand*. New York: Houghton Mifflin, 1975.

Chambers, Robert. *Walks in Edinburgh: A Guide to the Scottish Capital*. Edinburgh: 1829.

Chopin, Frédéric. *Correspondance de Frédéric Chopin*. Bronislas Sydow, Suzanne and Denise Chainaye, and Irene Sydow, eds. Paris: Richard-Masse 1953–1960.

Chopin, Fryderyk. *Selected Correspondance of Fryderyk Chopin*. Arthur Hedley, tr. and ed. London: Heinemann, 1962.

Chorley, H. F. *Thirty Years of Musical Recollections*. New York and London: Knopf, 1926.

Christiansen, Rupert. *Prima Donna*. New York: Viking, 1985.

Cobban, Alfred. *A History of Modern France*. Baltimore: Penguin, 1961.

Cole, Hugo. "Proud Look Back: The RPS and Its Orchestras." *Country Life*, January 12, 1984, p. 60.

Comettant, Jean Pierre Oscar. *Histoire de cent mille pianos et d'une salle de concert*. Paris: 1890.

Concert Hall, Manchester: Rules Passed at a Special Meeting of Subscribers on the 14th of December, 1848.
Czartkowski, Adam and Zofia Jeżewska. *Chopin Żywy.* Warsaw: 1958.
Dasent, Arthur I. *The History of St. James's Square.* London: Macmillan, 1895.
Davison, J. W. *The Mazurkas and Valses of Frederick Chopin with Memoir.* London and New York: Boosey, n.d.
Delacroix, Eugène. *The Journal of Eugène Delacroix.* Lucy Norton, tr. London: Phaidon, 1951.
Desanti, Dominique. *Daniel, ou Le visage secret d'une comtesse romantique, Marie d'Agoult.* Paris: Editions Stock, 1980.
Devries, Anik. *Salle Pleyel: Les 175 ans de la maison Pleyel.* Paris: 1983.
Dolge, Alfred. *Pianos and Their Makers.* New York: Dover, 1972.
Donnet, Alexis. *Architectonographie des théâtres.* Paris: 1857.
Droz, Jacques. *Europe Between Revolutions, 1815–1848.* Robert Baldick, tr. New York: Harper and Row, 1968.
Dulaure, Jacques-Antoine. *Histoire de Paris depuis les premiers temps historiques.* Paris: 1852.
Eigeldinger, J. J. *Chopin vu par ses élèves.* Neuchâtel: La Baconnière 1970.
Eitner, R. *Bibliographisch-bibliographisches Quellen-Lexicon der Musiker und Musikgelehrten.* Leipzig: Breitkopf und Härtel, 1900.
Ewen, David and Frederic. *Musical Vienna.* New York: McGraw-Hill, 1939.
Feicht, Hieronim. "Chopin we Wrocławiu." *Zeszyty Wrocławskie* (1949), 1–2, p. 13.
Ferra, Bartolomé. *Chopin and George Sand in Majorca.* James Webb, tr. Palma de Mallorca: 1936.
Fétis, F. J. *Biographie universelle des musiciens.* Paris: 1875–78.
Fourcaud, L., A. Pougin, and L. Pradel. *La Salle Pleyel.* Paris: 1893.
Galignani. *Picture of Paris.* Paris: 1816.
Galignani's New Paris Guide. 1841 and 1846.
Ganche, Édouard. *Frédéric Chopin: Sa vie et ses oeuvres.* Paris: Mercure de France, 1913.
Gartenberg, Egon. *Vienna: Its Musical Heritage.* University Park; Pennsylvania State University Press, 1968.
Gattey, Charles Neilson. *A Bird of Curious Plumage.* London: Constable, 1971.
Gavoty, Bernard. *Frédéric Chopin.* Martin Sokolinsky, tr. New York: Scribner's, 1977.

Gieysztor, Aleksander et al. *History of Poland.* Warsaw: Polish Scientific Publishers, 1979.

Gourret, J. *Dictionnaire de chanteurs de l'Opéra de Paris.* Paris: Editions Albatros, 1982.

Gronowicz, Antoni. *Chopin.* Jessie McEwen, tr. New York: Nelson, 1943.

Grove's Dictionary of Music and Musicians. 3d ed. H. C. Colles, ed. New York: Macmillan, 1935–1942.

Guest, Ivor. *Fanny Elssler.* London: Adam and Charles Black, 1970.

Guichard, Léon. *La musique et les lettres au temps du romantisme.* Paris: 1955.

Guide Chopin illustré. Warsaw: Towarzystwo Fryderyka Chopina, 1960.

Habel, Heinrich. *Das Odeon in München und die Frühzeit des öffentlichen Konzertsaalhaus.* Berlin: Walter de Gruyter, 1967.

Hadden, J. C. *Chopin.* London: J.M. Dent, 1906.

Halecki, Oscar. *A History of Poland.* Monica M. Gardner and Mary Corbridge-Patkaniowska, trs. New York: McKay, 1976.

Harasowski, Adam. *The Skein of Legends Around Chopin.* New York: Da Capo Press, 1980.

Hedley, Arthur. *Chopin.* London and New York: Farrar, Straus and Cudahy, 1947.

Hervey, Charles. *The Theatres of Paris.* Paris and London: 1846.

Hueffer, Francis. *Half a Century of Music in England.* London: 1889.

Huneker, James. *Chopin: The Man and His Music.* New York: Scribner, 1924.

Jackson, Lady Catherine Charlotte. *The Court of the Tuileries from the Restoration to the Flight of Louis Philippe.* Boston: Page, 1897.

Jameson, Mrs. *Memoirs and Essays, Illustrative of Art, Literature, and Social Morals.* London: 1846.

"Journal de Chopin, Le." *Le Guide Musicale.* September 8 and 15, 1907.

Kański, J. and A. Zborski. *Chopin i Jego Ziemia.* Warsaw: Wydawnictwo Interpress, 1975.

Karlowicz, Mieczysław. *Souvenirs inédits.* Paris and Leipzig: 1904.

Kendall, Alan. *Paganini: A Biography.* London: Chappell, Elm Tree Books, 1982.

Kobylańska, Krystyna. *Chopin in His Own Land.* Cracow: Polskie Wydawnictwo Muzyczne, 1955.

Krasiński, Józef. *Guide du voyageur en Pologne.* Warsaw: 1820.

Kraushar, Alexander. *Dawne Pałace Warszawskie: Rzeczypospolitej, Ka-*

zimierzowski, Radzwiłłowski i Błękitny. Poznan, Warsaw, Wilno, and Lublin: 1925.

Kraushar, Alexander. *Resursa Kupiecka w Warszawie.* Warsaw: 1928.

Kraushar, Alexander. *Widoki Warszawy i jej Okolic, Karola Albertiego.* Warsaw: 1912.

Kwiatkowska, Maria. *Kościół Ewangelicko-Augsburski.* Warsaw: 1982.

Lenz, Wilhelm von. *The Great Piano Virtuosos of Our Time from Personal Acquaintance: Liszt, Chopin, Tausig, Henselt.* Madeleine R. Baker, tr. New York: Schirmer, 1899.

Liszt, Franz. *Frédéric Chopin.* Edward N. Waters, tr. New York: Free Press of Glencoe, 1963.

Loesser, Arthur. *Men, Women, and Pianos: A Social History.* New York: Simon and Schuster, 1954.

Marcinek, Kazimierz and Wacław Prorok. *Duszniki Zdrój, Polanica Zdrój i Okolice.* Warsaw: 1984.

Marek, George. *Gentle Genius: The Story of Felix Mendelssohn.* New York: Crowell, 1972.

Marek, George and Maria Gordon-Smith. *Chopin.* New York: Harper and Row, 1978.

Marmontel, Antoine François. *Les pianistes célèbres.* Paris: 1888.

Maurois, André. *Lélia: The Life of George Sand.* Gerard Hopkins, tr. New York: Harper, 1954.

Méreaux, Amédée. *Variétes littéraires et musicales.* Paris: 1878.

Methuen-Campbell, James. *Chopin Playing, from the Composer to the Present Day.* New York: Taplinger, 1981.

Mizwa, Stephen. *Frederic Chopin, 1810–1849.* New York: Macmillan, 1949.

Moscheles, Charlotte. *Life of Moscheles.* A. D. Coleridge, ed. and tr. London: Hurst and Blackett, 1873.

Muhlstein, Anka. *Baron James: The Rise of the French Rothschilds.* New York and Paris: Vendome Press, 1982.

Murdoch, William. *Chopin: His Life.* New York: Macmillan, 1935.

Nicolson, Harold. *The Congress of Vienna: A Study in Allied Unity, 1812–1822.* New York: Viking, 1946.

Niecks, Frederick. *Frederick Chopin as a Man and Musician.* London and New York: Novello, Ewer, 1888.

Nodier, Charles. *Paris historique: Promenade dans les rues de Paris.* Paris: 1839.

Orga, Ates. *Chopin: His Life and Times.* Tunbridge Wells, Eng.: Midas, 1976.

Osborne, G. A. "Reminiscences of Frederick Chopin." *Proceedings of the Royal Musical Association,* 1879, p. 91.

Oxford Companion to the Theatre. Phyllis Hartnoll, ed. London: 1967.

Patschovsky, Wilhelm. *Führer durch Bad Kudowa und Umgebung.* Schweidnitz, Ger.: 1925.

Perényi, Eleanor. *Liszt: The Artist as Romantic Hero.* Boston and Toronto: Little, Brown, 1974.

Pleasants, Henry. *The Great Singers from the Dawn of Opera to Our Own Time.* New York: Simon and Schuster, 1966.

Procházka, J. *Chopin and Bohemia.* Prague: Artia, 1969.

Raynor, Henry. *Music and Society Since 1815.* New York: Schocken Books, 1976.

Rocheblave, S. "Une amitié romanesque: George Sand et Mme. d'Agoult." *La Revue de Paris,* December 15, 1894, p. 814.

Rowan, Alistair. "Keir, Perthshire." *Country Life,* August 7, 1975, p. 326, and August 14, 1975, p. 390.

Sand, George. *Correspondance.* Georges Lubin, ed. Vols. 1–9. Paris: Garnier, 1964–1972.

Sand, George. *Histoire de ma vie.* Paris: 1928.

Sand, George. *Les Majorcains.* Paris: 1843.

Sand, George. *Winter in Majorca.* Robert Graves, tr. Palma de Mallorca: Valldemosa Edition, 1956.

Schaden, Adolphe de. *Nouveau guide des étrangers dans Munich et ses environs.* Munich: 1835.

Schiller, Felix. *Munich: Its Treasures of Art and Science, Manners and Customs.* Munich: 1852.

Schoenberg, Harold. *The Great Pianists.* New York: Simon and Schuster, 1963.

Schumann, Robert. *On Music and Musicians.* Konrad Wolff, ed. Paul Rosenfeld, tr. New York: McGraw-Hill, 1964.

Simond, Charles. *La vie parisienne au XIX siècle: Paris de 1800 à 1900.* Paris: Plon, Nourrit et Cie, 1900–1901.

Slonimsky, Nicholas. *Lexicon of Musical Invective.* Seattle and London: University of Washington Press, 1969.

Smith, Ronald. *Alkan.* London: Kahn and Averill, 1976.

Stoekl, Agnes de. *King of the French: A Portrait of Louis-Philippe.* New York: Putnam, 1958.

Sutherland, Duke of. *The Story of Stafford House.* London: Geoffrey Bles, 1935.

Szenic, S. and J. Chudek. *Najstarszy Szlak Warszawy.* Warsaw: 1955.

Tessaro-Kosimova, Irena. *Warszawa w Starych Albumach.* Warsaw: 1978.
Thomson, David. *Europe Since Napoleon.* New York: Knopf, 1960.
Tomaszewska, Wanda. "Chopin w Dusznikach." *Muzyka* (1961), no. 4, p. 88.
Troyat, Henri. *Alexander of Russia: Napoleon's Conqueror.* Joan Pinkham, tr. New York: Dutton, 1982.
Walker, Alan. *Franz Liszt: The Virtuoso Years, 1811–1847.* New York: Knopf, 1983.
Walker, Alan, ed. *The Chopin Companion: Profiles of the Man and the Musician.* New York: Norton, 1973.
Weinstock, Herbert. *Chopin: The Man and His Music.* New York: Knopf, 1949.
Wierzyński, Casimir. *The Life and Death of Chopin.* Norbert Guterman, tr. New York: Simon and Schuster, 1949.
Zagiba, Franz. *Chopin und Wien.* Vienna: Bauer, 1951.
Zamoyski, Adam. *Chopin.* Garden City, N.Y.: Doubleday, 1980.
Zielony, Wiktor. *Polanica Zdrój, Duszniki Zdrój, Kudowa Zdrój.* Wrocław: 1979.

INDEX